DELIBERATE PRACTICE IN

COGNITIVE BEHAVIORAL THERAPY

Essentials of Deliberate Practice Series

Tony Rousmaniere and Alexandre Vaz, Series Editors

Deliberate Practice in Cognitive Behavioral Therapy
James F. Boswell and Michael J. Constantino

Deliberate Practice in Emotion-Focused Therapy
Rhonda N. Goldman, Alexandre Vaz, and Tony Rousmaniere

ESSENTIALS OF DELIBERATE PRACTICE SERIES

TONY ROUSMANIERE AND ALEXANDRE VAZ, SERIES EDITORS

DELIBERATE PRACTICE IN
COGNITIVE BEHAVIORAL THERAPY

JAMES F. BOSWELL

MICHAEL J. CONSTANTINO

AMERICAN PSYCHOLOGICAL ASSOCIATION

Published by
American Psychological Association
750 First Street, NE
Washington, DC 20002
https://www.apa.org

Order Department
https://www.apa.org/pubs/books
order@apa.org

In the U.K., Europe, Africa, and the Middle East, copies may be ordered from Eurospan
https://www.eurospanbookstore.com/apa
info@eurospangroup.com

Typeset in Cera Pro by Circle Graphics, Inc., Reisterstown, MD

Printer: Gasch Printing, Odenton, MD
Cover Designer: Naylor Design, Washington, DC

Library of Congress Cataloging-in-Publication Data

Names: Boswell, James F., author. | Constantino, Michael J., 1971- author.
Title: Deliberate practice in cognitive behavioral therapy / by James F. Boswell and
    Michael J. Constantino.
Description: Washington, DC : American Psychological Association, [2022] |
    Series: Essentials of deliberate practice | Includes bibliographical references
    and index.
Identifiers: LCCN 2021013084 (print) | LCCN 2021013085 (ebook) |
    ISBN 9781433835551 (paperback) | ISBN 9781433835568 (ebook)
Subjects: LCSH: Cognitive therapy. | Behavior therapy. | BISAC: PSYCHOLOGY /
    Education & Training | PSYCHOLOGY / Clinical Psychology
Classification: LCC RC489.C63 B68 2022 (print) | LCC RC489.C63 (ebook) |
    DDC 616.89/1425—dc23
LC record available at https://lccn.loc.gov/2021013084
LC ebook record available at https://lccn.loc.gov/2021013085

https://doi.org/10.1037/0000256-000

Printed in the United States of America

10 9 8 7 6 5 4 3 2 1

We dedicate this book to our mentor, Louis G. Castonguay. Un mentor est quelqu'un qui voit plus de talent et de capacité en vous, que vous ne voyez en vous-même, et qui aide à les faire sortir de vous. [A mentor is someone who sees more talent and ability within you, that you did not see in yourself, and helps bring it out of you.]

—James F. Boswell and Michael J. Constantino

Contents

Series Preface

Tony Rousmaniere and Alexandre Vaz

We are pleased to introduce the Essentials of Deliberate Practice series of training books. We are developing this book series to address a specific need that we see in many psychology training programs. The issue can be illustrated by the training experiences of Mary, a hypothetical second-year graduate school trainee. Mary has learned a lot about mental health theory, research, and psychotherapy techniques. Mary is a dedicated student; she has read dozens of textbooks, written excellent papers about psychotherapy, and receives near-perfect scores on her course exams. However, when Mary sits with her clients at her practicum site, she often has trouble performing the therapy skills that she can write and talk about so clearly. Furthermore, Mary has noticed herself getting anxious when her clients express strong reactions, such as getting very emotional, hopeless, or skeptical about therapy. Sometimes this anxiety is strong enough to make Mary freeze at key moments, limiting her ability to help those clients.

During her weekly individual and group supervision, Mary's supervisor gives her advice informed by empirically supported therapies and common factor methods. The supervisor often supplements that advice by leading Mary through role-plays, recommending additional reading, or providing examples from her own work with clients. Mary, a dedicated supervisee who shares tapes of her sessions with her supervisor, is open about her challenges, carefully writes down her supervisor's advice, and reads the suggested readings. However, when Mary sits back down with her clients, she often finds that her new knowledge seems to have flown out of her head, and she is unable to enact her supervisor's advice. Mary finds this problem to be particularly acute with the clients who are emotionally evocative.

Mary's supervisor, who has received formal training in supervision, uses supervisory best practices, including the use of video to review supervisees' work. She would rate Mary's overall competence level as consistent with expectations for a trainee at Mary's developmental level. But even though Mary's overall progress is positive, she experiences some recurring problems in her work. This is true even though the supervisor is confident that she and Mary have identified the changes that Mary should make in her work.

The problem with which Mary and her supervisor are wrestling—the disconnect between her knowledge about psychotherapy and her ability to reliably perform psychotherapy—is the focus of this book series. We started this series because most therapists experience this disconnect, to one degree or another, whether they are beginning trainees or highly experienced clinicians. In truth, we are all Mary.

To address this problem, we are focusing this series on the use of deliberate practice, a method of training specifically designed for improving reliable performance of complex skills in challenging work environments (Rousmaniere, 2016, 2019; Rousmaniere et al., 2017). Deliberate practice entails experiential, repeated training with a particular skill until it becomes automatic. In the context of psychotherapy, this involves two trainees role-playing as a client and a therapist, switching roles every so often, under the guidance of a supervisor. The trainee playing the therapist reacts to client statements, ranging in difficulty from beginner to intermediate to advanced, with improvised responses that reflect fundamental therapeutic skills.

To create these books, we approached leading trainers and researchers of major therapy models with these simple instructions: Identify 10 to 12 essential skills for your therapy model where trainees often experience a disconnect between cognitive knowledge and performance ability—in other words, skills that trainees could write a good paper about but often have challenges performing, especially with challenging clients. We then collaborated with the authors to create deliberate practice exercises specifically designed to improve reliable performance of these skills and overall responsive treatment (Hatcher, 2015; Stiles et al., 1998; Stiles & Horvath, 2017). Finally, we rigorously tested these exercises with trainees and trainers at multiple sites around the world and refined them based on extensive feedback.

Each book in this series focuses on a specific therapy model, but readers will notice that most exercises in these books touch on common factor variables and facilitative interpersonal skills that researchers have identified as having the most impact on client outcome, such as empathy, verbal fluency, emotional expression, persuasiveness, and problem focus (e.g., Anderson et al., 2009; Norcross et al., 2019). Thus, the exercises in every book should help with a broad range of clients. Despite the specific theoretical model(s) from which therapists work, most therapists place a strong emphasis on pantheoretical elements of the therapeutic relationship, many of which have robust empirical support as correlates or mechanisms of client improvement (e.g., Norcross et al., 2019). We also recognize that therapy models have already-established training programs with rich histories, so we present deliberate practice not as a replacement but as an adaptable, transtheoretical training method that can be integrated into these existing programs to improve skill retention and help ensure basic competency.

About This Book

This book in the series is on cognitive behavioral therapy (CBT), an umbrella term for a diverse set of treatments that draw from both basic and applied research on learning, cognition, and emotion (Dobson & Dozois, 2019). Despite the diversity of CBT-oriented approaches, a common maxim is the importance of "learning by doing." A broad and deep familiarity with the theoretical and empirical CBT literature is important, yet this knowledge can never replace direct, hands-on experiences with clients and in the training/supervision process. The importance of experiential learning in the training/supervision process is magnified by the reality that, especially for novice trainees who are just beginning to work with clients, there are relatively few opportunities to practice the wide range of clinical skills that are theoretically at one's disposal. This reality runs counter to key elements of the overall CBT philosophy, which stresses the importance of creating opportunities for exposure and repeated and generalizable practice.

In this book, we adopt deliberate practice methods to support experiential—learn by doing—training opportunities. The described methods and stimuli can facilitate practicing a range of important CBT skills. In addition, it supports fine-tuning the "how" of intervention delivery, including in a flexible manner across diverse clinical scenarios. Importantly, this book is not intended to replace core coursework and exposure to foundational CBT theory and principles of practice. Rather, this book is intended to augment other common training components.

For example, through coursework or other reading, a trainee might learn that avoidance is a common feature of anxiety disorders, and problem maintenance through negative reinforcement should be a target of treatment. The trainee can understand the concept of negative reinforcement and begin to learn about the types of CBT techniques that are commonly used to address it. This book is about providing opportunities for trainees to practice not only what they would say to an avoidant client but also how they would say it. In the case of avoidance, the focus is not only on the client's avoidance outside of the therapy context but also within the therapy context—when the client's avoidance is impacting their ability to make use of CBT. In essence, this book aims to help trainees (at all professional levels) learn how to responsively and fluidly apply foundational "tried-and-true" CBT concepts and strategies, which will add to their overall repertoire of clinical skills and principles. With such an expanded repertoire, therapists can maximize their ability to offer personally compelling treatment rationales and related interventions to each patient, including, in this case, of the CBT variety.

Acknowledgments

We would like to acknowledge Rodney Goodyear for his significant contribution to starting and organizing this book series. We are grateful to Susan Reynolds, David Becker, and Emily Ekle at American Psychological Association (APA) Books for providing expert guidance and insightful editing that has significantly improved the quality and accessibility of this book.

We are also deeply grateful to Jacqueline Persons for her careful and helpful feedback on earlier versions of the exercise content in this book. These exercises underwent extensive testing at training programs around the world. For all of the pilot site leaders and trainees who volunteered to "test run" this work and provided critically important feedback throughout the method refinement and writing process, we cannot thank you enough. In particular, we are deeply grateful to the following supervisors and trainees who tested exercises and/or provided invaluable feedback:

- Jennifer Oswald, Matteo Bugatti, Carly Schwartzman, Brittany King, and Adela Scharff at University at Albany, State University of New York

- Dong Xie, Kristina Ray, and Savannah Nolan at University of Central Arkansas, Conway

- Kim de Jong and Anne D. Krause-Utz at Leiden University, Leiden, The Netherlands

- Angelo Compare at University of Bergamo, Bergamo, Italy

- Jacqueline Persons at Oakland Cognitive Behavior Therapy Center, Oakland, California

- Garret G. Zieve at University of California, Berkeley

- Elon Gersh at University of Melbourne, Melbourne, Australia

- Nathan Castle, Meghan Odgers, and Ashley Bentley at Psychology Outcomes Pty Ltd, Melbourne, Australia

- Jeremy Ray, Tove Lindström, and Christian Grönvall at Gothenburg University, Gothenburg, Sweden

- Isabel Basto at University Institute of Maia-ISMAI, Maia, Portugal, and University of Porto, Porto, Portugal

- Christopher R. Martell, Heather Muir, Parker Longwell, Sungha Kang, Sherry Woods, Albert Lo, Minji Lee, Clara Defontes, Eleni Kapoulea, Averi Gaines, and Katie Gonzalez at University of Massachusetts, Amherst

Overview and Instructions

In Part I, we provide an overview of deliberate practice, including how it can be integrated into clinical training programs for cognitive behavioral therapy (CBT), and instructions for performing the deliberate practice exercises in Part II. **We encourage both trainers and trainees to read both Chapters 1 and 2 before performing the deliberate practice exercises for the first time.**

Chapter 1 provides a foundation for the rest of the book by introducing important concepts related to deliberate practice and its role in psychotherapy training more broadly and CBT training more specifically. We review the three broad categories of CBT skills—structural skills, general problem-focused skills, and what we term *flexibility within fidelity*—that are covered by the deliberate practice exercises in Part II. We also individually review the 10 skills from these exercises.

Chapter 2 lays out the basic, most essential instructions for performing the CBT deliberate practice exercises in Part II. They are designed to be quick and simple and provide you with just enough information to get started without being overwhelmed by too much information. Chapter 3 in Part III provides more in-depth guidance, which we encourage you to read once you are comfortable with the basic instructions in Chapter 2.

Introduction and Overview of Deliberate Practice and Cognitive Behavioral Therapy

The metaphor of a "toolbox" is often used when describing the techniques available to a psychotherapist. Among the systems of psychotherapy, this metaphor may be most apt for cognitive behavioral therapies (CBTs), as technical factors have been, historically, the primary focus. Indeed, there is an inherent technical eclecticism to CBT. As a clinician, it is reassuring to know that one is working with a relatively large toolbox that holds a diverse set of tools. As a trainee, it is exciting to learn and think about selecting and applying these tools with one's clients.

The learning curve is steep in clinical training. One is rapidly exposed to a wide variety of technical components and principles, largely in the context of assigned readings and discussions. Although transdiagnostic CBT models have emerged in recent decades (Sauer-Zavala et al., 2017), discrete interventions and treatment packages often also remain connected to specific *Diagnostic and Statistical Manual of Mental Disorders* (American Psychiatric Association, 2013) diagnoses. For example, it isn't just learning about exposure; it is learning about exposure for panic disorder, and social anxiety disorder, and obsessive–compulsive disorder, and so on. In other words, trainees are tasked with learning a wide variety of technical components, as well as the decision guidelines for when or when not to apply those components. Rather early in the training process, in most cases, trainees begin sitting across from real clients. In our own graduate training, the expectation was that we would continuously carry a minimum individual psychotherapy caseload of three weekly clients. Outside of a more dedicated clinical assistant position, it was rare for even a more advanced student to carry a weekly caseload of more than five individual clients. Since completing our graduate education, we have observed that this is a relatively common scenario in PhD programs.

Something rather obvious about the typical training scenario did not consciously dawn on us until we were faculty members who supervised doctoral students. That is, training based on work performance alone means rarely—and in numerous cases never—using many of the tools in the toolbox, with there being even fewer opportunities to use similar tools with different types of clients. Despite the best intentions

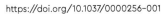

https://doi.org/10.1037/0000256-001

Deliberate Practice in Cognitive Behavioral Therapy, by J. F. Boswell and M. J. Constantino

of supervisors and training clinic directors, it can be extremely difficult to assign a variety (in terms of presenting problems and characteristics) of training cases. Even when some diversity of cases exists, there are only so many hours of doing psychotherapy in a given week or month during training. In addition, premature termination rates have been shown to be the highest in university-based training clinics, relative to other community treatment settings (Swift & Greenberg, 2012). Many clients do not stick around, which further limits opportunities to implement strategies that tend to coincide with more advanced stages of a course of CBT.

All of this understandably leaves trainees wondering if they will ever be able to practice implementing many of the tools in the vast toolbox they've been reading about, as well as questioning their competence when they've only been able to implement a given tool on one or two occasions. Many tools gather dust, so to speak, impeding skill development, which requires experience with actual selection and implementation of the tools.

Working with clients is critical; however, in our view, such work performance alone is insufficient to develop a broad and deep set of skills. What is missing are opportunities for behavioral rehearsal with targeted performance assessment and feedback. Use of deliberate practice methods during our training would have facilitated a greater frequency and variety of tool implementation opportunities for us. Deliberate practice methods hold promise for addressing certain gaps in training and professional development through a focus on the rehearsal of discrete skills in any or all of the potentially relevant simulated environments for a psychotherapist (trainee or otherwise). Although it is not a substitute for work performance with real clients, deliberate practice increases one's exposure to the tools in the toolbox. For example, a trainee is not necessarily dependent upon being assigned just the right client to begin developing competence in the evidence-based strategies they have been introduced to in their coursework or in guidebooks and manuals. Similar to other types of parallel processes in psychotherapy, as trainers, supervisors, and clinicians, we are excited about the emergence of deliberate practice in our own training toolboxes.

Overview of the Deliberate Practice Exercises

The main focus of the book is a series of 12 exercises that have been thoroughly tested and modified based on feedback from CBT trainers and trainees. The first 10 exercises each represents an essential CBT skill. The last two exercises are more comprehensive, consisting of annotated CBT transcripts and improvised mock therapy sessions that teach practitioners how to integrate some or all of these skills into more expansive clinical scenarios. Table 1.1 presents the 10 skills that are covered in these exercises.

Throughout all of the exercises, trainees work in pairs under the guidance of a supervisor and role-play as a client and a therapist, switching back and forth between the two roles. Each of the 10 skill-focused exercises consists of multiple client statements grouped by difficulty—beginner, intermediate, and advanced—that calls for that specific skill. Trainees are asked to read through and absorb the description of the skill, its criteria, and some examples of its implementation. The trainee playing the client then reads the statements, which present possible problems and emotional states, or client markers. The trainee playing the therapist then responds in a way that demonstrates the appropriate skill. Trainee therapists will have the option of practicing a response using the one supplied in the exercise or immediately improvising and supplying their own.

After each client statement and therapist response couplet is practiced several times, the trainees will stop to receive feedback from the supervisor. Guided by the

TABLE 1.1. The 10 Cognitive Behavioral Therapy Skills Presented in the Deliberate Practice Exercises

Beginner Skills	Intermediate Skills	Advanced Skills
1. Explaining the treatment rationale for cognitive behavioral therapy 2. Establishing goals 3. Negotiating a session agenda 4. Assigning and reviewing between-session activities	5. Working with cognitions 6. Working with behaviors 7. Working with emotions	8. Adherence flexibility 9. Responding to therapeutic alliance ruptures 10. Responding to client resistance

supervisor, the trainees will be instructed to try statement–response couplets several times, working their way down the list. In consultation with the supervisor, trainees will go through the exercises, starting with the least challenging and moving through to more advanced levels. The triad (supervisor–client–therapist) will have the opportunity to discuss whether exercises present too much or too little challenge and adjust up or down depending on the assessment. Some exercises provide optional modifications so that trainees role-playing as clients can improvise based on personal experience, rather than using a scripted statement.

Trainees, in consultation with supervisors, can decide which skills they wish to work on and for how long. On the basis of our testing experience, we have found that practice sessions should last about 1 to 1.25 hours to receive maximum benefit. After this, trainees become saturated and need a break.

Ideally, CBT learners will both gain confidence and achieve competence through practicing these exercises. Competence is defined here as the ability to perform a CBT skill in a manner that is flexible and responsive to the client. Skills have been chosen that are considered essential to CBT or that practitioners often find challenging to implement.

The skills identified in this book are not comprehensive in the sense of representing all of the tools in the CBT toolbox. Rather, the book covers many of the important core skills of CBT, some of which will present particular challenges for trainees. Indeed, when selecting the skills, we were guided by our perceptions of essential skills for competent CBT practice and the skills that trainees, particularly novice trainees, have trouble applying with real clients. We also provide a short history of CBT and a brief description of the deliberate practice methodology to explain how we have arrived at the union between them.

The Goals of This Book

The primary goal of this book is to help trainees achieve competence in core CBT skills. Therefore, the expression of that skill or competency may look somewhat different across clients or even within a session with the same client.

The CBT deliberate practice exercises are designed to achieve the following:

1. Help therapists develop the ability to apply CBT skills in a range of clinical situations.

2. Move the CBT skills into procedural memory (Squire, 2004) so that therapists can access them even when they are tired, stressed, overwhelmed, or discouraged.

3. Provide therapists in training with an opportunity to exercise the particular CBT skill using a style and language that is congruent with who they are.

4. Provide the opportunity to use the CBT skills in response to varying client statements and affect. This is designed to build confidence to adopt skills in a broad range of circumstances within different client contexts.

5. Provide therapists in training with many opportunities to "fail" and then correct their "failed" CBT response on the basis of feedback. This helps build confidence and persistence.

6. Help trainees discover their own personal learning style so they can continue their professional development long after their formal training is concluded.

Who Can Benefit From This Book?

This book is designed to be used in multiple contexts, including in graduate-level courses, supervision, postgraduate training, and continuing education programs. It assumes the following:

1. The trainer is knowledgeable about and competent in CBT.

2. The trainer is able to provide good demonstrations of how to use CBT skills across a range of therapeutic situations, via role-play or the many psychotherapy video examples available (see, e.g., J. Beck, 2006; Dobson, 2011; Newman, 2016; Olatunji, 2011; Persons, 2007).

3. The trainer is able to provide feedback to students regarding how to craft or improve their application of CBT skills.

4. Trainees will have accompanying reading, such as books and articles, that explain the theory, research, and rationale of CBT and each particular skill. Recommended reading for each skill is provided in the sample syllabus (Appendix C).

The exercises covered in this book were piloted in 16 trainings sites from across four continents (North America, Europe, Australia, and Asia). Some training sites chose to translate the exercises into their native language to adapt them for use with their trainees. This book is designed for trainers and trainees from different cultural backgrounds worldwide.

This book is also designed for those who are training at all career stages, from beginning trainees, including those who have never worked with real clients, to seasoned therapists. All exercises feature guidance for assessing and adjusting the difficulty to target precisely the needs of each individual learner. The term *trainee* in this book is used broadly, referring to anyone in the field of professional mental health who is endeavoring to acquire CBT psychotherapy skills.

Deliberate Practice in Psychotherapy Training

How does one become an expert in their professional field? What is trainable, and what is simply beyond our reach, due to innate or uncontrollable factors? Questions such as these touch on our fascination with expert performers and their development.

A mixture of awe, admiration, and even confusion surround people such as Mozart, Leonardo da Vinci, or more contemporary top performers such as basketball legend LeBron James and chess virtuoso Garry Kasparov. What accounts for their consistently superior professional results? Evidence suggests that the amount of time and the quality of time spent on a particular type of training are key factors in developing expertise in virtually all domains. "Deliberate practice" is an evidence-based method that can improve performance in an effective and reliable manner.

The concept of deliberate practice has its origins in a classic study by K. Anders Ericsson and colleagues (1993). They found that the amount of time practicing a skill and the quality of the time spent doing so were key factors predicting mastery and acquisition. They identified five key activities in learning and mastering skills: (a) observing one's own work, (b) getting expert feedback, (c) setting small incremental learning goals just beyond the performer's ability, (d) engaging in repetitive behavioral rehearsal of specific skills, and (e) continuously assessing performance. Ericsson and his colleagues termed this process "deliberate practice," a cyclical process that is illustrated in Figure 1.1.

Research has shown that lengthy engagement in deliberate practice is associated with expert performance across a variety of professional fields, such as medicine, sports, music, chess, computer programming, and mathematics (Ericsson et al., 2018). People may associate deliberate practice with the widely known "10,000-hour rule," popularized by Malcolm Gladwell in his 2008 book *Outliers*. Although a useful heuristic, Gladwell's work has perpetuated two misunderstandings. First, that 10,000 is the number of deliberate practice hours that everyone needs to attain expertise, no matter the domain. In fact, there can be considerable variability in how many hours are required (Ericsson & Pool, 2016).

The second misunderstanding is that engagement in 10,000 hours of work performance will invariably lead one to become an expert in that domain. This misunderstanding

FIGURE 1.1. Cycle of Deliberate Practice

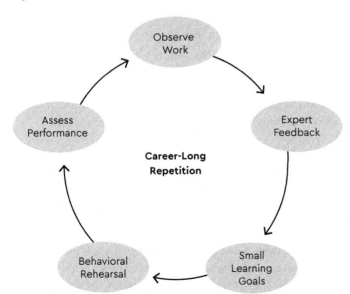

Note. Reprinted from *Deliberate Practice in Emotion-Focused Therapy* (p. 7), by R. N. Goldman, A. Vaz, and T. Rousmaniere, 2021, American Psychological Association (https://doi.org/10.1037/0000227-000). Copyright 2021 by the American Psychological Association.

holds considerable significance for the field of psychotherapy, where hours of work experience with clients has traditionally been used as a measure of proficiency (Rousmaniere, 2016). But, in fact, we know that amount of experience alone does not predict therapist effectiveness (Goldberg, Babins-Wagner, et al., 2016; Goldberg, Rousmaniere, et al., 2016). It may be that the *quality* of deliberate practice is a key factor.

Psychotherapy scholars, recognizing the value of deliberate practice in other fields, have recently called for this method to be incorporated into training for mental health professionals (e.g., Bailey & Ogles, 2019; Hill et al., 2020; Rousmaniere et al., 2017; Taylor & Neimeyer, 2017; Tracey et al., 2015). There are, though, good reasons to question analogies made between psychotherapy and other professional fields, like sports or music, because by comparison, psychotherapy is so complex and free-form. Sports have clearly defined goals, and classical music follows a written score. In contrast, the goals of psychotherapy shift with the unique presentation of each client at each session. Therapists do not have the luxury of following a score.

Instead, good psychotherapy is more like improvisational jazz (Noa Kageyama, cited in Rousmaniere, 2016). In jazz improvisations, a complex mixture of group collaboration, creativity, and interaction is coconstructed among band members. Like psychotherapy, no two jazz improvisations are identical. However, improvisations are not a random collection of notes. They are grounded in a comprehensive theoretical understanding and technical proficiency that is only developed through continuous deliberate practice. For example, prominent jazz instructor Jerry Coker (1990) listed 18 different skill areas that students must master, each of which has multiple discrete skills, including tone quality, intervals, chord arpeggios, scales, patterns, and licks. In this sense, more creative and artful improvisations are actually a reflection of a previous commitment to repetitive skill practice and acquisition. As legendary jazz musician Miles Davis put it, "You have to play a long time to be able to play like yourself."

The main idea that we would like to stress here is that we want deliberate practice to help therapists using CBT skills to become themselves. The goal is to learn the skills so that you have them on hand when you want them. Practice the skills to make them your own. Incorporate those aspects that feel right for you. Ongoing and effortful deliberate practice should not be an impediment to flexibility and creativity. Ideally, it should enhance it. We recognize and celebrate that psychotherapy is an ever-shifting encounter and by no means want it to become or feel formulaic. Strong CBT therapists mix an eloquent integration of previously acquired skills with properly attuned flexibility. The core CBT responses provided are meant as templates or possibilities rather than "answers." Please interpret and apply them as you see fit, in a way that makes sense to you and, most important, to your individual clients. We encourage flexible and improvisational play.

Simulation-Based Mastery Learning

Deliberate practice uses simulation-based mastery learning (Ericsson, 2004; McGaghie et al., 2014). That is, the stimulus material for training consists of "contrived social situations that mimic problems, events, or conditions that arise in professional encounters" (McGaghie et al., 2014, p. 375). A key component of this approach is that the stimuli being used in training are sufficiently similar to the real-world experiences. This facilitates *state-dependent learning*, in which professionals acquire skills in the same psychological environment where they will have to perform the skills (R. P. Fisher & Craik, 1977; Smith, 1979). For example, pilots train with flight simulators that present mechanical failures and dangerous weather conditions, and surgeons practice with surgical simulators that present medical complications. Training in simulations with challenging stimuli increases professionals' capacity to perform effectively under stress. For the psychotherapy training exercises in this book, the "simulators" are typical client statements that might actually be presented in the course of therapy sessions and call on the use of the particular skill.

Declarative Versus Procedural Knowledge

Declarative knowledge is what a person can understand, write, or speak about. It often refers to factual information that can be consciously recalled through memory and is often acquired relatively quickly. In contrast, procedural learning is implicit in memory, and "usually requires *repetition of an activity*, and associated learning is demonstrated through *improved task performance*" (Koziol & Budding, 2012, p. 2694, emphasis added). *Procedural knowledge* is what a person can perform, especially under stress (Squire, 2004). There can be a wide difference between their declarative and procedural knowledge. For example, an "armchair quarterback" is a person who understands and talks about athletics well but would have trouble performing it at a professional ability. Likewise, most dance, music, or theater critics have a very high ability to write about their subjects but would be flummoxed if asked to perform them.

In CBT training, the gap between declarative and procedural knowledge appears when a trainee or therapist is capable of reciting the textbook rationale for and implementation "nuts and bolts" of exposure, yet the actual implementation begins to fall to pieces when working with a highly anxious or resistant client in the moment. **The sweet spot for deliberate practice is the gap between declarative and procedural knowledge.** In other words, effortful practice should target those skills that the trainee could write a good paper about but would have trouble actually performing with a real client. We start with declarative knowledge, learning skills theoretically and observing others perform them. Once learned, with the help of deliberate practice, we work toward the development of procedural learning, with the aim of therapists having "automatic" access to each of the skills that they can draw on when necessary.

Let us turn to a little theoretical background on CBT (declarative knowledge) to help contextualize the skills of the book and how they fit into the greater training model.

Cognitive Behavioral Therapy

CBT is an umbrella for treatments that involve behavioral therapy theory and techniques, cognitive therapy theory and techniques, or a combination of these. Behavior therapy developed from basic and applied research on learning theory. Clinical applications followed lab-based experimentation with animals (e.g., Wolpe, 1952). The so-called cognitive revolution followed, with a focus on cognition as the key mediating factor to explain behavior (A. T. Beck, 1976; A. Ellis, 1962; Goldfried & Davison, 1976; Miechenbaum, 1977). Since the introduction of these clinical frameworks, and their often-inherent integration to some degree, considerable research has focused on understanding the etiology and maintenance of mental health problems through the lens of behavioral/ learning and cognitive theory (Barlow, 2008).

CBT Theory

Unsurprisingly, cognitive and behavioral (C/B) theories emphasize the importance of associations among cognitions, behaviors, and emotions. Psychopathology is understood to represent learned schemes (or schemata) that comprise these components and produce less adaptive behaviors and suffering (e.g., depression, anxiety; Barlow, 2008). Most CBT interventions aim to interrupt or modify maladaptive behavioral, cognitive, emotional, and physiological processes or alter the pathological beliefs, emotions, and behaviors that are involved in the maintenance of problem behaviors (Boswell et al., 2011).

Early behavioral theories (e.g., Mowrer, 1939; Watson & Raynor, 1920) posited that psychopathology (understood as less adaptive behaviors) could be explained through classical and operant conditioning principles. Although still connected with learning theory, cognitive theories focused on understanding and elaborating the construct of cognitive schema. Problems, such as major depressive disorder, were explained by negative, rigid cognitive schemata, which prime individuals to interpret experience through a negative, rigid lens. Behavior therapy, therefore, focuses on counterconditioning and manipulating contingencies; cognitive therapy, therefore, focuses on restructuring rigid, dysfunctional interpretations and negative core beliefs (A. T. Beck, 1976). Within the C/B paradigm, theories progressed to create diagnosis-specific models that attempted to explain core symptom clusters through the interaction of particular cognitive, behavioral, and physiological patterns (Barlow, 2008; Clark, 1986).

The empirical tradition of CBT can be observed in the unyielding attempts to test and refine C/B theories. Many such updates include contemporary knowledge of familiar foundational elements and processes, such as extinction (Craske et al., 2008), as well as findings from emotion science (Barlow, 2002; Barlow et al., 2004; Boswell, 2013; Power & Dalgleish, 2008). The empirical status of C/B theories is robust and still actively developing, based on accumulating findings from diverse areas of basic psychology, experimental psychopathology, and applied clinical research.

CBT Process

Although CBT is considered technique-focused, it is important to emphasize the importance of the working alliance in this treatment approach. The importance of developing and maintaining a positive CBT working relationship has been acknowledged explicitly for many decades (A. T. Beck et al., 1979; Foa et al., 1983). Research has also demonstrated that the quality of the working alliance in CBT is quite positive (Fluckiger et al., 2018; Keijsers et al., 2000). Interpersonally, a CBT therapist stance is genuine, empathic, and collaborative (Castonguay et al., 2011). In general, the CBT therapist style is more active and directive, and this makes transparency important; specifically, the CBT therapist provides a clear framework and set of expectations for the focus of the treatment and what will take place within and across sessions. In terms of collaboration, the stance of "collaborative empiricism" is a defining feature, in which the CBT therapist works with the client to develop a scientific attitude toward experience and new learning. Although CBT is less likely to view the quality of the working alliance as a *primary* mechanism of change in therapy, the working alliance is indeed important in CBT and is seen as a critical facilitative factor (Castonguay et al., 2011).

Schemata and fear structures (Foa & Kozak, 1986) are assumed to comprise dynamically interacting information process systems related to behavior, physical sensations, cognitions, and emotions. Any or all of these systems can be a target of treatment, and it is generally assumed that changes in one component of experience will affect changes in others (e.g., behavioral interventions can promote cognitive change;

Goldfried & Davison, 1976). Consistent with its behavioral roots, an understanding of the environment or context in which less adaptive behaviors and experiences occur is critical. The pattern of responses traces the environment and contextualized antecedents, to the mediating cognitions (appraisals and beliefs), and then the behavioral responses. Avoidance behaviors (e.g., fleeing a situation at the onset of panic attack symptoms), presumed to serve a negative reinforcement function, are of particular interest. The process of developing a working model of such patterns is commonly referred to as a functional analysis of behavior. Once the unique pattern has been "diagnosed," most contemporary CBT approaches involve inviting the client to enter or attend to the problematic situation, while evoking and experiencing relevant emotions (e.g., anxiety or fear; to facilitate "hot cognitions" or "emotional processing"; e.g., Barlow et al., 2017), and eliminating avoidance behavior. This more exposure-focused work is often done in conjunction with cognitive appraisal and reappraisal strategies (reevaluating the thoughts that occurred in the situation), as well as brainstorming alternative behaviors (e.g., exposure to feared experience and conversely, avoiding avoidance).

CBT approaches emphasize learning through experience and the therapist works to create opportunities for corrective learning experiences (see Castonguay & Hill, 2012). The nature of the corrective learning might vary as a function of the specific CBT protocol. Behaviorally oriented therapists will emphasize exposure and the elimination of avoidance (behavioral, cognitive, emotional); cognitive therapists will emphasize testing predictions and thoughts with cognitive reappraisal and behavioral experiments to test negative expectancies (e.g., Did the imagined worst-case scenario actually happen?). In practice, there is considerable overlap in terms of what the therapist does and how change is assumed to occur, hence the use of the broader label of CBT. For example, counterconditioning is likely to occur in both exposure and behavioral experiments, as are violations of expectancies (Craske et al., 2008).

Although variability exists among specific CBT protocols, most forms of CBT involve core components, such as psychoeducation, experience monitoring, cognitive reappraisal, exposure, and homework assignments. The type of exposure (e.g., in vivo vs. imaginal) and use of other commonly used strategies, such as behavioral activation, will depend more on the client and the nature of the presenting problem. Returning to the toolbox metaphor, the selection of specific techniques is tailored to the client. Decisions are guided by the working case formulation (functional analysis), with particular attention to the maintaining factors (A. J. Fisher & Boswell, 2016). The importance of an individualized case formulation should be emphasized. The use of treatment manuals, which are commonly associated with the CBT tradition, has been critiqued because of the perception that manuals promote a rigidly standardized, one-size-fits-all approach to treatment. Manuals can provide a coherent structure and serve as a useful guide, yet CBT techniques are intended to be applied idiographically to the individual client.

It has become somewhat cliché, but it is very much the case that the CBT approach promotes the client's capacity to be their own therapist. Consequently, it is important for the client to be able to apply the concepts and skills that they have learned within the session (and with the therapist) in their day-to-day lives outside of therapy. In addition, the generalizability of in-session learning is potentially limited if opportunities for application in varied routine contexts does not occur. Practice in real-world environments is essential, and this underscores the importance of between-session activities (i.e., homework). Research has demonstrated a significant positive association between the use of homework and outcome in CBT (Kazantzis et al., 2016, 2000). As we stated elsewhere (Boswell et al., 2011),

> the use of homework in CBT is similar to that of learning a new language. One needs to immerse oneself in the language if one is to be fluent enough to use it in difficult situations. Although the therapy sessions may provide the basics of grammar and vocabulary for the language, only by using it in every opportunity can one truly master it and be able to use it independently even long after treatment. (p. 107)

The CBT paradigm has accumulated significant empirical support over the past 60-plus years. Although varied in emphasis (e.g., behavioral, cognitive, or a combination) and the specific constellation of techniques, the extant evidence supports the use of CBT for a wide spectrum of presenting problems (Nathan & Gorman, 2007). There also remains a constant effort toward evaluating what is working within CBT and how it can be improved. To that end, we conclude this section by providing some additional context for the skills addressed in this book.

To remain consistent with its epistemological roots, it is only natural for CBT to evolve in response to theoretical, empirical, and practical developments. The development and testing of transdiagnostic CBT approaches is one example. Although most of the core elements of "traditional" CBT protocols are integrated into transdiagnostic approaches, some elements are arguably less traditional and the whole is greater than, or at least somewhat different from, the sum of its parts. For example, mindfulness strategies have been integrated into more recently developed CBT protocols. In some instances, mindfulness theory and practice is more seamlessly integrated into a broadly CBT oriented model, such as with dialectical behavioral therapy (Linehan, 1993). In other instances, mindfulness can be treated as an "add-on" component or module to an otherwise standard CBT protocol. More recently, researchers have developed and tested the integration of motivational interviewing strategies in CBT (Westra et al., 2016). This work has raised awareness of constructs that have historically received less attention in CBT, such as client resistance and change ambivalence, and the therapist's responsive use of client-centered stances and strategies.

In addition, the importance of the working alliance has received more explicit and nuanced attention from CBT researchers and clinicians in recent years. In fact, many of the developments in alliance-rupture repair work and alliance-focused training have taken place within the context of CBT (Eubanks et al., 2018). Finally, Samoilov and Goldfried (2000) argued for the importance of emotion in CBT and suggested that the 2000s would be the decade of emotion for this orientation. In hindsight, this was quite prescient, as CBT has become more explicitly emotion focused in recent decades. A prime example is the Unified Protocol for Treatment of Emotional Disorders (UP; Barlow et al., 2011, 2017). The UP is transdiagnostic, integrates mindfulness, adopts a modular approach to treatment (including a module dedicated to motivation enhancement), and focuses heavily on emotion.

This is not intended to be an exhaustive list or breakdown of contemporary versions or elements of CBT. Rather, these examples are intended to provide context for the remainder of this book. Although this book is very much intended to be, at its core, CBT, "this is not your grandparents' CBT." We have adopted a contemporary CBT "spirit" that is emotion focused and does not shy away from terms like resistance, ambivalence, responsiveness, and the alliance. We view these concepts and elements as ultimately compatible with the CBT paradigm, and we view them as pathways for enhancing its impact.

Deliberate practice methods are particularly well-suited to the CBT paradigm, so developments in this area are exciting. Perhaps more so than any other system of psychotherapy, CBT scholars and practitioners have worked to distill and codify technical skills and associated competence domains. The eclectic nature of this paradigm's technical repertoire also fits a learning approach that prioritizes breaking things down into digestible, meaningful elements (of course, ultimately in a cohesive manner that is consistent with the treatment rationale and plan). The elemental nature of a specific skill falls nicely in line with core features of deliberate practice, such as setting incremental goals that are within one's zone of proximal development and engaging in repetitive behavioral rehearsal. These are common features of any learning process, and CBT clinicians need look no farther than their typical outpatient session to underscore this point. Therapists don't throw the CBT-based kitchen sink at a client during session one, assign remodeling the kitchen as homework, and then move on to refinish the bathroom the next week. Rather, concepts and skills are broken down into digestible units, as repetition promotes and strengthens learning. Moreover, adjustments to intensity and complexity are made for a given client based on careful observation and feedback. The same principles can be applied to therapist training, making it an excellent match for deliberate practice methods.

From a different perspective, one can contrast deliberate practice methods with common training approaches. To be clear, we do not view different approaches to learning CBT as mutually exclusive; rather, we view them as complementary. For example, even with a solid foundation in CBT coursework and application, speaking from personal experience, it can be quite difficult to "learn" CBT from treatment manuals. I (JFB) am admittedly fond of treatment manuals and use them extensively. Most manuals are written first to be applied with actual clients; they are not written first to train therapists, particularly novice therapists (this is not intended to be a critique because our sense is that this statement would not be viewed as controversial by manual developers). However, our experience is that manuals are often used as a core training tool and that the testing and trial-and-error phase of applying the elements of the manual occurs with actual clients. The deliberate practice approach offers a paradigm for taking these same elements and applying them in training simulations that allow for repetition, feedback, and adjustments. Specifically related to this book, there are also opportunities to practice how to respond when things do not go perfectly as planned, which is often the case, outside of "primetime" (see Chapter 3).

Cognitive Behavioral Skills in Deliberate Practice

We have thus far provided a brief introduction to CBT and highlighted how deliberate practice methods are particularly well-suited to the CBT paradigm. In the following sections, we describe the categorization of different CBT skills and outline the skills that will be the focus of the deliberate practice exercises in this book. In addition, we address the importance of basic communication features in CBT, such as emotional expression and nonverbal behavior.

Categorizing CBT Skills

Under the broad label of CBT technical factors, previous work has suggested that skills can be divided into different categories. In cognitive therapy for depression, DeRubeis and Feeley (1990; Feeley et al., 1999), distinguished between *concrete* and *abstract* cognitive therapy features. Concrete features included, but were not limited to, setting and following an agenda, assigning and reviewing homework, labeling cognitive errors, examining evidence for beliefs, and asking clients to self-monitor and record thoughts. Abstract features included, but were not limited to, addressing the relation between thoughts and feelings, cognitive therapy rationale, exploring underlying assumptions, and negotiating the content of the session. These features were extracted from the Collaborative Study Psychotherapy Rating Scale (CSPRS; Hollon et al., 1988), which was designed to distinguish between sessions of cognitive therapy and alternative psychotherapy models.

Similar assessments of CBT adherence and competence provided additional guidance. Muse and McManus (2013) identified more than 60 measures of CBT fidelity in their comprehensive literature review. By far, the most commonly used measure was the Cognitive Therapy Rating Scale (CTRS; Young & Beck, 1980). With this measure, there is some precedence for dividing skills categories into (a) general therapy skills (e.g., interpersonal effectiveness/collaboration) and (b) CBT-specific skills (e.g., focusing on key cognitions and behaviors, cognitive conceptualization). Vallis et al. (1986) found support for a general competence factor yet also observed a second factor that seemed more related to session "structure," such as setting an agenda, time and session management, and assigning and reviewing homework assignments.

Ultimately, theory and research have failed to deliver a universally agreed on factor model for the CTRS, yet more recent work indicates that a single, global cognitive therapy competence factor is the best fit for examining cognitive therapy competence at the between-therapist level, which is arguably most relevant for training and certification efforts (Goldberg et al., 2020).

Despite these mixed findings, we used previous competence assessment work to guide our skill selection and categorization, while considering additional factors. For example, although the CTRS has been used extensively in both CT and CBT research, practice, and training, it was initially developed for CT and the items, understandably, more directly align with this specific approach. Most of the existing CBT fidelity measures were developed specifically for CT, BT, or CBT, and focus on a particular diagnosis or a set of diagnoses within the same general class (e.g., anxiety disorders). To enhance generalizability, our goals were to focus on skills that spanned CT, BT, and CBT (both more traditional and contemporary styles), and to adopt a transdiagnostic approach.

Ultimately, we were conceptually inclined toward a distinction among (a) beginner foundational/structural CBT skills, (b) intermediate general problem-focused CBT skills, and (c) advanced flexibility within CBT fidelity-oriented skills (Kendall et al., 2008). With this in mind, we considered (a) explaining the treatment rationale for CBT, (b) establishing treatment goals, (c) negotiating a session agenda, and (d) assigning and reviewing between-session activities (i.e., homework) to be structural skills. These structural skills are nearly universally included in measures of CBT fidelity in controlled trials and training and certification activities.

In turn, we considered (a) working with cognitions, (b) working with behaviors, and (c) working with emotions to be general problem-focused CBT skills. You will likely notice that these skills are framed around the *focus* of the therapist rather than a specific technique. For the purposes of this book, these skill labels are intentionally broader than specific skills, such as exposure, Socratic dialogue, relaxation training, or mindfulness. It is notable that within the deliberate practice approach, even these specific skills are likely too broad. For example, "doing an exposure" is a rather complex intervention. It includes, among other features, providing a rationale, establishing a hierarchy, delineating expectancies, repeated implementation of stimuli, monitoring, and debriefing. We describe each of these skill exercises (working with cognitions, working with behaviors, and working with emotions) in more detail later. We note here, however, that the diversity of circumstances to implement more specific skills (e.g., guided discovery) is represented in the diversity of client stimuli in each of the exercises in this book. That is, rather than create a separate exercise for exposure therapy, many of the stimuli in the working with behaviors exercise call for an exposure-oriented response, in addition to other types of behaviorally oriented responses (e.g., stimulus control, activity scheduling).

Our tongue-in-cheek description of the third category of skills in this book, flexibility within fidelity (all considered to be advanced skills), is what to do when CBT starts going off the rails. More specifically, the skills within this category focus on CBT implementation in the face of impasses and implementation roadblocks and include (a) implementing adherence flexibility, (b) responding to therapeutic alliance ruptures, and (c) responding to client resistance. The ultimate focus of these skills is to help trainees learn how to maintain a consistent, collaborative CBT framework with clients in the face of difficulties, while exercising flexibility and tailored responsiveness that meets the clients where they are in the session or a given treatment.

The CBT Skills Presented in Exercises 1 Through 10

This section briefly describes the skills presented in the deliberate practice exercises and highlights any important takeaways for each skill that will be helpful for trainers and trainees to keep in mind. The skills are grouped by difficulty (beginner, intermediate, and advanced), and their order matches the order of the exercises in Part II.

Beginner Skills

Exercise 1: Explaining the Treatment Rationale for Cognitive Behavioral Therapy. Explaining the rationale for CBT is an essential skill that helps get therapy off on the right foot (King & Boswell, 2019). In our experience, after some basic coursework in CBT theory and application, trainees are able to give a nice textbook explanation of the CBT model and rationale. It is quite another thing to provide a convincing treatment rationale when interacting with an actual client. Importantly, the skill of providing a rationale is not limited to the first session with a client; therapists should be sensitive to rationale throughout therapy, in order to help facilitate a collaborative therapeutic relationship and evolving treatment plan (Coyne et al., 2019).

Although the development of a collaborative spirit is critical, early sessions are a bit more didactic. This includes a description of the broad CBT model and an initial working formulation from this perspective, which leads to a preliminary description and discussion of the treatment tasks and goals. The focus on treatment tasks includes the basic structure of the treatment session(s)—what the client and therapist's time together will look like—for example, setting up the expectation that sessions will begin by setting an agenda (in collaboration with the client). Establishing a rationale and goal-oriented framework in the first session(s) capitalizes on the importance of perceived treatment credibility, as well as the facilitation of task and positive treatment outcome expectancies.

Therapists can use this skill unprompted or in response to client inquiries about how CBT works, what methods CBT therapists use, and what will happen in the sessions. Like much of CBT, explaining a treatment rationale is not a singular event; rather, it should be used as needed, perhaps especially when a client expresses confusion about, or doubt in, elements of the CBT model. Provision of a treatment rationale, establishing a clear framework, and appeals to research evidence are universal hallmarks of evidence-based CBT protocols. Findings from meta-analyses also highlight the importance of promoting clients' early positive treatment outcome expectancies (Constantino, Vîslă, et al., 2018) and perceptions of treatment credibility (Constantino, Coyne, et al., 2018) for treatment outcome.

Exercise 2: Establishing Goals. CBT is a goal-oriented approach. Establishing shared treatment goals and tasks early in treatment not only facilitates a positive working alliance and congruent expectancies (both of which can facilitate good outcomes), but also provides a personalized treatment roadmap. It is difficult to navigate the journey when one does not know the destination. Such navigation to long-term goals is aided by establishing short- and middle-term goals. In addition, some research has shown that early participant agreement on goals and tasks is particularly important for CBT outcome (Webb et al., 2011).

Although therapists should use this skill at the outset of CBT, similar to providing a rationale, attending to and negotiating goals and tasks is not a singular or solely early treatment event. Even if not explicitly addressed in a given session, goals and tasks are invariably in the background. Moreover, they might require close attention as treatment unfolds, such as when a client masters a skill and prefers to refocus on something else, or when progress has stalled or failed to develop. In addition, goal-setting is not a skill that the therapist unidirectionally "delivers"; rather, it is typically (and most usefully) a collaborative exercise. A big part of the skill is to negotiate with the client personalized CBT goals that they value, as well as a corresponding framework (personalized ratio-nale) and goal-consistent tasks.

Exercise 3: Negotiating a Session Agenda. Negotiating a session agenda is an essen-tial skill that helps get the session off on the right foot, clarifies expectations for the appointment, and fosters continued collaboration on specific goals and tasks. In addi-tion, some research has shown that techniques, such as agenda setting, are uniquely associated with symptom reduction in CBT (DeRubeis & Feeley, 1990).

Therapists should use this skill at the beginning of most CBT sessions. However, like much of CBT, setting a session agenda is not a singular event; rather, it is founda-tional to overall session and time management and requires attention at various points in a session. Moreover, it is typically (and most usefully) a collaborative exercise. The client's input on the agenda should be directly solicited. A big part of the skill is to negotiate with the client personalized CBT agendas that they value and includes goals that they are at least to some degree motivated to work toward in the moment. When agenda negotiations seem to be moving in a direction that is inconsistent with the established treatment framework and plan, therapists may need to rely on some of the more advanced skills covered in this book (see Exercises 8–10).

Exercise 4: Assigning and Reviewing Between-Session Activities. Between-session practice and activity (i.e., homework) is a core feature of CBT. Homework's importance has been researched relatively thoroughly and shown to be a significant predictor of outcome in CBT (Kazantzis et al., 2000, 2016). Between-session activities facilitate the corrective learning process—both in and outside of CBT sessions. Furthermore, work outside of the sessions assists with generalization and helping the client to become their own therapist. Although completing homework can certainly be challenging for clients, there is a general expectation that some form of homework be incorporated across most sessions. Thus, when socializing clients to CBT, setting this expectation and discussing any questions or concerns that the client has is important. In particular, therapists should emphasize how homework can help generalize the skills learned in, and the experiences of, therapy to daily life outside of the therapy appointment.

Given its ubiquity, we view assigning and reviewing homework as a beginner or "basic" skill. When following a typical session agenda, time is budgeted at the end of each session to collaboratively identify between-session activities, such as experience monitoring, behavioral experiments, exposures, or relevant readings. In turn, time is budgeted at the beginning of the subsequent session to review the previous session's assigned homework. It is also important to tailor assignments to the individual client.

Intermediate Skills

Exercise 5: Working With Cognitions. As established, CBT involves a mix of C/B strategies. Even in more strictly behavioral treatment approaches, such as behavioral activation, cognitions remain important. Guided discovery is an essential process of cognitive work in which the therapist assists the clients in finding their own understandings of, and solutions to, personal concerns. To facilitate this process, CBT clinicians often use the cognitive method of Socratic questioning.

In our experience, it can be easier to first describe guided discovery (and Socratic questioning) by what it is not (or, at least, not intended to be). Guided discovery is not, for example, telling clients that their thinking is wrong or convincing them to change their beliefs. It is also not a series of "why" questions that imply a current problem or irrationality in thoughts, emotions, or behaviors. Rather, in the spirit of collaborative empiricism, guided discovery involves helping clients gather relevant information, examine it in different ways (without judgment from the therapist), and develop a personalized plan for what to do with it. In other words, the goal of working with cognitions is not to simply tell clients to think differently or point out flaws; rather, it is to teach clients a process for evaluating their own experience and determining subsequent actions based on this self-reflection. Consistent with more contemporary CBT perspectives on working with cognitions (e.g., Barlow et al., 2017), we view facilitating the client's cognitive flexibility as a central aim of working with cognitions.

In addition, because a mix of cognitive and behaviorally oriented strategies is common in most treatments, it is important for trainees and trainers to keep the context of the deliberate practice exercise in mind. Depending on the nature of the individual treatment, as well as the preferences and expectations of the client and therapist, the same client statement could conceivably be met with a cognitive-, behavior-, or emotion-focused therapist response—all remaining under the broad CBT umbrella. It is not, therefore, "wrong" for a trainee to focus instinctively on behavior when working on the cognitive skill exercise. However, we strongly encourage trainees and trainers to work within the skill of interest; that is, even if one's general preference or instinct is to focus on behaviors, it is important to prioritize a focus on cognitions when practicing the working with cognitions stimuli. The recognition that practicing such a narrow focus is more difficult for some trainees is important information; perhaps they are developing their style as a more behaviorally focused CBT therapist. That is great! Concomitantly, this means that these trainees need to build up their cognitive "muscle" in the interest of becoming a more well-rounded CBT therapist.

Exercise 6: Working With Behaviors. Even in more strictly cognitive treatment approaches, explicitly working with behaviors remains important (e.g., conduct of behavioral experiments). Behavioral work relies on principles of classical and operant conditioning, which translate to a relatively eclectic toolbox of strategies. Behavioral interventions can focus on antecedents, the behavioral repertoire itself (including skill deficits), contingencies, and consequences, depending on the nature of the presenting problem. Behavioral strategies can include exposure, stimulus control, activity scheduling, contingency management, and behavioral skill training, among others.

Selection of the appropriate behavioral target and intervention can vary greatly among clients, even within ostensibly similar presenting problem domains, thus requiring an idiographic approach. Given the need for an idiographic approach and the diversity of skills and strategies that can be placed under the behavioral umbrella, we are unable to address them all in this book. Rather, we focus on working with (or targeting) behaviors more broadly, as well as the application of learning principles to facilitate change processes more broadly.

Once again, it is important for trainees and trainers to keep the context of the specific deliberate practice exercise in mind. Depending on the nature of the individual treatment, as well as the preferences and expectations of the client and therapist, the same client statement could conceivably be met with a cognitive-, behavior-, or emotion-focused therapist response—all remaining under the broad CBT umbrella. It is not, therefore, "wrong" for a trainee to focus instinctively on cognition when working on the behavior skill exercise. However, we strongly encourage trainees and trainers to work within the skill of interest; that is, even if one's general preference or instinct is to focus on cognitions, it is important to prioritize a focus on behaviors when practicing the working with behaviors stimuli. The recognition that practicing such a narrow focus is more difficult for some trainees is important information; perhaps they are developing their style as a more cognitively focused CBT therapist. That is great! Concomitantly, this means that these trainees need to build up their behavior "muscle" in the interest of becoming a more well-rounded CBT therapist.

Exercise 7: Working With Emotions. A therapist's ability to evoke, tolerate, and work effectively with client emotions are critically important in CBT. Moreover, "working with" implies helping the client to tolerate their emotions and emotion-related distress, such as in the case of exposure. Exposure is a potent, yet often intense intervention, both for the client and therapist. In addition, beyond exposure-based interventions, contemporary CBT models attend explicitly to emotions in varied ways, often with a goal of reducing emotion-related avoidance (Barlow et al., 2017; Boswell, 2013). It may be more intuitive to think about this skill as focusing on helping clients work on their emotional experience and processing, yet the emotions serve both inter- and intrapersonal functions, and research demonstrates that both client and therapist emotional expression are associated with treatment outcome (Peluso & Freund, 2018).

As such, the decision to implement exposure or to work with emotions and address emotion avoidance in other ways is predicated on the therapist's skill of tolerating the inherent discomfort often affiliated with such foci. Difficulty with this skill can translate to the therapist maladaptively avoiding the use of this potentially potent intervention and/or reinforcing client avoidance and, thereby, maintaining the problem(s). Thus, practicing this skill can help therapists circumvent this fairly typical, understandable, and inadvertent negative reinforcement process.

Advanced Skills

Exercise 8: Adherence Flexibility. Although extant evidence fails to demonstrate a consistent, linear relationship between adherence and treatment outcome, there is both direct and indirect evidence for the importance of maintaining a coherent treatment framework (Boswell et al., 2010). Furthermore, among the wide variety of CBT techniques included in evidence-based treatments, the evidence supporting the importance of any specific technique is mixed (Cuijpers et al., 2019). There is some evidence that adherence aligns with the story of Goldilocks (McCarthy et al., 2016). The extreme ends of the adherence continuum appear to be problematic—that is, rigid adherence or haphazard eclecticism (or the absence of working from a coherent framework). The "just right" findings underscore the importance of flexibility within fidelity (Kendall et al., 2008). When considering flexible practice, others have made the distinction between fidelity-consistent and fidelity-inconsistent modifications to a specific treatment protocol. When following a CBT manual, for example, a therapist might adopt a technique that is not specifically included in the designed protocol, yet the adopted technique is still consistent with the broader CBT model (fidelity-consistent modification). Conversely, fidelity-inconsistent modifications represent the adoption of techniques that are inconsistent with the broader CBT model. Setting aside arguments that, on closer inspection, some techniques that initially appear to be unique to a particular model may not be (Castonguay, 2011), in this skill, we focus on what we would consider fidelity-consistent modification or flexibility. That is, responding in a flexible manner to the needs and circumstances of the individual client, while remaining anchored in the broad CBT model.

Exercise 9: Responding to Therapeutic Alliance Ruptures. Therapist flexibility and the ongoing tailoring of CBT to the specific client and context represents evidence-based practice in its most complex and fullest form. Complementing the skill of CBT fidelity-consistent modification and flexibility, there is also growing evidence that CBT is more effective when therapists fully, although temporarily, "depart" from standard CBT skills in the face of certain in-session process markers or moments (see Constantino et al., 2021). Depending on the marker, the therapist can use specific and evidence-informed CBT fidelity-inconsistent strategies until the salient (and often hindering) process has been addressed; such resolution would then precipitate a return to standard CBT. In this skill, we focus on the responsive use of *humanistic and interpersonal* skills to address alliance ruptures that may emerge in the client–therapist relationship during a course of CBT.

A quality therapeutic alliance is commonly and pantheoretically defined as comprising three interrelated components: (a) client and therapist agreement on treatment goals; (b) client and therapist agreement on the tasks that will be used to achieve those goals; and (c) a dyadic bond that the client and therapist experience as secure, warm, and friendly. Such relational qualities can wax and wane during therapy, especially considering the natural strains of therapeutic work or other dyadic misattunements that might rupture (in one participant, the other, or both) a sense of coordinated collaboration or close connection. When such ruptures occur, they can relate to maladaptive treatment processes and outcomes (Eubanks et al., 2018). Importantly, though, they can also represent potential change opportunities that, if handled skillfully, can be therapeutic. That is, rupture repair can be a therapy change mechanism that operates instead of, or alongside, the putative mechanisms of the treatment being delivered. In this case, rather than persist with CBT in the face of rupture markers, which might involve trying to convince the client of CBT's merits, research supports a contextual shift from CBT to a more humanistic and interpersonal stance and strategy.

To responsively apply such strategies first requires noticing markers of alliance rupture, which (when originating with the client) can be generally classified into two types. The first, *withdrawal markers*, represent the pursuit of relatedness at the expense of one's need for self-definition or assertion (i.e., being reluctant to confront because of fear of losing the relationship). The second, *confrontation markers*, represent the expression of self-definition at the expense of relatedness. Whatever the type, the marker represents an important message about the state of the relationship and treatment that a clinician would be wise to explore via the interpersonal strategy of metacommunication or bringing immediate awareness to bear on the relational process as it unfolds (Muran & Eubanks, 2020). Such temporary and contextual departure from CBT can be facilitative, both on its own as a corrective interpersonal experience and by restoring the working relationship to the point of returning to the CBT plan.

Exercise 10: Responding to Client Resistance. As noted, therapist flexibility and the ongoing tailoring of CBT to the specific client and context represents evidence-based practice in its complex, fullest form, including deviating from CBT when clinically indicated. For this departure skill, we focus on the responsive use of *client-centered* skills to address client *resistance* that may emerge during a course of CBT (Leahy, 2003).

Namely, research supports a contextual shift from CBT to motivational interviewing (MI) strategies and "spirit" when a client demonstrates resistance to the direction of the treatment or provider (e.g., Westra et al., 2016). Resistance, a regularly occurring clinical process, can stem from a few common precipitants. For example, it may reflect a client's diminishing belief in the personally relevant logic or efficacy of CBT, despite being motivated to reduce symptoms and improve functioning. Alternatively, resistance may be the manifestation of a client's understandable ambivalence about change and moving away from what is familiar (even if it is maladaptive). Such resistances can take different direct forms (e.g., homework noncompliance, explicitly disagreeing with the treatment rationale, criticizing the therapist) or indirect forms (e.g., missing sessions; in-session withdrawing, interrupting, or sidetracking), but the general experience is palpable client opposition to the current session agenda or general direction of treatment. Importantly, though, resistance is usually a valid client message that the treatment is misaligned with their ideas about improvement, that they are ambivalent about changing, that the therapeutic relationship is misattuned, or a combination of these. Whatever the reason, persisting with the current plan is unlikely to help, whereas engaging more client-centered, MI principles, precisely in this context, can be facilitative (see Westra, 2012; Westra & Constantino, 2019).

A Note About Vocal Tone, Facial Expression, and Body Posture

Among the overarching aims of CBT deliberate practice, the hope is that learners will develop the ability to apply skills in a range of clinical situations and use this is an opportunity to exercise the skills using a style and language that is congruent with who they are. Just as we encourage those who are role-playing as the client to adjust the difficulty of the stimuli (e.g., their tone and the quality and intensity of affect), we also encourage therapists to adjust and experiment with their vocal tone, facial expressions, and body postures, as appropriate. Of course, basic principles should be generally followed, such as engaging in nonverbal behaviors that communicate active listening and engagement. However, even factors such as maintaining consistent eye contact may need to be adjusted, depending on the characteristics of the individual client. Relatedly, on multiple occasions, supervisees have asked about whether it is best to try to match the client's vocal tone and affect or to maintain a neutral tone and posture, regardless of the circumstances. The admittedly frustrating answer is it depends. As noted, research demonstrates that therapist emotional expression is associated with treatment outcome (Peluso & Freund, 2018). However, this is an overall effect, and the association between emotional expression and outcome at the individual client–therapist dyad level is complex. Therefore, we encourage learners to be mindful of their emotional expressions and nonverbal behaviors while engaging in the deliberate practice exercises.

The Role of Deliberate Practice in CBT Training

In this chapter and before each exercise in this book, we provide a brief introduction to the skill(s) that includes some attention to theory, research, and generally accepted application principles. However, neither this book nor the deliberate practice method in general is intended to be sufficient for obtaining competence in CBT on its own. Although we envision this book as being useful for CBT training and professional development at all levels, our working model has been a method that can be integrated into a one- or two-semester practicum or other application-oriented courses (see the sample syllabus in Appendix C). With this in mind, trainees should have prior and/or parallel exposure to CBT theory and application in dedicated coursework and readings. In line with what we said earlier in this chapter, this loosely reflects the distinction between declarative and procedural knowledge. The CBT deliberate practice methods outlined in this book are not intended to be a primary source of declarative knowledge. In addition, they are not intended to replace or stand in for work performance or work with actual clients or training cases and case-based supervision (e.g., with review of actual session audio or video).

Deliberate practice methods should play a complementary role in CBT training, in the service of augmenting core readings and work performance with real clients. For example, deliberate practice methods could provide the first opportunity for a trainee to translate their textbook definition of CBT learned in a seminar to the provision of a treatment rationale with an actual client. The simulated environment mimics the clinical interaction, while providing opportunities for behavioral rehearsal and feedback. Later in this chapter, and throughout this book, we recommend resources that provide more information about CBT principles, skills, and training.

Overview of the Book's Structure

This book is organized into three parts. Part I contains this chapter and Chapter 2, which provide basic instructions on how to perform these exercises. We found through testing that providing too many instructions up-front overwhelmed trainers and trainees, and they ended up skipping past them as a result. Therefore, we kept these instructions as brief and simple as possible to focus on only the most essential information that trainers and trainees will need to get started with the exercises. Further guidelines for getting the most about deliberate practice are provided in Chapter 3, and additional instructions for monitoring and adjusting the difficulty of the exercises are provided in Appendix A. **Do not skip the instructions in Chapter 2, and be sure to read the additional guidelines and instructions in Chapter 3 and Appendix A once you are comfortable with the basic instructions.**

Part II contains the 10 skill-focused exercises, which are ordered based on their difficulty: beginner, intermediate, and advanced (see Table 1.1). They each contain a brief overview of the exercise, example client–therapist interactions to help guide trainees, step-by-step instructions for conducting that exercise, and a list of criteria for mastering the relevant skill. The client statements and sample therapist responses are then presented, also organized by difficulty (beginner, intermediate, and advanced). The statements and responses are presented separately so that the trainee playing the therapist has more freedom to improvise responses without being influenced by the sample responses, which should only be turned to if the trainee has difficulty improvising their own responses. The last two exercises in Part II provide opportunities to practice the 10 skills within simulated psychotherapy sessions. Exercise 11 (Annotated Cognitive Behavioral Therapy Practice Session Transcripts) provides sample psychotherapy session transcripts in which the CBT skills are used and clearly labeled, thereby demonstrating how they might flow together in an actual therapy session. CBT trainees are invited to run through the sample transcript with one playing the therapist and the other playing the client to get a feel for how a session might unfold. Exercise 12 (Mock Cognitive Behavioral Therapy Sessions) provides suggestions for undertaking actual mock sessions, as well as client profiles ordered by difficulty (beginner, intermediate, and advanced) that trainees can use for improvised role-plays.

Part III contains Chapter 3, which provides additional guidance for trainers and trainees. While Chapter 2 is more procedural, Chapter 3 covers big-picture issues. It highlights six key points for getting the most out of deliberate practice and describes the importance of appropriate responsiveness, attending to trainee well-being and respecting their privacy, and trainer self-evaluation, among other topics.

Three appendixes conclude this book. Appendix A provides instructions for monitoring and adjusting the difficulty of each exercise as needed. It provides a Deliberate Practice Reaction Form for the trainee playing the therapist to complete to indicate whether the exercise is too easy or too difficult. Appendix B includes an optional deliberate practice diary form, which provides a format for trainees to explore and record their experiences while engaging in deliberate practice between focused training sessions with a supervisor. Appendix C presents a sample syllabus demonstrating how the 12 deliberate practice exercises and other support material can be integrated into a wider CBT training course. Instructors may choose to modify the syllabus or pick elements of it to integrate into their own courses.

For supplemental materials related to this book, see Clinician and Practitioner Resources at https://www.apa.org/pubs/books/deliberate-practice-cognitive-behavioral-therapy, which features the three appendixes from this book.

Instructions for the Cognitive Behavioral Therapy Deliberate Practice Exercises

This chapter provides basic instructions that are common to all the exercises in this book. More specific instructions are provided for each exercise. Chapter 3 also provides important guidance for trainees and trainers that will help them get the most out of deliberate practice. Appendix A offers additional instructions for monitoring and adjusting the difficulty of the exercises as needed after getting through all the client statements in a single difficulty level, including a Deliberate Practice Reaction Form the trainee playing the therapist can complete to indicate whether they found the statements too easy or too difficult. **Difficulty assessment is an important part of the deliberate practice process and should not be skipped.**

Overview

The deliberate practice exercises in this book involve role-plays of hypothetical situations in therapy. The role-play involves three people: One trainee role-plays the therapist, another trainee role-plays the client, and a trainer (professor/supervisor) observes and provides feedback. Alternately, a peer can observe and provide feedback.

This book provides a script for each role-play, each with a client statement and also with an example therapist response. The client statements are graded in difficulty from beginning to advanced, although these grades are only estimates. The actual perceived difficulty of client statements is subjective and varies widely by trainee. For example, some trainees may experience a stimulus of a client being angry to be easy to respond to, whereas another trainee may experience it as very difficult. Thus, it is important for trainees to provide difficulty assessments and adjustments to ensure that they are practicing at the right difficulty level: neither too easy nor too hard.

https://doi.org/10.1037/0000256–002

Deliberate Practice in Cognitive Behavioral Therapy, by J. F. Boswell and M. J. Constantino

Time Frame

We recommend a 90-minute time block for every exercise, structured roughly as follows:

- First 20 minutes: Orientation. The trainer explains the cognitive behavioral therapy (CBT) skill and demonstrates the exercise procedure with a volunteer trainee.

- Middle 50 minutes: Trainees perform the exercise in pairs. The trainer or a peer provides feedback throughout this process and monitors or adjusts the exercise's difficulty, as needed, after each set of statements (see Appendix A for more information about difficulty assessment).

- Final 20 minutes: Evaluation/feedback and discussion.

Preparation

1. Every trainee will need their own copy of this book.

2. Each exercise requires forms that are available to download or print at https://www. apa.org/pubs/books/deliberate-practice-cognitive-behavioral-therapy (see Clinician and Practitioner Resources).

3. Trainees are grouped into pairs. One volunteers to role-play the therapist and the other to role-play the client (they will switch roles after 15 minutes of practice). As noted previously, an observer who might be either the trainer or a fellow trainee will work with each pair.

The Role of the Trainer

The primary responsibilities of the trainer are as follows:

1. Provide corrective feedback, which includes both information about how well the trainees' response met expected criteria and any necessary guidance about how to improve the response.

2. Remind trainees to do difficulty assessments and adjustments after each level of client statements is completed (beginning, intermediate, and advanced).

How to Practice

Each exercise includes its own step-by-step instructions. Trainees should follow these instructions carefully, as every step is important.

Skill Criteria

Each of the first 10 exercises focuses on one essential CBT skill with three to five skill criteria that describe the important components or principles for that skill.

The goal of the role-play is for trainees to practice improvising responses to the client statement in a manner that (a) is attuned to the client, (b) meets skill criteria as much as possible, and (c) feels authentic for the trainee. Trainees are provided scripts with example therapist responses to give them a sense of how to incorporate the skill criteria into a response. **It is important, however, that trainees do not read the example responses verbatim in the role-plays!** Therapy is highly personal and improvisational; the goal of deliberate practice is to develop trainees' ability to improvise within a consistent framework. Memorizing scripted responses would be counterproductive for helping trainees learn to perform therapy that is responsive, authentic, and attuned to each individual client.

Both authors wrote the scripted example responses. However, trainees' personal style of therapy may differ slightly or greatly from that in the example scripts. It is essential that, over time, trainees develop their own style and voice, while simultaneously being able to intervene according to the model's principles and strategies. To facilitate this, the exercises in this book were designed to maximize opportunities for improvisational responses informed by the skill criteria and ongoing feedback. Trainees will note that some of the scripted responses do not meet all the skill criteria: These responses are provided as examples of flexible application of CBT skills in a manner that prioritizes attunement with the client.

In addition, the focus of each scripted response was written explicitly for that specific skill exercise. For example, depending on the context of the therapy, nature of the client, working CBT formulation, and preference of the therapist, a therapist could conceivably (and competently) respond to a given client response with a behaviorally focused or cognitively focused intervention. In Working With Behaviors (Exercise 6), scripted example responses were designed to focus more on behaviors. In Working With Cognitions (Exercise 5), scripted example responses were designed to focus more on cognitions. The context of working on that particular skill in a given practice session should be kept in mind. A trainee might instinctively offer a response that focuses on cognition while practicing working with behaviors or vice versa. We do not necessarily view this as a problem; in fact, it provides an interesting twist to the exercise by considering alternative responses to the stimuli, and "trying on" different kinds of therapist responses that fit under the CBT umbrella. We simply highlight this for additional context when comparing one's improvised response to the scripted therapist response.

The goal for the role-plays is for trainees to practice improvising responses to the client statements in a manner that

- is attuned to the client,
- meets as many of the skill criteria as possible, and
- feels authentic for the trainee.

Feedback

The review and feedback sequence after each role-play has these two elements:

- First, the trainee who played the client **briefly** shares how it felt to be on the receiving end of the therapist response. This can help assess how well trainees are attuning with the client.

- Second, the trainer provides **brief** feedback (less than 1 minute) based on the skill criteria for each exercise. Keep feedback specific, behavioral, and brief to preserve time for skill rehearsal. If one trainer is teaching multiple pairs of trainees, the trainer walks around room, observing the pairs and offering brief feedback. When the trainer is not available, the trainee playing the client gives peer feedback to the therapist, based on the skill criteria and how it felt to be on the receiving end of the intervention. Alternately, a third trainee can observe and provide feedback.

Trainers (or peers) should remember to keep all feedback specific and brief and not to veer into discussions of theory. There are many other settings for extended discussion of CBT theory and research. In deliberate practice, it is of utmost importance to maximize time for continuous behavioral rehearsal via role-plays.

Final Evaluation

After both trainees have role-played the client and the therapist, the trainer provides an evaluation. Participants should engage in a short group discussion based on this evaluation. This discussion can provide ideas for where to focus homework and future deliberate practice sessions. To this end, Appendix B presents a deliberate practice therapist diary form, which can also be downloaded from the series companion website (see Clinician and Practitioner Resources at https://www.apa.org/pubs/books/deliberate-practice-cognitive-behavioral-therapy). This form can be used by trainees as a template to help them explore and record their experiences of deliberate practice activities between focused training sessions with a supervisor.

Deliberate Practice Exercises for Cognitive Behavioral Therapy Skills

This section of the book provides 10 core deliberate practice exercises for essential cognitive behavioral therapy (CBT) skills. These exercises are organized in a developmental sequence, from those that are more appropriate to someone just beginning CBT training to those who have progressed to a more advanced level. Although we anticipate that most trainers would use these exercises in the order we have suggested, some trainers may find it more appropriate to their training circumstances to use a different order. We also provide two comprehensive exercises that bring together the CBT skills using annotated session transcripts and mock CBT sessions.

Explaining the Treatment Rationale for Cognitive Behavioral Therapy

Preparations for Exercise 1

1. Read the instructions in Chapter 2.

2. Download the Deliberate Practice Reaction Form at https://www.apa.org/pubs/ books/deliberate-practice-cognitive-behavioral-therapy (refer to Clinician and Practitioner Resources; also available in Appendix A). The optional diary form in Appendix B can also be downloaded from this site.

Skill Description

Skill Difficulty Level: Beginner

Explaining the rationale for cognitive behavioral therapy (CBT) is an essential skill that helps get therapy off on the right foot (King & Boswell, 2019). It should also be used throughout therapy to help facilitate a collaborative therapeutic relationship and evolving treatment plan. Early CBT treatment sessions tend to be more didactic, yet it is also important to adopt a collaborative style. The more didactic elements involve describing the CBT model and transparently offering a CBT-consistent formulation of the problem and impending treatment, which includes a description and discussion of what the treatment will look like and what it will aim to achieve. Within the discussion of the rationale and tasks, basic information about the expected structure of the session and treatment is important (e.g., establishing the expectation that sessions will involve setting an agenda and that between-session activities will be encouraged). As King and Boswell (2019) stated,

> Establishing a rationale and goal-oriented framework in the first session(s) capitalizes on the importance of perceived treatment credibility, as well as the facilitation of task and positive treatment outcome expectancies. Part of this process often includes an appeal to the research evidence. (p. 36)

https://doi.org/10.1037/0000256-003

Deliberate Practice in Cognitive Behavioral Therapy, by J. F. Boswell and M. J. Constantino

Therapists can use this skill unprompted and/or in response to client inquiries about how CBT works, what methods CBT therapists use, and what will happen in the sessions. Like much of CBT, explaining a treatment rationale is not a singular event; rather it can be used as needed, perhaps especially when a client expresses confusion about, or doubt in, elements of the CBT model. Establishing a treatment rationale and a clear framework, as well as appeals to research evidence, are hallmarks of evidence-based CBT protocols (King & Boswell, 2019). Both client early positive treatment outcome expectancies (Constantino, Vîslă, et al., 2018) and perceptions of treatment credibility (Constantino, Coyne, et al., 2018) are correlated with better treatment outcomes.

Examples of Therapists Explaining the Treatment Rationale for CBT

Example 1

CLIENT: [*curious*] Is this approach helpful for people like me?

THERAPIST: Yes, this approach is generally quite helpful for people like you. This is a well-researched approach with substantial support for its effectiveness across a broad range of clients and problems. Of course, each person is unique and experiences things differently. So, we'll tailor what we do to best fit your needs and preferences and make sure that we prioritize checking in to see what seems to be working or not working for you.

Example 2

CLIENT: [*nervous*] I've never been in therapy before. What do we talk about here?

THERAPIST: We'll likely talk about a variety of things. Ultimately, we want to focus on what's most important to you. We'll set goals for treatment; I'll teach you skills for noticing and modifying thoughts and behaviors; you'll do homework to practice; we'll set an agenda at the beginning of each session and take up concrete, specific things you want help with; and we'll monitor progress as we proceed, making adjustments if we do not get the progress we want.

Example 3

CLIENT: [*concerned*] I really need to know *why* I am the way I am now. I think understanding my past and childhood is really important, but it sounds like this approach doesn't get into any of that?

THERAPIST: This is an important point of clarification. I actually agree that the past is important, and past experience is still relevant to this approach. Although we tend to focus on the present and what is going on now, your past is by no means "off limits." In fact, we will probably need to discuss your past experiences to better understand your present life. If and when that seems most relevant, we will go there, while making sure that we connect things to what is most helpful for you now. Does that seem like a good fit for your interests?

INSTRUCTIONS FOR EXERCISE 1
Step 1: Role-Play and Feedback
• The client says the first beginner client statement. The therapist improvises a response based on the skill criteria. • The trainer (or, if not available, the client) provides *brief* feedback based on the skill criteria. • The client then repeats the same statement, and the therapist again improvises a response. The trainer (or client) again provide brief feedback.
Step 2: Repeat
• Repeat Step 1 for all the statements in the current difficulty level (beginner, intermediate, or advanced).
Step 3: Assess and Adjust Difficulty
• The therapist completes the Deliberate Practice Reaction Form (see Appendix A) and decides whether to make the exercise easier or harder or to stay at the same difficulty level.
Step 4: Repeat for Approximately 15 Minutes
• Repeat Steps 1 to 3 for at least 15 minutes. • The trainees then switch therapist and client roles and start over.

Optional Variation for Exercise 1

In the final round of the exercise, the person playing the client improvises by raising a question or concern about this CBT model that they have been struggling with as a trainee or have heard directly from a real training case, and the person playing the therapist attempts to address the CBT rationale concern. The client can then share if the therapist's response was experienced as compelling or persuasive. Note that the client should be careful to talk only about topics that they feel comfortable sharing.

SKILL CRITERIA FOR EXERCISE 1
1. Validate the client's experience. 2. Explain the logic of how CBT can be used to address concerns. 3. Instill hope for using CBT effectively. 4. Set appropriate expectations for the nature and impact of CBT. 5. Engage in ample eye contact and forward lean.

Now it's your turn! Follow Steps 1 and 2 from the instructions.

Remember: The goal of the role-play is for trainees to practice improvising responses to the client statements in a manner that (a) uses the skill criteria and (b) feels authentic for the trainee. **Example therapist responses for each client statement are provided at the end of this exercise. Trainees should attempt to improvise their own responses before reading the example responses.**

BEGINNER-LEVEL CLIENT STATEMENTS FOR EXERCISE 1
Beginner Client Statement 1
[**Curious**] Is this approach helpful for people like me?
Beginner Client Statement 2
[**Curious**] How does therapy work?
Beginner Client Statement 3
[**Nervous**] I've never been in therapy before. What do we talk about here?
Beginner Client Statement 4
[**Nervous**] I've never been in therapy before. Do we just talk about my past or upbringing?

 Assess and adjust the difficulty here (see Step 3 in the exercise instructions).

INTERMEDIATE-LEVEL CLIENT STATEMENTS FOR EXERCISE 1
Intermediate Client Statement 1
[**Confused**] I'm not sure I understand how talking about my feelings will help.
Intermediate Client Statement 2
[**Nervous**] I have a hard time with organization, so I'm worried about doing all of the homework correctly.
Intermediate Client Statement 3
[**Dismissive**] I'm not sure this is the right thing for me.
Intermediate Client Statement 4
[**Nervous**] The things that you're saying make sense. I can see how this way of working would be helpful to other people, but I'm not sure it is a good fit for me.
Intermediate Client Statement 5
[**Afraid**] I've had bad experiences in therapy before, and I'm unsure if it's really helpful. How is this going to be different?
Intermediate Client Statement 6
[**Impatient**] How long will it take for this to work? I don't have a lot of time or money.

🛑 **Assess and adjust the difficulty here (see Step 3 in the exercise instructions).**

ADVANCED-LEVEL CLIENT STATEMENTS FOR EXERCISE 1

Advanced Client Statement 1

[**Afraid**] I've had bad experiences in therapy before. My last therapist tried to make me talk about and visualize my past traumas. I ended up in the hospital! How can I know that I can trust you?

Advanced Client Statement 2

[**Helpless**] I was abused when I was a child, and recently I can't stop thinking about it. My boyfriend tries to help me be positive, but I can't stop feeling depressed. Sometimes I think it would be easier for everyone if I was dead.[1]

Advanced Client Statement 3

[**Angry**] My doctor said I have to come see you about my "anger problem." Sometimes when I get really angry, I lose control and hit people. I just get so angry when people say stupid things! Are you sure that you will be able to help me with this?

Advanced Client Statement 4

[**Concerned**] I really need to know *why* I am the way I am now. I think understanding my past and childhood is really important, but it sounds like this approach doesn't get into any of that?

 Assess and adjust the difficulty here (see Step 3 in the exercise instructions). If appropriate, follow the instructions to make the exercise even more challenging (see Appendix A).

---

1. Expressions like "Sometimes I think it would be easier for everyone if I was dead" may reflect a feeling and not an intent to harm oneself. However, therapists should use multiple contextual client indicators to determine suicidal intent. Trainees should seek close supervision for clients who may be at risk of self-harm or suicide. If a client is at risk of suicide, therapists should consider a suicide assessment and a possible referral or option for suicide-focused treatment, such as the collaborative assessment and management of suicidality (https://cams-care.com).

Example Therapist Responses: Explaining the Treatment Rationale for CBT

Remember: Trainees should attempt to improvise their own responses before reading the example responses. **Do not read the following responses verbatim unless you are having trouble coming up with your own responses!**

EXAMPLE RESPONSES TO BEGINNER-LEVEL CLIENT STATEMENTS FOR EXERCISE 1
Example Response to Beginner Client Statement 1
Yes, this approach is generally quite helpful for people like you. This is a well-researched approach with substantial support for its effectiveness across a broad range of clients and problems. Of course, each person is unique and experiences things differently. So, we'll tailor what we do to best fit your needs and preferences, and make sure that we prioritize checking in to see what seems to be working or not working for you.
Example Response to Beginner Client Statement 2
That's a great question! In cognitive behavioral therapy, we'll be looking at your cognitions—that is, your thoughts and your behaviors—to identify whether I can teach you some skills for managing them that will help you address some of the problems you are wanting help with. Does that help answer your question?
Example Response to Beginner Client Statement 3
We'll likely talk about a variety of things. Ultimately, we want to focus on what's most important to you. We'll set goals for treatment; I'll teach you skills for noticing and modifying thoughts and behaviors; you'll do homework to practice; we'll set an agenda at the beginning of each session and take up concrete, specific things you want help with; and we'll monitor progress as we proceed, making adjustments if we do not get the progress we want.
Example Response to Beginner Client Statement 4
I can appreciate that therapy may be a bit of a mystery to you. I am interested in your history. In general, CBT emphasizes *current* and *future* experiences, though we may need to discuss your past experiences to help us contextualize the present.

EXAMPLE RESPONSES TO INTERMEDIATE-LEVEL CLIENT STATEMENTS FOR EXERCISE 1

Example Response to Intermediate Client Statement 1

This is very common concern, and I appreciate you sharing it. Our intention won't be to talk about your feelings simply for the sake of talking about your feelings. Rather, we want to help you experience your feelings in new ways. This will help you reflect on them more objectively and respond to them in a more adaptive way to get your needs met and live the type of life that you want to live.

Example Response to Intermediate Client Statement 2

I understand your concern and would like, first, to clarify the exact nature of it. In general, before we send you out the door with an assignment, we'll spend some time thinking about what might make it hard for you to do and figure out a strategy or two to help with that. How does that sound?

Example Response to Intermediate Client Statement 3

I think that's really important to acknowledge. I'd like to better understand what's behind your concerns. I can say it's pretty common for people to be uncertain about whether therapy is the right option for them, whether therapy in general or of a particular type. Based on what I've heard thus far, I believe that therapy *could* help you, but I want to help you make an informed choice that is going to best meet *your* needs at this time.

Example Response to Intermediate Client Statement 4

I appreciate that you're sharing your uncertainty. If it's OK with you, I'd like to spend some time exploring what, in particular, seems like less of a fit. It seems like it would be good for us to lay out or talk about a range of types of therapies so you can make a decision about which might be the best fit. I suggest we put that on our agenda for our session today. How does that sound?

Example Response to Intermediate Client Statement 5

Given your bad experiences, I can see why you might be skeptical. Frankly, I think every course of therapy is different, and there's a lot of potential for this to be different for you. I think it would be important to discuss your previous experiences with therapy, in particular what was unhelpful, and what, if anything, was at least somewhat helpful. How does that sound?

Example Response to Intermediate Client Statement 6

That's an important question that's somewhat difficult to answer. I realize this might be frustrating to hear, but it depends. This approach to therapy is generally built on a shorter term model that has a track record of effectiveness, but each person is unique. We'll be monitoring progress at every session and would expect to see improvement by six or eight sessions. If we don't, we'll want to discuss whether any changes are needed.

EXAMPLE RESPONSES TO ADVANCED-LEVEL CLIENT STATEMENTS FOR EXERCISE 1

Example Response to Advanced Client Statement 1

I'm sorry to hear that you've had negative experiences. That sounds really difficult, and I think it's understandable for you to ask that question. First, I think it's important to be clear that you'll never be "forced" to do anything in our work together. Without necessarily going into the content of your past traumatic experiences, it would be helpful to hear a bit more about the nature of the work that you were doing with your previous therapist and the circumstances around your hospitalization. I also suggest that we prioritize today discussing how to develop and maintain trust in our work. How does that sound?

Example Response to Advanced Client Statement 2

I imagine that feels pretty overwhelming. Sometimes you think it would be easier for everyone if you were dead. I don't want to put words in your mouth, but it sounds like there may be other times when there is still some hope—for example, the part that brought you here today. Can we examine the thought that it might be easier for everyone if you were dead?[1]

Example Response to Advanced Client Statement 3

It sounds like you're angry now. Let's talk about your concerns about whether you are going to get the help you want. We can put that on our agenda for today. I'd also like to talk with you about how we can make a plan for if or when you feel angry in here. Could we talk about that today too? First, though, I'd like to get a better sense for the degree to which *you* think you have an anger problem?

Example Response to Advanced Client Statement 4

This is an important point of clarification. I actually agree that the past is important, and past experience is still relevant to this approach. Although we tend to focus on the present and what is going on now, your past is by no means "off limits." In fact, we will probably need to discuss your past experiences to better understand your present life. If and when that seems most relevant, we will go there, while making sure that we connect things to what is most helpful for you now. Does that seem like a good fit for your interests?

Establishing Goals

Preparations for Exercise 2

1. Read the instructions in Chapter 2.

2. Download the Deliberate Practice Reaction Form at https://www.apa.org/pubs/books/deliberate-practice-cognitive-behavioral-therapy (refer to Clinician and Practitioner Resources; also available in Appendix A). The optional diary form in Appendix B can also be downloaded from this site.

Skill Description

Skill Difficulty Level: Beginner

Cognitive behavioral therapy (CBT) is a structured, action and goal-oriented approach. Establishing shared treatment goals and tasks early in treatment not only facilitates a positive working alliance and congruent expectancies (both of which can facilitate good outcomes) but also provides a personalized treatment roadmap. Put simply, it is difficult to navigate the journey when one does not know the destination. Such navigation to long-term goals is aided by establishing short- and middle-term goals. In addition, some research has shown that early participant agreement on goals and tasks is particularly important for CBT outcome (Webb et al., 2011).

Although therapists should use this skill at the outset of CBT, attending to and negotiating goals and tasks is not a singular or solely early treatment event. Even if not explicitly addressed in a given session, goals and tasks are invariably in the background. Moreover, they might require close attention as treatment unfolds, such as when a client masters a skill and prefers to refocus on something else, or when progress has stalled or failed to develop. In addition, similar to establishing a session agenda, it is not a skill that the therapist unidirectionally "delivers"; rather, it is typically (and most usefully) a collaborative exercise. A big part of the skill is to negotiate with the client *personalized* CBT goals that *they value*, as well as a corresponding framework (personalized rationale) and goal-consistent tasks.

https://doi.org/10.1037/0000256-004

Deliberate Practice in Cognitive Behavioral Therapy, by J. F. Boswell and M. J. Constantino

Examples of Therapists Establishing Goals

Example 1

CLIENT: [*calm*] I just want to be happier.

THERAPIST: Being happier sounds like a reasonable goal to me. I wonder, though, if we can break it down a bit into something more concrete. For example, what would it look like to be happier? How, precisely, might your life be different?

Example 2

CLIENT: [*nervous*] I just don't want to feel anxious anymore. I'm tired of it.

THERAPIST: I know it's exhausting, and no one can blame you for having that goal. In cases like yours, we want to get the anxiety to more manageable levels. Is it more accurate to say that you have a goal of *reducing* anxiety? Or, do you want to *eliminate* it altogether; *never* feeling anxious?

Example 3

CLIENT: [*weeping*] I just can't imagine anything changing. I feel so hopeless.

THERAPIST: I can see how it's hard to picture how things might be different, and at this point there might be a part of you that's overwhelmed by the work that's ahead. And there is another part that brought you here today, and that reality is not trivial and gives me hope *for* you. Perhaps this feeling of hopelessness is itself a problem worth working on (i.e., to reduce or overcome) as a goal in here. Do you have thoughts on that?

INSTRUCTIONS FOR EXERCISE 2
Step 1: Role-Play and Feedback
• The client says the first beginner client statement. The therapist improvises a response based on the skill criteria. • The trainer (or, if not available, the client) provides brief feedback based on the skill criteria. • The client then repeats the same statement, and the therapist again improvises a response. The trainer (or client) again provide brief feedback.
Step 2: Repeat
• Repeat Step 1 for all the statements in the current difficulty level (beginner, intermediate, or advanced).
Step 3: Assess and Adjust Difficulty
• The therapist completes the Deliberate Practice Reaction Form (see Appendix A) and decides whether to make the exercise easier or harder or to stay at the same difficulty level.
Step 4: Repeat for Approximately 15 Minutes
• Repeat Steps 1 to 3 for at least 15 minutes. • The trainees then switch therapist and client roles and start over.

Optional Variation for Exercise 2

In the final round of the exercise, the person playing the client improvises by raising a goal-related concern or impasse that they have heard directly from a real training case, and the person playing the therapist then attempts to address the CBT goal concern. The client can then share if the therapist's response was experienced as persuasive and collaborative. Note that the client should be careful only to talk about topics that they feel comfortable sharing.

SKILL CRITERIA FOR EXERCISE 2
1. Suggest CBT-consistent goals and tasks that align with an individualized CBT case formulation.
2. Invite the client's input on and agreement with the goals and tasks.
3. Demonstrate flexibility.
4. Emphasize concrete, actionable, and measurable goals.

Now it's your turn! Follow Steps 1 and 2 from the instructions.

Remember: The goal of the role-play is for trainees to practice improvising responses to the client statements in a manner that (a) uses the skill criteria and (b) feels authentic for the trainee. **Example therapist responses for each client statement are provided at the end of this exercise. Trainees should attempt to improvise their own responses before reading the example responses.**

BEGINNER-LEVEL CLIENT STATEMENTS FOR EXERCISE 2
Beginner Client Statement 1
[**Calm**] I just want to be happier.
Beginner Client Statement 2
[**Curious**] Geez. I don't even know where to start in picturing my happiness.
Beginner Client Statement 3
[**Nervous**] I just don't want to feel anxious anymore. I'm tired of it.
Beginner Client Statement 4
[**Curious**] How long will this take?
Beginner Client Statement 5
[**Nervous**] You're the expert, so I'll defer to what you think is best.

 Assess and adjust the difficulty here (see Step 3 in the exercise instructions).

INTERMEDIATE-LEVEL CLIENT STATEMENTS FOR EXERCISE 2
Intermediate Client Statement 1
[**Nervous**] I guess I was expecting that we'd just talk about whatever came to my mind on a given week.
Intermediate Client Statement 2
[**Confused**] I'm not sure I want to do homework or exercises in here.
Intermediate Client Statement 3
[**Weeping**] I just can't imagine anything changing. I feel so hopeless.
Intermediate Client Statement 4
[**Anxious**] I don't think I want to do any exposure.
Intermediate Client Statement 5
[**Agitated**] Honestly, my main problem is my partner.
Intermediate Client Statement 6
[**Anxious**] I want to get a job, find a new partner, lose weight, be happier and less anxious, be more outgoing, and work on some my grief issues.

 Assess and adjust the difficulty here (see Step 3 in the exercise instructions).

ADVANCED-LEVEL CLIENT STATEMENTS FOR EXERCISE 2
Advanced Client Statement 1
[**Impatient**] I think there's a problem with my brain and I might just need medication.
Advanced Client Statement 2
[**Irritated**] I can't commit to coming in here each week. My schedule is unpredictable, and I don't have a car.
Advanced Client Statement 3
[**Irritated**] I don't think this is going to work, so I'm not sure setting goals matters.
Advanced Client Statement 4
[**Angry**] You just need goals to write down for the insurance companies so you get paid for this.
Advanced Client Statement 5
[**Angry**] It's hard to come up with goals because I'm not really sure what we're doing in here.

Assess and adjust the difficulty here (see Step 3 in the exercise instructions). If appropriate, follow the instructions to make the exercise even more challenging (see Appendix A).

Example Therapist Responses: Establishing Goals

Remember: Trainees should attempt to improvise their own responses before reading the example responses. **Do not read the following responses verbatim unless you are having trouble coming up with your own responses!**

EXAMPLE RESPONSES TO BEGINNER-LEVEL CLIENT STATEMENTS FOR EXERCISE 2
Example Response to Beginner Client Statement 1
Being happier sounds like a reasonable goal to me. I wonder, though, if we can break it down a bit into something more concrete. For example, what would it look like to be happier? How, precisely, might your life be different?
Example Response to Beginner Client Statement 2
I can appreciate that. Perhaps we can start by narrowing the focus a bit. How will we know if you're happier, say, one month from now? What would be a good indication of that?
Example Response to Beginner Client Statement 3
I know it's exhausting, and no one can blame you for having that goal. In cases like yours, we want to get the anxiety to more manageable levels. Is it more accurate to say that you have a goal of *reducing* anxiety? Or do you want to *eliminate* it altogether—*never* feel anxious?
Example Response to Beginner Client Statement 4
That's an important question, and the answer is, it depends, in part based on your goals and preferences. I *can* say that this therapy will not be indefinite because we'll work to give you the skills to become your own therapist and carry forward the work independently. Tell me more about your question. Are you worried about being here forever?
Example Response to Beginner Client Statement 5
I suppose in *some* ways I'm an expert, but I want to avoid unilaterally dictating your goals and how we go about achieving them. Further, you're the expert on you, including what you need and your preferences for our work together. I have some ideas about this but think it would be best to discuss and plan together. Sound OK to you?

EXAMPLE RESPONSES TO INTERMEDIATE-LEVEL CLIENT STATEMENTS FOR EXERCISE 2

Example Response to Intermediate Client Statement 1

We do want to prioritize what's most important for you. In fact, we'll work together today to develop a general road map for your therapy, while collaboratively establishing an agenda each session. We might find that some recurring themes emerge and drive our work (more so than just what comes to mind). Does that make sense?

Example Response to Intermediate Client Statement 2

As we've discussed, the CBT approach tends to emphasize learning by doing—in particular, trying things out in between sessions, in your daily life. Although each person is different, it can be difficult to translate or generalize the work we do in here to your day-to-day life without trying out new things and applying them outside of here. Now, that can look a lot of different ways, depending on your preferences and the given week. Perhaps we can discuss some of your concerns and expectations regarding homework?

Example Response to Intermediate Client Statement 3

I can see how it's hard to picture how things might be different, and at this point, there might be a part of you that's overwhelmed by the work that's ahead. And there is another part that brought you here today, and that reality is not trivial and gives me hope *for* you. Perhaps this feeling of hopelessness is itself a problem worth working on (i.e., to reduce or overcome) as a goal in here. Do you have thoughts on that?

Example Response to Intermediate Client Statement 4

I hear that. If it's OK with you, we can spend some time talking about what exposure work would look like and discuss your concerns. We also have other options to discuss.

Example Response to Intermediate Client Statement 5

I'd like to hear more details about that. If relationship issues are most concerning to you, we can focus our work on that area. In our individual work together, we'll need to focus on things that you can change. Part of our session today can be brainstorming what some of those things might be.

Example Response to Intermediate Client Statement 6

Those all sound like worthwhile goals to me. Is there a way to identify some common threads and/or prioritize one or two of these to start? I wonder if some overlap or relate to each other?

EXAMPLE RESPONSES TO ADVANCED-LEVEL CLIENT STATEMENTS FOR EXERCISE 2
Example Response to Advanced Client Statement 1
Some people with similar problems do benefit from medication, or a combination of CBT and medication. Although biology is important, I'm not sure I'd frame this as a problem with your brain. Even if we did stipulate this, CBT can also change your brain. Shall we spend a few minutes discussing your options?
Example Response to Advanced Client Statement 2
That's important to know. The evidence seems to show that more consistent, weekly sessions is best, on average. Can we discuss your concerns in more detail and brainstorm a plan to support your ability to make it to sessions, as well as how we'll communicate about this as things come up?
Example Response to Advanced Client Statement 3
I think we should explore your valid concerns about therapy, and what it might mean for therapy to "work" or "not work." Are you open to discussing this further?
Example Response to Advanced Client Statement 4
OK, so if I'm understanding you, you're suggesting that I'm asking to set goals for reasons other than that they'll be helpful to you. Is that right? It seems like you're concerned about me being really committed to you. You deserve to feel confident your therapist is really concerned about you, not just getting paid, so let's put this on the agenda and talk about it. Would that be OK?
Example Response to Advanced Client Statement 5
That's important to hear, and I can see how that might make it hard to come up with goals! Just to clarify, is the uncertainty about therapy in general or the CBT model that we've started to introduce? It might seem a bit backward, but identifying potential goals can also inform what we do in here.

Negotiating a Session Agenda

Preparations for Exercise 3

1. Read the instructions in Chapter 2.

2. Download the Deliberate Practice Reaction Form at https://www.apa.org/pubs/ books/deliberate-practice-cognitive-behavioral-therapy (refer to Clinician and Practitioner Resources; also available in Appendix A). The optional diary form in Appendix B can also be downloaded from this site.

Skill Description

Skill Difficulty Level: Beginner

Negotiating a session agenda is an essential skill that helps get the session off on the right foot, clarifies expectations for the appointment, and fosters continued collaboration on specific goals and tasks. In addition, some research has shown that techniques such as agenda-setting are associated with symptom reduction in CBT (DeRubeis & Feeley, 1990). Therapists can use this skill at the beginning of most cognitive behavioral therapy (CBT) sessions. However, like much of CBT, setting a session agenda is not a singular event; rather, it is foundational to overall session and time management and requires attention at various points in a session. Moreover, it is not a skill that the therapist unidirectionally "delivers"; rather, it is typically (and most usefully) a collaborative exercise. The client's input on the agenda should be directly solicited. A big part of the skill is to negotiate with the client personalized CBT agendas that they value, and includes goals that they are at least to some degree motivated to work toward in the moment. When agenda negotiations seem to be moving in a direction that is inconsistent with the established treatment framework and plan, therapists may need to rely on some of the more advanced skills covered later in this book (see Exercises 8–10).

https://doi.org/10.1037/0000256-005

Deliberate Practice in Cognitive Behavioral Therapy, by J. F. Boswell and M. J. Constantino

Examples of Therapists Negotiating a Session Agenda

Example 1

CLIENT: [*calm*] I'm not sure what to talk about today.

THERAPIST: OK. I have a tentative agenda for today's session based on how we have initially framed your concerns. What if we start by reviewing that and getting your input? We might also start by reviewing the homework, seeing if that suggests any other agenda items. How does that sound?

Example 2

CLIENT: [*nervous*] I don't think I'm ready for working on this today.

THERAPIST: OK. We can revisit and possibly modify our plan for today. How about we first take a step back and explore your thinking about this? What thoughts are you noticing as we discuss the agenda?

Example 3

CLIENT: [*nervous*] I know that the plan was to talk about exposure today, but something's come up that I'd like to talk about first.

THERAPIST: So, here's my thought. My experience is that exposure can be scary and challenging, and I've found that if we get started on the road of putting it off because something else came up, then it becomes easier and easier to keep putting off. Then we find ourselves off our agreed-upon path. So, my suggestion would be this: Let's do some exposure first, and aim to save some time for the other topic. Does that plan work for you?

INSTRUCTIONS FOR EXERCISE 3
Step 1: Role-Play and Feedback
• The client says the first beginner client statement. The therapist improvises a response based on the skill criteria. • The trainer (or, if not available, the client) provides brief feedback based on the skill criteria. • The client then repeats the same statement, and the therapist again improvises a response. The trainer (or client) again provide brief feedback.
Step 2: Repeat
• Repeat Step 1 for all the statements in the current difficulty level (beginner, intermediate, or advanced).
Step 3: Assess and Adjust Difficulty
• The therapist completes the Deliberate Practice Reaction Form (see Appendix A) and decides whether to make the exercise easier or harder or to stay at the same difficulty level.
Step 4: Repeat for Approximately 15 Minutes
• Repeat Steps 1 to 3 for at least 15 minutes. • The trainees then switch therapist and client roles and start over.

Optional Variation for Exercise 3

In the final round of the exercise, the person playing the client improvises by raising an agenda-related concern or impasse that they have heard directly from a real training case, and the person playing the therapist then attempts to address the CBT agenda concern. The client can then share if the therapist's response was experienced as collaborative and CBT-consistent. Note that the client should be careful only to talk about topics that they feel comfortable sharing.

SKILL CRITERIA FOR EXERCISE 3
1. Suggest a CBT-consistent agenda that aligns with the CBT case formulation. 2. Invite the client's input on and agreement with the agenda. 3. Demonstrate flexibility. 4. Maintain some degree of frame or structure (i.e., the agenda can shift, but generally maintain a more or less explicit attempt to delineate expectations for session goals and tasks).

Now it's your turn! Follow Steps 1 and 2 from the instructions.

Remember: The goal of the role-play is for trainees to practice improvising responses to the client statements in a manner that (a) uses the skill criteria and (b) feels authentic for the trainee. **Example therapist responses for each client statement are provided at the end of this exercise. Trainees should attempt to improvise their own responses before reading the example responses.**

BEGINNER-LEVEL CLIENT STATEMENTS FOR EXERCISE 3
Beginner Client Statement 1
[**Calm**] I'm not sure what to talk about today.
Beginner Client Statement 2
[**Curious**] So, what's our agenda for today?
Beginner Client Statement 3
[**Nervous**] I don't think I'm ready for working on this today.
Beginner Client Statement 4
[**Flustered**] Sorry I'm so late. I had the wrong time in my calendar.
Beginner Client Statement 5
[**Curious**] I'm not sure about an agenda. With my other therapist, I just kind of talked about whatever was on my mind.

 Assess and adjust the difficulty here (see Step 3 in the exercise instructions).

INTERMEDIATE-LEVEL CLIENT STATEMENTS FOR EXERCISE 3
Intermediate Client Statement 1
[**Nervous**] You're the expert, so just tell me what to do today.
Intermediate Client Statement 2
[**Nervous**] I know that the plan was to talk about exposure today, but something's come up that I'd like to talk about first.
Intermediate Client Statement 3
[**Nervous**] My partner wants us to talk about something today.
Intermediate Client Statement 4
[**Dismissive**] I'm not sure this is the best use of my time today.
Intermediate Client Statement 5
[**Agitated**] Wow. You won't believe what happened this week. It's a really long story . . .

 Assess and adjust the difficulty here (see Step 3 in the exercise instructions).

ADVANCED-LEVEL CLIENT STATEMENTS FOR EXERCISE 3
Advanced Client Statement 1
[**Irritated**] This week has been terrible, and I don't feel like talking today.
Advanced Client Statement 2
[**Sad**] I think our sessions have been very helpful. However, my depression is getting worse. On my drive to this session today. I pictured myself driving off a bridge. It honestly felt like a relief to imagine not having to work so hard to feel better anymore.
Advanced Client Statement 3
[**Irritated**] The agenda sounds fine, I suppose. I don't know. I don't think this is working, so I'm not sure it matters.
Advanced Client Statement 4
[**Frustrated**] To be honest, the last couple of sessions I've been confused by our focus on my challenges. My family says I should just stay positive, smile more, and not think about anything negative. Do we have to discuss my challenges?
Advanced Client Statement 5
[**Curious**] I read an article on the internet that a new energy-healing technique can help people 10 times faster than CBT and is easy for therapists to learn. I brought a printout of the article with instructions. Can we talk about possibly trying that today?

 Assess and adjust the difficulty here (see Step 3 in the exercise instructions). If appropriate, follow the instructions to make the exercise even more challenging (see Appendix A).

Example Therapist Responses: Negotiating a Session Agenda

Remember: Trainees should attempt to improvise their own responses before reading the example responses. **Do not read the following responses verbatim unless you are having trouble coming up with your own responses!**

EXAMPLE RESPONSES TO BEGINNER-LEVEL CLIENT STATEMENTS FOR EXERCISE 3
Example Response to Beginner Client Statement 1
OK. I have a tentative agenda for today's session based on how we have initially framed your concerns. What if we start by reviewing that and getting your input? We might also start by reviewing the homework, seeing if that suggests any other agenda items. How does that sound?
Example Response to Beginner Client Statement 2
Let's start by figuring that out together, OK? I was thinking that we would begin by reviewing your experience with the homework over the past week, including any questions that came up for you. That should then be a nice segue to something I'd like to introduce and practice a bit in here today. We can spend most of the session on that and then save some time to make a plan for the next week. Of course, I also want to make sure that we budget time for anything else that you'd like to discuss today. Is there anything you'd like to add?
Example Response to Beginner Client Statement 3
OK. We can revisit and possibly modify our plan for today. How about we first take a step back and explore your thinking about this? What thoughts are you noticing as we discuss the agenda?
Example Response to Beginner Client Statement 4
Mistakes happen, and we can adjust. What do you think about the following plan? We can spend a few minutes reviewing what you've worked on since the last session, and then we can discuss what is going to be most helpful between today and our next appointment— for example, continuing on with a similar plan or making some adjustments.
Example Response to Beginner Client Statement 5
Yes, some therapies are less structured than others. The approach that we're taking is more on the structured side. Regardless, I want to make sure that we focus on the things that are most important to you. In my experience, it can be helpful to do this in the context of a general plan connected to your goals to keep things on track and continue to move our work forward. If it's OK with you, I'd like to hear more about your thoughts about being more structured in here.

EXAMPLE RESPONSES TO INTERMEDIATE-LEVEL CLIENT STATEMENTS FOR EXERCISE 3
Example Response to Intermediate Client Statement 1
I suppose in some ways I'm the expert, but I want to avoid unilaterally dictating how we spend our time today. Further, you're the expert on you. I have some ideas for our agenda but think it would be best to discuss and plan it together. I'm very interested in hearing your thoughts and preferences. Does this make sense?
Example Response to Intermediate Client Statement 2
So, here's my thought. My experience is that exposure can be scary and challenging, and I've found if we get started on the road of putting it off because something else came up, then it becomes easier and easier to keep putting off. Then we find ourselves off our agreed-on path. So, my suggestion would be let's do some exposure first and aim to save some time for the other topic. Does that plan work for you?
Example Response to Intermediate Client Statement 3
OK. I'd like to hear more about that, and, most important, if this is something that *you* want us to put on the agenda today. Perhaps we can visit that after we review what you've been working on over the past week?
Example Response to Intermediate Client Statement 4
I think that's important to acknowledge, and I'm glad that you're sharing that concern with me. We want to make sure that we're making the best use of your time. I'd like to better understand what's behind your concerns and discuss our options for today.
Example Response to Intermediate Client Statement 5
It sounds like there's a lot on your mind, and I'd like to hear about it. Would it be OK to take a second to discuss our agenda for the day first, including where discussing this past week might fit in, as well as anything else you want to take up here today? I want to make sure that we budget our time accordingly. Shall we start with a homework check-in and then tackle the story?

EXAMPLE RESPONSES TO ADVANCED-LEVEL CLIENT STATEMENTS FOR EXERCISE 3

Example Response to Advanced Client Statement 1

Wow. It sounds like you've had a really hard week. I'd like to get a better sense of what has been terrible. I was thinking that we would start with a brief homework review, and that might lead naturally into continuing to practice what we introduced last week. But first, it might help to clarify if you don't feel like talking at all, or talking specifically about what has been terrible about this week?

Example Response to Advanced Client Statement 2

It sounds like you're still feeling pretty overwhelmed. The fantasy of driving off a bridge and the impact that it apparently had seem pretty powerful and important. I suggest we put this at the top of our agenda today. I'd like to understand that feeling of relief when imagining this scenario, including what you were experiencing before this.[1]

Example Response to Advanced Client Statement 3

That's really important, and I'm glad you're sharing these concerns with me. I suggest we put that issue on our agenda today—explore your concerns about therapy and what is contributing to this sense that it isn't "working." Is that OK with you?

Example Response to Advanced Client Statement 4

I see. You're bringing up an important point. I agree that it's important to also focus on strengths and be mindful of and build on what is positive, so this is helpful feedback. I also wonder about *your* perspective on this. How about we put this issue on our agenda today?

Example Response to Advanced Client Statement 5

Sure, we can add this discussion to the agenda today. Thanks, for sharing this with me; I'm not familiar with this technique and would need a bit more time to understand it. First, though, I'm curious about what's drawn you to it. The possibility of feeling better faster seems generally appealing. I wonder if you have concerns about our pace in here because that seems like an important piece of this discussion. Would you prefer to begin there or come back to this?

---

1. Expressions like "I pictured myself driving off a bridge" may reflect a feeling and not an intent to harm oneself. However, therapists should use multiple contextual client indicators to determine suicidal intent. Trainees should seek close supervision for clients who may be at risk of self-harm or suicide. If a client is at risk of suicide, therapists should consider a suicide assessment and a possible referral or an option for suicide-focused treatment, such as the collaborative assessment and management of suicidality (https://cams-care.com).

Assigning and Reviewing Between-Session Activities

Preparations for Exercise 4

1. Read the instructions in Chapter 2.

2. Download the Deliberate Practice Reaction Form at https://www.apa.org/pubs/books/deliberate-practice-cognitive-behavioral-therapy (refer to Clinician and Practitioner Resources; also available in Appendix A). The optional diary form in Appendix B can also be downloaded from this site.

Skill Description

Skill Difficulty Level: Beginner

Between-session practice and activity (i.e., homework) is a core feature of cognitive behavioral therapy (CBT). Relative to the remainder of clients' lives, the time spent in direct contact with a therapist is a drop in the bucket. Between-session activities facilitate the corrective learning process—both in and outside of CBT sessions. Furthermore, work outside of the sessions assists with generalization and helping the client to become their own therapist.

Although completing homework can certainly be challenging for clients, there is a general expectation that some form of homework be incorporated across most sessions. Thus, when socializing clients to CBT (at the outset and as needed throughout treatment), setting this expectation and discussing any questions or concerns that the client has is important (see also Exercise 1: Explaining the Treatment Rationale for Cognitive Behavioral Therapy). In particular, therapists should emphasize how homework

https://doi.org/10.1037/0000256-006

Deliberate Practice in Cognitive Behavioral Therapy, by J. F. Boswell and M. J. Constantino

can help generalize the skills learned in, and the experiences of, therapy to daily life outside of the therapy appointment. As we considered elsewhere,

> Conceptually, the use of homework in CBT is similar to that of learning a new language. One needs to immerse oneself in the language if one is to be fluent enough to use it in difficult situations. Although the therapy sessions may provide the basics of grammar and vocabulary for the language, only by using it in every opportunity can one truly master it and be able to use it independently even long after treatment. (Boswell et al., 2011, p. 107)

This metaphor can be provided directly to the client as a homework rationale.

Given its ubiquity, we view assigning and reviewing homework as a "basic" skill. When following a typical session agenda, time is budgeted at the end of each session to collaboratively identify between-session activities, such as experience monitoring, behavioral experiments, exposures, or relevant readings (e.g., from a companion workbook). In turn, time is budgeted at the beginning of the subsequent session to review the previous session's assigned homework, an aspect of CBT that has been associated with symptom reduction (DeRubeis & Feeley, 1990). It is important to tailor assignments to the individual client and to keep in mind that quantity should not be prioritized over quality.

Examples of Therapists Assigning and Reviewing Between-Session Activities

Example 1

CLIENT: [curious] I'm still trying to get the hang of identifying my thoughts. Should I plan for anything next week?

THERAPIST: Sure, I hear you are still learning to identify your thoughts. Here's an idea: If I give you a thought record, would you be able to focus on an upsetting situation and write down the emotions and thoughts you have in that situation, just like we've done in here together?

Example 2

CLIENT: [nervous] What do we do next with this exposure thing?

THERAPIST: We've talked about how we want to translate or extend what we do in session to your life outside of here. If it works for you, I suggest we spend our remaining minutes thinking about and planning for the next week. Let's find something on your hierarchy that you can aim for in between today and our next session. It can be useful to have a few related options that slightly vary in expected difficulty. You might surprise yourself! Sound good?

Example 3

CLIENT: [anxious] I'm not sure I'm ready to do this on my own.

THERAPIST: I totally get it. This is new and far from easy, so I'm not surprised that you're unsure. If this was a "slam dunk," we probably wouldn't spend too much of your time on it. On the one hand, we want to push beyond your comfort zone a bit, but we also don't want to blow right past it if that isn't going to be helpful. Let's take a moment to discuss some of your concerns and come up with a plan that seems workable. I would especially like to discuss what *you* would most like to work on before next session.

INSTRUCTIONS FOR EXERCISE 4

Step 1: Role-Play and Feedback

- The client says the first beginner client statement. The therapist improvises a response based on the skill criteria.
- The trainer (or, if not available, the client) provides brief feedback based on the skill criteria.
- The client then repeats the same statement, and the therapist again improvises a response. The trainer (or client) again provide brief feedback.

Step 2: Repeat

- Repeat Step 1 for all the statements in the current difficulty level (beginner, intermediate, or advanced).

Step 3: Assess and Adjust Difficulty

- The therapist completes the Deliberate Practice Reaction Form (see Appendix A) and decides whether to make the exercise easier or harder or to stay at the same difficulty level.

Step 4: Repeat for Approximately 15 Minutes

- Repeat Steps 1 to 3 for at least 15 minutes.
- The trainees then switch therapist and client roles and start over.

Optional Variation for Exercise 4

In the final round of the exercise, the person playing the client improvises by raising a homework-related concern or impasse that they have heard directly from a real training case, and the person playing the therapist then attempts to address the CBT homework concern. The client can then share whether the therapist's response was experienced as validating and collaborative. Note that the client should be careful only to talk about topics that they feel comfortable sharing.

SKILL CRITERIA FOR EXERCISE 4

1. Provide a basic rationale for the homework assignment.
2. Tailor the homework assignment to the client's concerns and needs.
3. Ensure that there is adequate agreement on and understanding of the homework assignment.
4. Encourage and validate good-faith efforts.

Now it's your turn! Follow Steps 1 and 2 from the instructions.

Remember: The goal of the role-play is for trainees to practice improvising responses to the client statements in a manner that (a) uses the skill criteria and (b) feels authentic for the trainee. **Example therapist responses for each client statement are provided at the end of this exercise. Trainees should attempt to improvise their own responses before reading the example responses.**

BEGINNER-LEVEL CLIENT STATEMENTS FOR EXERCISE 4
Beginner Client Statement 1
[**Pleased**] I feel like I'm getting the hang of objective monitoring.
Beginner Client Statement 2
[**Curious**] I'm still trying to get the hang of identifying my thoughts. Should I plan for anything next week?
Beginner Client Statement 3
[**Curious**] OK, what do we do now that we've created an exposure hierarchy?
Beginner Client Statement 4
[**Nervous**] What do we do next with this exposure thing?
Beginner Client Statement 5
[**Curious, after emotion monitoring homework was assigned at the end of the previous session**] Where should we start today?

 Assess and adjust the difficulty here (see Step 3 in the exercise instructions).

INTERMEDIATE-LEVEL CLIENT STATEMENTS FOR EXERCISE 4
Intermediate Client Statement 1
[**Anxious**] I'm not sure I'm ready to do this on my own.
Intermediate Client Statement 2
[**Anxious**] I have a hard time with organization, so I'm worried about doing all of the homework correctly.
Intermediate Client Statement 3
[**Flustered**] I actually need to be out the door right now. Is there anything that I should do before our next session?
Intermediate Client Statement 4
[**Ashamed**] I did some of what we talked about last week but forgot the forms.
Intermediate Client Statement 5
[**Ashamed**] I was only able to do part of what we talked about last week.
Intermediate Client Statement 6
[**Frustrated**] I don't expect this assignment to help.
Intermediate Client Statement 7
[**Agitated**] I'm too swamped; I don't think I'll have the time to do any homework.

 Assess and adjust the difficulty here (see Step 3 in the exercise instructions).

ADVANCED-LEVEL CLIENT STATEMENTS FOR EXERCISE 4
Advanced Client Statement 1
[**Frustrated**] I'm just not getting it. I don't understand what you're asking me to do for the homework.
Advanced Client Statement 2
[**Weeping**] I just don't think I can do this homework on my own.
Advanced Client Statement 3
[**Apprehensive**] I successfully did the homework! However, it made me very nervous, so I had a few drinks beforehand. This is OK, right? I hope you don't judge my drinking, like my wife and boss do.
Advanced Client Statement 4
[**Anxious**] Whenever I have trouble motivating to do the homework, I think of how happy I will feel telling you that I did it. Your approval means everything to me. I honestly think you're the best therapist I've ever met.
Advanced Client Statement 5
[**Dismissive**] I didn't do the homework. It didn't seem like it was that important, to be honest.

 Assess and adjust the difficulty here (see Step 3 in the exercise instructions). If appropriate, follow the instructions to make the exercise even more challenging (see Appendix A).

Example Therapist Responses: Assigning and Reviewing Between-Session Activities

Remember: Trainees should attempt to improvise their own responses before reading the example responses. **Do not read the following responses verbatim unless you are having trouble coming up with your own responses!**

EXAMPLE RESPONSES TO BEGINNER-LEVEL CLIENT STATEMENTS FOR EXERCISE 4
Example Response to Beginner Client Statement 1
That's great. It's important to keep in mind that this is a skill, and something that few of us do naturally. Now that we've spent some time on this together, what do you think about practicing this a bit more on your own, between now and our next session? As we've discussed, this is common practice in CBT, and people often find it very useful, even if sometimes challenging. Shall we come up with a plan for that?
Example Response to Beginner Client Statement 2
Sure, I hear you are still learning to identify your thoughts. Here's an idea: If I give you a thought record, would you be able to focus on an upsetting situation and write down the emotions and thoughts you have in that situation, just like we've done in here together?
Example Response to Beginner Client Statement 3
The next step is to actually start working on the items on the hierarchy. I think you're ready to try this on your own over the next week. Let's start with the first item. Does that seem like something you could try next week?
Example Response to Beginner Client Statement 4
We've talked about how we want to translate or extend what we do in here to your life outside of here. If it works for you, I suggest we spend our remaining minutes thinking about and planning for the next week. Let's find something on your hierarchy that you can aim for between today and our next session. It can be useful to have a few related options that slightly vary in expected difficulty. You might surprise yourself! Sound good?
Example Response to Beginner Client Statement 5
Toward the end of our last session, we made a plan for you to practice monitoring your emotions over the past week. I suggest we take some time to talk about how that went and what you noticed. How does that sound?

EXAMPLE RESPONSES TO INTERMEDIATE-LEVEL CLIENT STATEMENTS FOR EXERCISE 4

Example Response to Intermediate Client Statement 1

I totally get it. This is new and far from easy, so I'm not surprised that you're unsure. If this was a "slam dunk," we probably wouldn't spend too much of your time on it. On the one hand, we want to push beyond your comfort zone a bit, but on the other hand, we also don't want to blow right past it if that isn't going to be helpful. Let's take a moment to discuss some of your concerns and come up with a plan that seems workable. I would especially like to discuss what *you* would most like to work on before next session.

Example Response to Intermediate Client Statement 2

That's a pretty common concern. Let's come up with ways to help support your work this week. Regarding doing all of the homework correctly, although we want to be on the same page, honest mistakes invariably create useful learning opportunities. It might sound weird, but part of me actually wants you to make some mistakes because we often learn best from them.

Example Response to Intermediate Client Statement 3

OK. I apologize for not preserving enough time to discuss. I can work on that! For now, I would suggest either continuing to reflect on what we discussed today or repeating the work that you did for today's session. Repetition is a good thing. It's up to you—one or both of these would work. How does that sound?

Example Response to Intermediate Client Statement 4

That's great that you did some of what we talked about. We can go over it even without the forms. Also, I'm listening to your tone and wondering if you're beating yourself up about forgetting the forms. Is that happening?

Example Response to Intermediate Client Statement 5

We can work with part! I suggest we start with the part that you were able to do, and then we can discuss what was more difficult to get to. As always, we can adjust, and possibly address some or most of it in here today. Does that plan work for you?

Example Response to Intermediate Client Statement 6

It sounds like it isn't clear how doing this over the next week is going to be useful. There may be different versions of this that could be more or less helpful at this time. I'd like us to consider what is potentially most useful, as well as think about what it means for this to be helpful or not, if that is itself worth testing out.

Example Response to Intermediate Client Statement 7

OK, I appreciate that. We can be flexible and figure out a way to make this work over the next week, if possible. What about brainstorming what part or parts of this might be more feasible over the next week? I would suggest that we not abandon this completely because doing at least *some* homework has been shown to relate to improvement. But you can only do what you can fit in. So, again, let's think in terms of part or parts. Thoughts?

EXAMPLE RESPONSES TO ADVANCED-LEVEL CLIENT STATEMENTS FOR EXERCISE 4
Example Response to Advanced Client Statement 1
I'm glad you said that. It sounds like you're frustrated and possibly discouraged, and I was unclear about the homework, and you don't know what to do. It's important to be on the same page, and I certainly could have been clearer. Let's walk back a bit rather than rush ahead prematurely.
Example Response to Advanced Client Statement 2
It sounds like you're concerned about trying this on your own. We can take a few minutes to clear up anything that might be confusing logistically. Let's go into the details of the assignment to see how we can set something up that is more doable for you. It's also important to emphasize that this isn't something that you're either going to "pass" or "fail." The process is just as, or even more, important than the outcome.
Example Response to Advanced Client Statement 3
I appreciate that you shared this with me. It sounds like others have expressed concern about your drinking, and you're wondering if I might share that concern. Rather than labeling what happened as "OK" or "not OK," I'd rather discuss your experience of completing the homework and how drinking beforehand does or does not fit in with the spirit of the work you're during between our sessions. I'd also like to hear more about your impression that others, perhaps even me, are judging you for your drinking and the impact that seems to have on you.
Example Response to Advanced Client Statement 4
I'm glad to hear how much you're invested in this work and that you can find ways to stay motivated to continue the work between sessions, which can be difficult. I wonder if there are other potential sources of motivation. If we take me out of the equation, what would be most useful and meaningful to you?
Example Response to Advanced Client Statement 5
OK, well *that* seems important to me. Can we talk about that? Were you having doubts when we discussed this last session, or only after you thought about it more? In the end, we need to value the goals and tasks we are doing for them to bear fruit.

Working With Cognitions

Preparations for Exercise 5

1. Read the instructions in Chapter 2.

2. Download the Deliberate Practice Reaction Form at https://www.apa.org/pubs/books/deliberate-practice-cognitive-behavioral-therapy (refer to Clinician and Practitioner Resources; also available in Appendix A). The optional diary form in Appendix B can also be downloaded from this site.

Skill Description

Skill Difficulty Level: Intermediate

By definition, cognitive behavioral therapy (CBT) involves a mix of cognitive and behavioral strategies. Even in more strictly behavioral treatment approaches, cognitions remain important. Guided discovery is an essential process of cognitive work in which the therapist assists the clients in finding their own understandings of, and solutions to, personal concerns. To facilitate this process, CBT clinicians often use the cognitive method of Socratic questioning.

In our experience, it can be easier to first describe guided discovery (and Socratic questioning) by what it is not (or, at least, not intended to be). Guided discovery is not, for example, telling clients that their thinking is wrong or convincing them to change their beliefs. It is also not a series of "why" questions that imply a current problem or irrationality in thoughts, emotions, and/or behaviors.

Rather, in the spirit of collaborative empiricism, guided discovery involves helping clients gather relevant information, examine it in different ways (without judgment from the therapist), and develop a personalized plan for what to do with it. In other words, the goal of working with cognitions is not to simply tell clients to think differently or point out flaws; rather, it is to teach clients a process for evaluating their own experience

https://doi.org/10.1037/0000256-007

Deliberate Practice in Cognitive Behavioral Therapy, by J. F. Boswell and M. J. Constantino

and determining subsequent actions based on this self-reflection. Consistent with more contemporary CBT perspectives on working with cognitions (e.g., Barlow et al., 2017), we view facilitating the client's cognitive flexibility as a central aim of working with cognitions.

Examples of Therapists Working With Cognitions

Example 1

CLIENT: [*sad*] I know I'm a terrible mother.

THERAPIST: What do you mean when you say "terrible mother"? What information leads to that conclusion?

Example 2

CLIENT: [*impatient*] You talk about the importance of thoughts . . . I'm already very aware of my negative thoughts.

THERAPIST: You're absolutely right that you live this every day and these thoughts are in your awareness. I was thinking that was actually a good thing, as it will help us as we work to find new ways of responding to them. But you sound unhappy about being so aware of your thoughts, so there is something else important here. Tell me more.

Example 3

CLIENT: [*frustrated*] I don't know . . . when things get intense, I just act. I don't have any thoughts; I just act or react.

THERAPIST: I see. It happens so quickly that you just react. It's true that the thoughts connected to our emotions and behaviors aren't always so clear or explicit. Yet, if we train ourselves to step back for a moment and work backward from your reaction, I wonder if we might notice your thinking. In doing so, we might get a better sense of why you feel the way you do in these moments.

INSTRUCTIONS FOR EXERCISE 5

Step 1: Role-Play and Feedback

- The client says the first beginner client statement. The therapist improvises a response based on the skill criteria.
- The trainer (or, if not available, the client) provides brief feedback based on the skill criteria.
- The client then repeats the same statement, and the therapist again improvises a response. The trainer (or client) again provide brief feedback.

Step 2: Repeat

- Repeat Step 1 for all the statements in the current difficulty level (beginner, intermediate, or advanced).

Step 3: Assess and Adjust Difficulty

- The therapist completes the Deliberate Practice Reaction Form (see Appendix A) and decides whether to make the exercise easier or harder or to stay at the same difficulty level.

Step 4: Repeat for Approximately 15 Minutes

- Repeat Steps 1 to 3 for at least 15 minutes.
- The trainees then switch therapist and client roles and start over.

Optional Variation for Exercise 5

In the final round of the exercise, the person playing the client improvises a problem with thought monitoring or cognitive reappraisal (e.g., a firmly entrenched belief) that they have heard directly from a real training case, and the person playing the therapist then attempts to address the concern with a cognitively oriented response. The client can then share if the therapist's response was experienced as collaborative and facilitative of further exploration. Note that the client should be careful only to talk about topics that they feel comfortable sharing.

SKILL CRITERIA FOR EXERCISE 5

1. Encourage and facilitate client self-reflection on thoughts and beliefs.
2. Maintain an open, exploratory stance.
3. Orient the client's attention to thoughts or connections between thoughts and other experiences.
4. Emphasize cognitive flexibility, rather than simple thought replacement, and refrain from implying that a particular thought is "right or wrong."

Now it's your turn! Follow Steps 1 and 2 from the instructions.

Remember: The goal of the role-play is for trainees to practice improvising responses to the client statements in a manner that (a) uses the skill criteria and (b) feels authentic for the trainee. **Example therapist responses for each client statement are provided at the end of this exercise. Trainees should attempt to improvise their own responses before reading the example responses.**

BEGINNER-LEVEL CLIENT STATEMENTS FOR EXERCISE 5
Beginner Client Statement 1
[**Curious**] I'm still trying to get the hang of identifying my thoughts. What should I plan for next week?
Beginner Client Statement 2
[**Sad**] I know I'm a terrible mother.
Beginner Client Statement 3
[**Sad**] I'm a total failure.
Beginner Client Statement 4
[**Anxious**] I know the job interview is going to go poorly; they always do.
Beginner Client Statement 5
[**Anxious**] I don't really know anyone who will be at this party. I know I'll be miserable.

 Assess and adjust the difficulty here (see Step 3 in the exercise instructions).

INTERMEDIATE-LEVEL CLIENT STATEMENTS FOR EXERCISE 5
Intermediate Client Statement 1
[**Impatient**] You talk about the importance of thoughts . . . I'm already very aware of my negative thoughts.
Intermediate Client Statement 2
[**Irritated**] When we work through these thought records, it's not hard to come up with alternative evidence and thoughts, but it feels artificial and doesn't really make me feel better.
Intermediate Client Statement 3
[**Sad**] I was feeling hopeless and didn't want to come in today.
Intermediate Client Statement 4
[**Annoyed**] How will focusing more on these negative thoughts and feelings make me feel better rather than just feel worse?
Intermediate Client Statement 5
[**Frustrated**] I don't know . . . when things get intense, I just act. I don't have any thoughts; I just act or react.

🛑 **Assess and adjust the difficulty here (see Step 3 in the exercise instructions).**

ADVANCED-LEVEL CLIENT STATEMENTS FOR EXERCISE 5
Advanced Client Statement 1
[**Frustrated**] My boss's evaluation of me was devastating. I'm at a loss. There is no other perspective on this.
Advanced Client Statement 2
[**Angry**] You're telling me that if my partner died, I should be fine with it?!
Advanced Client Statement 3
[**Frustrated**] Why do you just keep asking questions, over and over again? It's really frustrating not to get anything more direct from you.
Advanced Client Statement 4
[**Happy**] I did what you suggested about my thoughts, and it really helped in the moment. Every time I had a negative thought, I just told myself the opposite.
Advanced Client Statement 5
[**Angry**] I don't like this or find it helpful. My thoughts aren't irrational or baseless, so I actually find it kind of invalidating and insulting.
Advanced Client Statement 6
[**Anxious**] I know I sometimes think in extremes, but what if the worst thing actually *did* happen? It could.

 Assess and adjust the difficulty here (see Step 3 in the exercise instructions). If appropriate, follow the instructions to make the exercise even more challenging (see Appendix A).

Example Therapist Responses: Working With Cognitions

Remember: Trainees should attempt to improvise their own responses before reading the example responses. **Do not read the following responses verbatim unless you are having trouble coming up with your own responses!**

EXAMPLE RESPONSES TO BEGINNER-LEVEL CLIENT STATEMENTS FOR EXERCISE 5
Example Response to Beginner Client Statement 1
Do keep in mind that this is something few of us do naturally. How about practicing thought records a bit more on your own, as I think this would be a good challenge? Shall we develop a practice plan?
Example Response to Beginner Client Statement 2
What do you mean when you say "terrible mother"? What information leads to that conclusion?
Example Response to Beginner Client Statement 3
Let's focus on that thought. I wonder what you might say to a friend who told you something similar?
Example Response to Beginner Client Statement 4
How do you typically determine whether or not an interview has gone poorly? Can you think of an instance when, perhaps to your surprise, an interview didn't go as poorly as you expected?
Example Response to Beginner Client Statement 5
It seems like you're certain of this. Setting aside the likelihood that you would, in fact, be miserable, what would that be like, concretely, for you? What would be some signs that you might actually be enjoying yourself, at least a little?

EXAMPLE RESPONSES TO INTERMEDIATE-LEVEL CLIENT STATEMENTS FOR EXERCISE 5

Example Response to Intermediate Client Statement 1

You're absolutely right that you live this every day and these thoughts are in your awareness. I was thinking that was actually a good thing, as it will help us as we work to find new ways of responding to them. But you sound unhappy about being so aware of your thoughts, so there is something else important here. Tell me more.

Example Response to Intermediate Client Statement 2

This is helpful, what you're telling me. I suggest we take a look at this thought record we just worked through and see if we can understand more about why it's not helping you. It sounds like the practice of identifying alternatives feels disingenuous compared to your typical automatic thoughts. We could start by asking for each of the alternative thoughts, "How much do you actually believe this thought?" We can also take a look to see if there are any action plans you can make for things you can do that might help you feel better about this situation. Or maybe we just need to bail out of thought records. Maybe they are not the right tool for you.

Example Response to Intermediate Client Statement 3

What was going through your mind when you noticed feeling hopeless? What ultimately led to your coming?

Example Response to Intermediate Client Statement 4

We want to help you focus on your thoughts in a new way, almost like a detective building a case for how true or untrue they are. We don't want you to just spend more time feeling bad or focusing on painful thoughts; rather, there are different ways to monitor your thoughts that can provide helpful information that you may typically overlook. Such reflection might help you see things more complexly, or from different angles, which can also help you experience things differently. Does that make sense?

Example Response to Intermediate Client Statement 5

I see. It happens so quickly that you just react. It's true that the thoughts connected to our emotions and behaviors aren't always so clear or explicit. Yet if we train ourselves to step back for a moment and work backward from your reaction, I wonder if we might notice your thinking. In doing so, we might get a better sense of why you feel the way you do in these moments.

EXAMPLE RESPONSES TO ADVANCED-LEVEL CLIENT STATEMENTS FOR EXERCISE 5

Example Response to Advanced Client Statement 1

It sounds like you might be feeling helpless. If I was convinced that my boss's evaluation of me was devastating, I might feel helpless too. Maybe we can see if there is or is not another perspective on this? Let's explore what happened in more detail.

Example Response to Advanced Client Statement 2

Oh, my goodness; no. I'm so sorry I was unclear. Let me try again. If we're tracking your experience, we can identify the situation "my partner died"; thoughts such as "This is horrible. My life is over, I'll never be happy again. I'll be alone forever"; and emotions of pain, grief, loss, hopelessness, helplessness. . . . OK, so now here is the question I have for you. Let's focus on these emotions. What is causing you to have them? Is it the situation? Or is it the thoughts?

Example Response to Advanced Client Statement 3

I think I understand your frustration, and some people can have this reaction to this type of work. I could have been more sensitive to this. The cognitive technique we're using is called guided Socratic discovery, and I can explain a bit more about how it works and why I'm asking all of these questions.

Example Response to Advanced Client Statement 4

It sounds like continued practice with identifying thoughts and coming up with alternative appraisals felt helpful, and I'm glad to hear that. I might reframe this work slightly, however. Considering the opposite can be a useful place to start, and we can also expand this to considering a number of alternative appraisals or interpretations that could enhance the flexibility of our thinking. Let's actually take an example from this past week, shall we?

Example Response to Advanced Client Statement 5

I appreciate you sharing this understandable feeling. It *would* be invalidating to have someone (including me) label your thoughts as irrational and baseless. To be sure, I'd like us both to assume that there is a way to understand the genuine bases of your thinking patterns, and how these are connected with other parts of your experience. Would you be open to exploring in more detail an example of when it felt like I was implying that your thoughts are invalid or baseless and work to find out what was contributing to that experience?

Example Response to Advanced Client Statement 6

I hear you. Sometimes our biggest fears or concerns do rear their ugly head. Can you give me an example of a "worst thing"? Let's say it did occur, what's the absolute worst effect on you? Any sense of how you might cope?

Working With Behaviors

Preparations for Exercise 6

1. Read the instructions in Chapter 2.

2. Download the Deliberate Practice Reaction Form at https://www.apa.org/pubs/ books/deliberate-practice-cognitive-behavioral-therapy (refer to Clinician and Practitioner Resources; also available in Appendix A). The optional diary form in Appendix B can also be downloaded from this site.

SKILL DESCRIPTION

Skill Difficulty Level: Intermediate

By definition, cognitive behavioral therapy (CBT) involves a mix of cognitive and behavioral strategies. Even in more strictly cognitive treatment approaches, explicitly working with behaviors remains important (e.g., conduct of behavioral experiments). Behavioral work relies on principles of classical and operant conditioning, which translate to a relatively eclectic toolbox of strategies. Behavioral interventions can focus on antecedents, the behavioral repertoire itself (including skill deficits), contingencies, and consequences, depending on the nature of the presenting problem. Behavioral strategies can include exposure, stimulus control, activity scheduling, contingency management, and behavioral skill training, among others.

Selection of the appropriate behavioral target and intervention can vary greatly among clients, even within ostensibly similar presenting problem domains, thus requiring an idiographic approach. Given the need for an idiographic approach and the diversity of skills and strategies that can be placed under the behavioral umbrella, we are unable to address them all in this exercise. Rather, we focus on working with (or targeting) behaviors more broadly, as well as the application of learning principles to facilitate change processes more broadly. For example, inviting the client to brainstorm what

https://doi.org/10.1037/0000256-008
Deliberate Practice in Cognitive Behavioral Therapy, by J. F. Boswell and M. J. Constantino

would feel good about doing an activity that they have been avoiding is not concretely intervening on a behavior in the moment. However, this discussion allows for the identification of viable response contingent positive reinforcers, which, in turn, informs subsequent behavioral assignments.

Examples of Therapists Working With Behaviors

Example 1

CLIENT: [*frustrated*] I don't know why I keep blowing up at people. I just do.

THERAPIST: Let's try to understand this together. Understanding your responses in context can help us achieve some clarity. Let's start with a recent example and try to identify what was happening just before the "blow up."

Example 2

CLIENT: [*discouraged*] I've still been pretty down, I guess. I spent most of the week in bed.

THERAPIST: I'm sorry to hear that. There are a lot of factors that likely make it difficult to get out of bed. I wonder if we can actually start by exploring some of the things for which it would be worth getting out of bed.

Example 3

CLIENT: [*frustrated*] I cut myself this week. I don't know why I harm myself like I do.

THERAPIST: Well, let's try to get a better understanding of this together. With behaviors like this, it's important to identify what tends to come before the behavior, and what comes after the behavior. Let's start with what happened this week.

INSTRUCTIONS FOR EXERCISE 6

Step 1: Role-Play and Feedback

- The client says the first beginner client statement. The therapist improvises a response based on the skill criteria.
- The trainer (or, if not available, the client) provides brief feedback based on the skill criteria.
- The client then repeats the same statement, and the therapist again improvises a response. The trainer (or client) again provide brief feedback.

Step 2: Repeat

- Repeat Step 1 for all the statements in the current difficulty level (beginner, intermediate, or advanced).

Step 3: Assess and Adjust Difficulty

- The therapist completes the Deliberate Practice Reaction Form (see Appendix A) and decides whether to make the exercise easier or harder or to stay at the same difficulty level.

Step 4: Repeat for Approximately 15 Minutes

- Repeat Steps 1 to 3 for at least 15 minutes.
- The trainees then switch therapist and client roles and start over.

Optional Variation for Exercise 6

In the final round of the exercise, the person playing the client improvises a problem with behavior modification or subtle negative reinforcement that they have heard directly from a real training case, and the person playing the therapist then attempts to address the concern with a behaviorally oriented response. The client can then share if the therapist's response was experienced as collaborative and consistent with a behavioral framework. Note that the client should be careful only to talk about topics that they feel comfortable sharing.

SKILL CRITERIA FOR EXERCISE 6

1. Maintain a collaborative and curious stance.
2. Be clear when suggesting a plan of action and expectations.
3. Be positive and supportive of both big and small positive changes.
4. Appeal to relevant core learning concepts, including conditioning, reinforcement, the importance of environment, antecedents, and consequences.

Now it's your turn! Follow Steps 1 and 2 from the instructions.

Remember: The goal of the role-play is for trainees to practice improvising responses to the client statements in a manner that (a) uses the skill criteria and (b) feels authentic for the trainee. **Example therapist responses for each client statement are provided at the end of this exercise. Trainees should attempt to improvise their own responses before reading the example responses.**

BEGINNER-LEVEL CLIENT STATEMENTS FOR EXERCISE 6
Beginner Client Statement 1
[**Ashamed**] I know we talked about me having that date last week. I ended up cancelling at the last minute. You know, I actually felt relieved.
Beginner Client Statement 2
[**Frustrated**] I don't know why I keep blowing up at people. I just do.
Beginner Client Statement 3
[**Discouraged**] I've still been pretty down, I guess. I spent most of the week in bed.
Beginner Client Statement 4
[**Anxious**] I've been working hard on keeping my drinking under control, but it's hard. I'm kind of nervous because my friend insists on having his birthday party at the bar this weekend.
Beginner Client Statement 5
[**Frustrated**] I'm still having trouble making appointments. I either completely miss them or end up being late. I just can't get it together.

 Assess and adjust the difficulty here (see Step 3 in the exercise instructions).

INTERMEDIATE-LEVEL CLIENT STATEMENTS FOR EXERCISE 6
Intermediate Client Statement 1
[**Impatient**] Wait a minute . . . you're saying if I can't fall asleep, then I need to get out of bed and stop trying to sleep?
Intermediate Client Statement 2
[**Ashamed**] Umm. After being sober for 6 months, as you know . . . I drank this week. I feel like such a failure.
Intermediate Client Statement 3
[**Sad, failing to make eye contact**] I guess I don't deserve better.
Intermediate Client Statement 4
[**Hopeless**] Before being diagnosed with multiple sclerosis, I loved hiking. I'm devastated because nothing is going to replace that. It's all over.
Intermediate Client Statement 5
[**Frustrated**] I cut myself this week. I don't know why I harm myself like I do.

🛑 **Assess and adjust the difficulty here (see Step 3 in the exercise instructions).**

ADVANCED-LEVEL CLIENT STATEMENTS FOR EXERCISE 6
Advanced Client Statement 1
[**Panicking**] After touching all of the bathroom walls with millions of germs—I am going to wash my hands immediately! I get the point of exposure, but it's crazy not to wash your hands after what we just did.
Advanced Client Statement 2
[**Frustrated**] You think I should set up some "little rewards" to start feeling less depressed. That seems kind of embarrassing and infantilizing.
Advanced Client Statement 3
[**Frustrated**] You don't understand. I can't do these things because I'm depressed. If I wasn't depressed, I could easily do these things, and I wouldn't need to be here in the first place.
Advanced Client Statement 4
[**Angry**] The exposure you assigned last week was a disaster. I had a panic attack on the train, and everyone stared at me. So embarrassing. It's your fault because you told me to do it.
Advanced Client Statement 5
[**Anxious**] I cut myself again, so my fiancé got worried and stayed home from work again.

Assess and adjust the difficulty here (see Step 3 in the exercise instructions). If appropriate, follow the instructions to make the exercise even more challenging (see Appendix A).

Example Therapist Responses: Working With Behaviors

Remember: Trainees should attempt to improvise their own responses before reading the example responses. **Do not read the following responses verbatim unless you are having trouble coming up with your own responses!**

EXAMPLE RESPONSES TO BEGINNER-LEVEL CLIENT STATEMENTS FOR EXERCISE 6
Example Response to Beginner Client Statement 1
Yes, that reduction in tension or anxiety can feel like a relief and feel good in the moment. Canceling a plan like that is a pretty effective way of reducing anxiety. Keeping this in mind, we should discuss a process that is called negative reinforcement, and how it can help us understand how anxiety is maintained or even strengthened over time. Let's think through what we learn from this.
Example Response to Beginner Client Statement 2
Let's try to understand this together. Understanding your responses in context can help us achieve some clarity. Let's start with a recent example and try to identify what was happening just before the "blow up."
Example Response to Beginner Client Statement 3
I'm sorry to hear that. There are a lot of factors that likely make it difficult to get out of bed. I wonder if we can actually start by exploring some of the things for which it would be worth getting out of bed.
Example Response to Beginner Client Statement 4
Tell me if this is off base, but it sounds like you're concerned about being around so much alcohol and other people drinking at this party. When we've discussed your alcohol use, it seems like there are some specific circumstances that are associated with your drinking. Although we don't want to cut you off from your friends or any place that might serve alcohol forever, there are situations that are going to be more or less helpful to you. I'm interested in hearing more about your concerns, and I suggest that we brainstorm a plan. How does that sound?
Example Response to Beginner Client Statement 5
That sounds understandably frustrating. Let's revisit potential barriers to remembering appointments and getting yourself there on time. Then we can brainstorm some methods to help with this, such as setting up reminders in the places you are least likely to miss them. How does this sound?

EXAMPLE RESPONSES TO INTERMEDIATE-LEVEL **CLIENT STATEMENTS FOR EXERCISE 6**
Example Response to Intermediate Client Statement 1
Yes, and that might sound counterintuitive. It's important for the bed and bedroom to be specifically associated with sleep. The reality is that you aren't sleeping anyway. When you leave the bedroom and come back when you are ready for sleep, you train your brain to learn that the bed is the place for sleep.
Example Response to Intermediate Client Statement 2
It seems like you're feeling discouraged. I can imagine the struggle this has been for you, and I appreciate your willingness to talk about it today. Can we explore the circumstances surrounding what happened?
Example Response to Intermediate Client Statement 3
I notice that when you say these things, it seems hard to even make eye contact with me. I think it would be important to understand how this behavior relates to your experience in here and outside of here.
Example Response to Intermediate Client Statement 4
I hear that it's frustrating. And at some level you're right; nothing else is going to perfectly "replace" what you used to do. It's possible this expectation makes it hard to take the first step toward finding new, meaningful activities. Perhaps we can brainstorm some concrete options that would still be of interest, without any particular expectations that they would be, at least immediately, as enjoyable or meaningful as hiking?
Example Response to Intermediate Client Statement 5
Well, let's try to get a better understanding of this together. With behaviors like this, it's important to identify what tends to come before the behavior, and what comes after the behavior. Let's start with what happened this week.[1]

---

1. When a client says that they have caused self-harm, trainees should seek close supervision for future risk of self-harm or suicide. If a client is at risk of suicide, therapists should consider a suicide assessment and a possible referral or option for suicide-focused treatment, such as the collaborative assessment and management of suicidality (https://cams-care.com).

EXAMPLE RESPONSES TO ADVANCED-LEVEL CLIENT STATEMENTS FOR EXERCISE 6
Example Response to Advanced Client Statement 1
I hear you. Recall that there are two parts to this work—the actual exposure and then preventing the behaviors that you typically engage in to respond to the perceived threat of the germs. We need to fully disrupt this process of negative reinforcement if you are going to overcome this problem; in other words, refraining from washing is also critical.
Example Response to Advanced Client Statement 2
It sounds like some of the suggested strategies seem too simple or even paternalistic. I can appreciate that reaction, and it isn't that uncommon at first. Each person is different, but in my experience simple changes can actually have a major impact. It also seems like there is a relative absence of *any* positive reinforcement in your life right now.
Example Response to Advanced Client Statement 3
I would like to understand better. It can be hard to imagine doing things when feeling so depressed, and that just further highlights the difficulty of what we're up against. We can develop concrete strategies to help you take the initial step.
Example Response to Advanced Client Statement 4
I can understand your frustration. Before saying more, I just want to acknowledge that I know it took a lot from you to put yourself in that difficult situation. I don't want to invalidate your frustration because it is real, yet I also see you getting on a train in the first place as significant progress. However, I would like to know more details about what happened, and I also think it would be important to revisit the goals of exposure. Further, I'm concerned that it felt like the plan that we discussed last week was coercive in some way. That seems important to discuss.
Example Response to Advanced Client Statement 5
It sounds like your fiancé is concerned about you and becomes more attentive when you engage in this behavior. I think it would be important to consider a pattern that might be emerging.[2]

2. See Footnote 1.

Working With Emotions

Preparations for Exercise 7

1. Read the instructions in Chapter 2.

2. Download the Deliberate Practice Reaction Form at https://www.apa.org/pubs/books/deliberate-practice-cognitive-behavioral-therapy (refer to Clinician and Practitioner Resources; also available in Appendix A). The optional diary form in Appendix B can also be downloaded from this site.

Skill Description

Skill Difficulty Level: Intermediate

Like any psychotherapy, a therapist's ability to evoke or tolerate, and work effectively with, client emotions is critically important in cognitive behavioral therapy (CBT). Moreover, "working with" implies helping the client to tolerate their emotions and emotion-related distress, such as in the case of exposure. Exposure is a potent, yet often intense, intervention, for both the client and therapist. In addition, beyond exposure-based interventions, contemporary CBT models attend explicitly to emotions in varied ways, often with a goal of reducing emotion-related avoidance (Barlow et al., 2017; Boswell, 2013). It may be more intuitive to think about this skill as focusing on helping clients work on their emotional experience and processing, yet the emotions serve both inter- and intrapersonal functions, and research demonstrates that both client and therapist emotional expression are associated with treatment outcome (Peluso & Freund, 2018).

As such, the decision to implement exposure, or to work with emotions and address emotion avoidance in other ways, is predicated on the therapist's skill of tolerating the inherent discomfort often affiliated with such foci. Difficulty with this skill can translate to the *therapist* maladaptively avoiding the use of this potentially potent intervention or reinforcing client avoidance and thereby maintaining the problem(s). Thus, practicing

https://doi.org/10.1037/0000256-009

Deliberate Practice in Cognitive Behavioral Therapy, by J. F. Boswell and M. J. Constantino

this skill can help therapists circumvent this fairly typical, understandable, and inadvertent negative reinforcement process.

Special Instructions for Exercise 7

Although emotions are more or less universally relevant in CBT, they are arguably uniquely relevant when a CBT therapist is engaging in strategies that are designed to evoke and promote tolerance and acceptance of difficult emotions and contexts associated with strong emotions, such as exposure. For the client stimuli in this exercise, it may be useful for the therapist to assume that the client statement is being made in the context of exposure (or a mood induction or behavioral experiment designed to evoke a strong response), either in preparation for or during an actual exercise. The majority of beginner and advanced stimuli were constructed with this in mind.

Examples of Therapists Working With Emotions

Example 1

CLIENT: [*panicking*] OK, I'm definitely feeling anxious now! Um, what's the point of this exposure again? What if it doesn't work? What if I can't stop feeling like this? Maybe we should stop now.

THERAPIST: OK, remember that you're in control of this. If you decide we need to stop, we absolutely will. But remember that sticking with this can help your brain and your body learn that you're actually safe right now. Remember that you won't feel anxious forever. So, with that in mind, I suggest we keep going. Are you up for that?

Example 2

CLIENT: [*shaking and weeping*] This is not something I can get into without hysterically crying. That's why I avoid it.

THERAPIST: Yes, I totally get it. And, like we discussed, avoiding it brings temporary relief. But, often at a longer term cost. By avoiding something to feel relief, it's like we tell ourselves that this to too big and powerful for me to deal with in any other way, which only strengthens the narrative and the emotion, giving it more control over you. Does that make sense? Do you remain motivated to see that we can lessen that power, even if it means tolerating discomfort to get there?

Example 3

CLIENT: [*disgusted, looking away*] Ugh. Ahh. That is disgusting! I am not looking at that or touching it!

THERAPIST: We shouldn't pretend it isn't disgusting. But you've been through so much, dealing with this. Try to think about the things that are dear to you, what kind of life you want to live. This is where you turn the corner.

INSTRUCTIONS FOR EXERCISE 7

Step 1: Role-Play and Feedback

- The client says the first beginner client statement. The therapist improvises a response based on the skill criteria.
- The trainer (or, if not available, the client) provides brief feedback based on the skill criteria.
- The client then repeats the same statement, and the therapist again improvises a response. The trainer (or client) again provide brief feedback.

Step 2: Repeat

- Repeat Step 1 for all the statements in the current difficulty level (beginner, intermediate, or advanced).

Step 3: Assess and Adjust Difficulty

- The therapist completes the Deliberate Practice Reaction Form (see Appendix A) and decides whether to make the exercise easier or harder or to stay at the same difficulty level.

Step 4: Repeat for Approximately 15 Minutes

- Repeat Steps 1 to 3 for at least 15 minutes.
- The trainees then switch therapist and client roles and start over.

Optional Variation for Exercise 7

In the final round of the exercise, the person playing the client improvises a problem with experiential avoidance (or emotional over- or undercontrol) that they have heard directly from a real training case, and the person playing the therapist then attempts to address the concern with an emotion-focused response. The client can then share if the therapist's response was experienced as empathic and emotion-focused (within a broader CBT framework). Note that the client should be careful only to talk about topics that they feel comfortable sharing.

SKILL CRITERIA FOR EXERCISE 7

1. Empathically inquire about clients' emotional experience.
2. Actively listen and maintain a supportive tone to clients' emotional disclosures.
3. Model tolerance of affect and an approach orientation to clients' strong emotional experience.
4. Use psychoeducation to support the importance of clients experiencing versus avoiding their emotion and the maladaptive consequences of negative reinforcement.

Now it's your turn! Follow Steps 1 and 2 from the instructions.

Remember: The goal of the role-play is for trainees to practice improvising responses to the client statements in a manner that (a) uses the skill criteria and (b) feels authentic for the trainee. **Example therapist responses for each client statement are provided at the end of this exercise. Trainees should attempt to improvise their own responses before reading the example responses.**

BEGINNER-LEVEL CLIENT STATEMENTS FOR EXERCISE 7
Beginner Client Statement 1
[**Nervous**] I don't think I'm ready to work on this today.
Beginner Client Statement 2
[**Weeping**] I'm so embarrassed. I'm an ugly crier.
Beginner Client Statement 3
[**Nervous, deflecting from exposure task**] Oh, I forgot to tell you that I might be switching jobs. Maybe we should talk about that instead today?
Beginner Client Statement 4
[**Panicking**] OK, I'm definitely feeling anxious now! Um, what's the point of this exposure again? What if it doesn't work? What if I can't stop feeling like this? Maybe we should stop now.
Beginner Client Statement 5
[**Tearing up**] I don't even know if I'm getting any better in here. I mean, I've been in therapy for weeks and I feel the same.

 Assess and adjust the difficulty here (see Step 3 in the exercise instructions).

INTERMEDIATE-LEVEL CLIENT STATEMENTS FOR EXERCISE 7
Intermediate Client Statement 1
[**Angry**] I think I'm done with therapy . . . things aren't that bad, and maybe I don't want to change! I've been dealing with this my whole life and I've managed.
Intermediate Client Statement 2
[**Shaking and teary**] I'm really embarrassed . . . I kind of lied to you about what I thought I could handle in here. I didn't want to disappoint you or make you feel like this is a waste of time.
Intermediate Client Statement 3
[**Crying**] My partner broke up with me today. I know it's stupid, but I really thought we were going to get married.
Intermediate Client Statement 4
[**Shaking and weeping**] This is not something I can get into without hysterically crying. That's why I avoid it.
Intermediate Client Statement 5
[**Head in hands, sobbing without speaking**]

Assess and adjust the difficulty here (see Step 3 in the exercise instructions).

ADVANCED-LEVEL CLIENT STATEMENTS FOR EXERCISE 7
Advanced Client Statement 1
[**Angry**] What we're doing in here is so stupid!
Advanced Client Statement 2
[**Very anxious**] I feel like I'm going to have a panic attack or faint!
Advanced Client Statement 3
[**Disgusted, looking away**] Ugh. Ahh. That is disgusting! I am not looking at that or touching it!
Advanced Client Statement 4
[**Crying, raised voice**] I can't do this!
Advanced Client Statement 5
[**Angry**] You don't understand. I want to stop feeling sad, not practice feeling sad. I'm already pretty freaking great at feeling bad. So, I really don't need more practice at that!
Advanced Client Statement 6
[**Panicking**] Oh my god . . . Oh my god . . . I'm dying! I can't breathe! Help me!
Advanced Client Statement 7
[**Angry**] I don't think you really care about me! You just pretend to like me because it's your job!

 Assess and adjust the difficulty here (see Step 3 in the exercise instructions). If appropriate, follow the instructions to make the exercise even more challenging (see Appendix A).

Example Therapist Responses: Working With Emotions

Remember: Trainees should attempt to improvise their own responses before reading the example responses. **Do not read the following responses verbatim unless you are having trouble coming up with your own responses!**

EXAMPLE RESPONSES TO BEGINNER-LEVEL CLIENT STATEMENTS FOR EXERCISE 7
Example Response to Beginner Client Statement 1
OK. It sounds like there's some uncertainty about moving forward with this today. Let's discuss your concerns. Some degree of anxiety is always expected—and part of the point, right? But this isn't easy. We can also revisit the plan for today.
Example Response to Beginner Client Statement 2
It sounds like you feel like your sadness and tears are ugly. I actually think they're important and important to listen to.
Example Response to Beginner Client Statement 3
We can definitely talk some about your work, as I know that's important. I'm wondering, though, if you might be feeling a little bit nervous about doing the exposures we discussed? This would make sense, as they can be uncomfortable. Can we start by identifying and exploring your internal experience right now?
Example Response to Beginner Client Statement 4
[**Speaking slowly and calmly, making eye contact**] OK, remember that you're in control of this. If you decide we need to stop, we absolutely will. But remember that sticking with this can help your brain and your body learn that you're actually safe right now. Remember that you won't feel anxious forever. So, with that in mind, I suggest we keep going. Are you up for that?
Example Response to Beginner Client Statement 5
If you feel you aren't making progress, that's important. Let's revisit your goals and see what we think about progress. If you aren't making the progress you want, we can do some brainstorming about how to enhance or change your treatment to get more progress. How does that sound to you? Or, another option is we could do a thought record to identify what thoughts you are having to cause you to feel so hopeless. Which of these do you want to do?

EXAMPLE RESPONSES TO INTERMEDIATE-LEVEL CLIENT STATEMENTS FOR EXERCISE 7

Example Response to Intermediate Client Statement 1

You have, and that's a testimony to your strength! But something made you decide to start therapy, and something made you come to this session today. I'm curious if what you're feeling is that you don't want things to change . . . or that you can't change.

Example Response to Intermediate Client Statement 2

I'm so glad you're telling me. We can always adjust our plan next session, but right now, I'm curious as to why not disappointing me is so important to you.

Example Response to Intermediate Client Statement 3

[**Nodding, leaning forward**] I'm so sorry to hear that. I know how much that relationship meant to you. I am wondering about your statement that this is "stupid." What contributes to that?

Example Response to Intermediate Client Statement 4

Yes, I totally get it. And, like we discussed, avoiding it brings temporary relief. But, often at a longer term cost. By avoiding something to feel relief, it's like we tell ourselves that "this is too big and powerful for me to deal with in any other way," which only strengthens the narrative and the emotion, giving it more control over you. Does that make sense? Do you remain motivated to see that we can lessen such power, even if it means tolerating discomfort to get there?

Example Response to Intermediate Client Statement 5

[**Silence; allow client to cry and simply be present with an engaged nod and gaze. Do not speak first or shut down the emotion experiencing.**]

EXAMPLE RESPONSES TO ADVANCED-LEVEL CLIENT STATEMENTS FOR EXERCISE 7

Example Response to Advanced Client Statement 1

I'm hearing that you find this unhelpful. I really do hear you, and I appreciate your candor. I'd like to know more about what's stupid about it.

Example Response to Advanced Client Statement 2

This is hard work. Let's sit with those feelings and anchor into your breath. I'm here with you. Let's stick with it and try not to fight it.

Example Response to Advanced Client Statement 3

We shouldn't pretend it isn't disgusting. But you've been through so much, dealing with this. Try to think about the things that are dear to you, what kind of life you want to live. This is where you turn the corner.

Example Response to Advanced Client Statement 4

I know it *feels* like you can't do this, that it's impossible today. I wouldn't suggest this if I didn't think you were ready or able. This takes a leap of faith, to trust me and yourself. I'm here with you. Let's take a minute to revisit what doing this means to you and the kind of life that you want to live.

Example Response to Advanced Client Statement 5

I'm really glad you told me how this feels for you! It sounds like I really missed the boat here and haven't been understanding what you've been telling me. I apologize. It must have been very frustrating to come in here every week and feel like you're doing the opposite of what you want to accomplish. I'm wondering if we can talk about this more and figure out a solution together?

Example Response to Advanced Client Statement 6

[**Speaking calmly, establishing eye contact**] Remember that you're breathing right now, even though it feels like you can't. Try to just focus on your breathing. We'll do it together. Just breathe with me. You can do this.

Example Response to Advanced Client Statement 7

You're right: This is my job. It's OK to question other people's motives, including mine, and to feel upset with me if I conveyed that I only pretend to be invested in you and your treatment. Can we discuss what's contributing to these doubts about whether I genuinely care about you?

Adherence Flexibility

Preparations for Exercise 8

1. Read the instructions in Chapter 2.

2. Download the Deliberate Practice Reaction Form at https://www.apa.org/pubs/
   books/deliberate-practice-cognitive-behavioral-therapy (refer to Clinician and
   Practitioner Resources; also available in Appendix A). The optional diary form in
   Appendix B can also be downloaded from this site.

Skill Description

Skill Difficulty Level: Advanced

Although extant evidence fails to demonstrate a consistent, linear relationship between
adherence and treatment outcome, there is direct and indirect evidence for the importance of maintaining a coherent framework. Furthermore, among the wide variety of
cognitive behavioral therapy (CBT) techniques included in evidence-based treatments,
the evidence supporting the universal importance of any specific technique is mixed
(Cuijpers et al., 2019). There is some evidence that adherence aligns with the story
of Goldilocks (McCarthy et al., 2016). The extreme ends of the adherence continuum
appear to be problematic—rigid adherence or haphazard adherence (or the absence
of working from a coherent framework). The "just right" findings underscore the importance of flexibility within fidelity (Kendall & Frank, 2018). When considering flexible
practice, others have made the distinction between fidelity-consistent and fidelity-
inconsistent modifications to a treatment approach. When following a CBT manual, for
example, a therapist might adopt a technique that is not specifically included in the
designed protocol, yet the adopted technique is still consistent with the broader CBT
model (fidelity-consistent modification). Conversely, fidelity-inconsistent modifications
represent the adoption of techniques that are inconsistent with the broader CBT

https://doi.org/10.1037/0000256-010

model. Setting aside arguments that, upon closer inspection, some techniques that initially appear to be unique may not be that unique (Castonguay, 2011), in this skill, we focus on what we would consider fidelity-consistent modification or flexibility—that is, responding in a flexible manner to the needs and circumstances of the individual client while remaining anchored in the broad CBT model.

Examples of Therapist Adherence Flexibility

Example 1

CLIENT: [*anxious*] I'm not ready to try the next item on my exposure hierarchy.

THERAPIST: OK. As we discussed, the plan is not completely encased in stone. Before we consider an adjustment, can we explore what might be concerning you about this?

Example 2

CLIENT: [*anxious*] I know the plan was to review my monitoring, but I learned yesterday that I might lose my job.

THERAPIST: I'm very sorry to hear that. I want to be sure that we give you space to talk about that in here. We can table some or most of what we planned for today, and we might actually find a way to incorporate aspects in our discussion.

Example 3

CLIENT: [*frustrated*] I don't think I can commit to coming here every week.

THERAPIST: OK. Let's consider our options and the potential costs and benefits for your treatment. We might be able to come up with a plan that facilitates continuing to meet weekly.

INSTRUCTIONS FOR EXERCISE 8
Step 1: Role-Play and Feedback
• The client says the first beginner client statement. The therapist improvises a response based on the skill criteria. • The trainer (or, if not available, the client) provides brief feedback based on the skill criteria. • The client then repeats the same statement, and the therapist again improvises a response. The trainer (or client) again provide brief feedback.
Step 2: Repeat
• Repeat Step 1 for all the statements in the current difficulty level (beginner, intermediate, or advanced).
Step 3: Assess and Adjust Difficulty
• The therapist completes the Deliberate Practice Reaction Form (see Appendix A) and decides whether to make the exercise easier or harder or to stay at the same difficulty level.
Step 4: Repeat for Approximately 15 Minutes
• Repeat Steps 1 to 3 for at least 15 minutes. • The trainees then switch therapist and client roles and start over.

Optional Variation for Exercise 8

In the final round of the exercise, the person playing the client improvises a problem with the CBT plan or activity that they have heard directly from a real training case, and the person playing the therapist then attempts to address the concern with a flexible yet CBT-consistent response. The client can then share if the therapist's response was indeed experienced as flexible while remaining generally consistent with the general CBT frame. Note that the client should be careful only to talk about topics that they feel comfortable sharing.

SKILL CRITERIA FOR EXERCISE 8
1. Maintain a collaborative and transparent stance.
2. Demonstrate empathy.
3. Demonstrate openness to explore before determining if a modification is indeed warranted.
4. Maintain consistency with a broad CBT orientation.

Now it's your turn! Follow Steps 1 and 2 from the instructions.

Remember: The goal of the role-play is for trainees to practice improvising responses to the client statements in a manner that (a) uses the skill criteria and (b) feels authentic for the trainee. **Example therapist responses for each client statement are provided at the end of this exercise. Trainees should attempt to improvise their own responses before reading the example responses.**

BEGINNER-LEVEL CLIENT STATEMENTS FOR EXERCISE 8
Beginner Client Statement 1
[**Anxious**] I'm not ready to try the next item on my exposure hierarchy.
Beginner Client Statement 2
[**Anxious**] I don't think I'm ready to do all of what you're asking me to do before the next session.
Beginner Client Statement 3
[**Frustrated**] I don't like this breathing stuff. The experience monitoring was more helpful.
Beginner Client Statement 4
[**Excited**] You won't believe what happened this week!
Beginner Client Statement 5
[**Frustrated**] I know I said I would go to the event and start a conversation with new people, but I only managed to say "hello" to one person.

 Assess and adjust the difficulty here (see Step 3 in the exercise instructions).

INTERMEDIATE-LEVEL CLIENT STATEMENTS FOR EXERCISE 8
Intermediate Client Statement 1
[**Anxious**] I know the plan was to review my monitoring, but I learned yesterday that I might lose my job.
Intermediate Client Statement 2
[**Agitated**] I'd go into what happened back then, but I know that we focus on the present in this therapy.
Intermediate Client Statement 3
[**Anxious**] I guess I haven't brought up religion in here yet; I've been unsure about doing that.
Intermediate Client Statement 4
[**Anxious**] I'm uneasy about doing the homework, living with my extended family in such a small place. It makes me uncomfortable.
Intermediate Client Statement 5
[**Hopeless, after completing a progress monitoring measure**] I think the scores on the measure you asked me to complete are consistent with my experience so far. It feels like things might actually be getting worse.
Intermediate Client Statement 6
[**Anxious**] I've learned some new things. But I still feel tense all the time. I can't have a conversation with anyone without lashing out. I feel on edge and still can't really relax.[1]

 Assess and adjust the difficulty here (see Step 3 in the exercise instructions).

---

1. This client statement and the subsequent example therapist response were originally described in Boswell and Schwartzman (2018). This example was taken from a transcript of an actual therapy session in which I (JFB) served as the therapist. We have reproduced this content from the original, more comprehensive case vignette because it conveys a common therapeutic scenario that is ideal for training in applying CBT in an adherent yet flexible manner.

ADVANCED-LEVEL CLIENT STATEMENTS FOR EXERCISE 8
Advanced Client Statement 1
[**Matter of fact**] I think my problems partly stem from the racism and disrespect that I experience at work.
Advanced Client Statement 2
[**Frustrated**] I don't think I can commit to coming here every week.
Advanced Client Statement 3
[**Depressed**] I wasn't able to do the trauma homework. I've been feeling more depressed and sleeping a lot. I've been late to work a few days this week.
Advanced Client Statement 4
[**Excited**] I found this article about a breakthrough medication for anxiety, and it seems like something I could try.
Advanced Client Statement 5
[**Hopeless**] To be honest, things haven't improved as much as I expected.

✋ **Assess and adjust the difficulty here (see Step 3 in the exercise instructions). If appropriate, follow the instructions to make the exercise even more challenging (see Appendix A).**

Example Therapist Responses: Adherence Flexibility

Remember: Trainees should attempt to improvise their own responses before reading the example responses. **Do not read the following responses verbatim unless you are having trouble coming up with your own responses!**

EXAMPLE RESPONSES TO BEGINNER-LEVEL CLIENT STATEMENTS FOR EXERCISE 8
Example Response to Beginner Client Statement 1
OK. As we discussed, the plan is not completely encased in stone. Before we consider an adjustment, can we explore what might be concerning you about this?
Example Response to Beginner Client Statement 2
Thanks for letting me know. Let's figure out something that will be more manageable and helpful for you.
Example Response to Beginner Client Statement 3
OK. Each person is different, and some things are experienced as more helpful than others. I'd like to hear more about what you don't like about the breathing work. We can certainly adjust to focus more on the experience monitoring if that is more helpful.
Example Response to Beginner Client Statement 4
It sounds like you've been going through a lot recently. I wonder if we can find a way to discuss what's going on, and also have time to keep working on the things we've identified to work on so you can get better in the long run. In terms of an agenda, how about if we take some of our time today to review the recent events and some of our time to keep working on the skills we've been discussing?
Example Response to Beginner Client Statement 5
It seems like you might be a bit disappointed by this, but I see this as significant progress. It was a big accomplishment to show up to the event in the first place and then say hello to someone you don't know. Let's talk about what that was like.

EXAMPLE RESPONSES TO INTERMEDIATE-LEVEL CLIENT STATEMENTS FOR EXERCISE 8
Example Response to Intermediate Client Statement 1
I'm very sorry to hear that. I want to be sure that we give you space to talk about that in here. We can table some or most of what we planned for today, and we might actually find a way to incorporate aspects in our discussion.
Example Response to Intermediate Client Statement 2
You're right that we focus more on the present in this approach, but that doesn't mean that your past experience is irrelevant. If it seems important to you, I'd like to hear more about what happened, and we can tie that back to what is going on now.
Example Response to Intermediate Client Statement 3
Do you have any spiritual or religious beliefs that are important to tell me about? I'd like to clarify that this is not off-limits in here. We can be sure to attend to that area as part of the work that we're doing if that is meaningful to you.
Example Response to Intermediate Client Statement 4
That's important to know, thanks. Let's brainstorm some adjustments that are likely to be more workable.
Example Response to Intermediate Client Statement 5
That's important to acknowledge, even more so because it's being communicated in multiple ways. I also understand that this might feel discouraging. Let's revisit our plan and talk about what, specifically, isn't working and what, if anything, might be working.
Example Response to Intermediate Client Statement 6
I'm glad we're having this conversation. My sense is that it will be useful to continue following our general plan, but there are some other options that clients find helpful that could help reduce some of your tension and are worth considering. If you're OK with this, I'd like us to spend the rest of today's session on some more targeted relaxation strategies.[2]

---

2. See Footnote 1.

EXAMPLE RESPONSES TO ADVANCED-LEVEL CLIENT STATEMENTS FOR EXERCISE 8
Example Response to Advanced Client Statement 1
First, I'm sorry to hear that you've experienced that. Rather than compartmentalize or treat that as something outside of the scope of therapy, we need to recognize the impact and integrate that reality into the work we're doing.
Example Response to Advanced Client Statement 2
OK. Let's consider our options, and the potential costs and benefits for your treatment. We might be able to come up with a plan that facilitates continuing to meet weekly.
Example Response to Advanced Client Statement 3
Being late for work is pretty unusual for you. It seems important to prioritize discussing your mood today, and we can circle back to discussing the homework if that seems most useful.
Example Response to Advanced Client Statement 4
It sounds like the article was of great interest, and part of you is curious if this option might work for you. In general, it seems like it might be important to discuss the option of a medication consultation and how that might fit with the work that we are doing in here.
Example Response to Advanced Client Statement 5
I hear and appreciate that. Let's revisit our plan. Although we don't want to just keep doing more of the same if it feels less helpful, we might simply need to adjust the initial expectations regarding the number of sessions.

Responding to Therapeutic Alliance Ruptures

Preparations for Exercise 9

1. Read the instructions in Chapter 2.

2. Download the Deliberate Practice Reaction Form at https://www.apa.org/pubs/books/deliberate-practice-cognitive-behavioral-therapy (refer to Clinician and Practitioner Resources; also available in Appendix A). The optional diary form in Appendix B can also be downloaded from this site.

Skill Description

Skill Difficulty Level: Advanced

Therapist flexibility and the ongoing tailoring of cognitive behavioral therapy (CBT) to the specific client and context represents evidence-based practice in its most complex, fullest form (see Chapter 3 on responsivity in CBT for a full discussion and synthesis of the research literature). Complementing the skill of CBT fidelity-consistent modification and flexibility (Exercise 8), there is also growing evidence that CBT is more effective when therapists fully, although temporarily, "depart" from standard CBT skills in the face of certain in-session process markers and moments. Instead, depending on the marker, the therapist can use specific and evidence-informed CBT fidelity-*inconsistent* strategies until the salient (and often hindering) process has been adequately addressed; such resolution would then precipitate a return to standard CBT. In this skill, we focus on the responsive use of *humanistic/interpersonal* skills to address *alliance ruptures* that may emerge in the client–therapist relationship during a course of CBT.

A quality therapeutic alliance is commonly and pantheoretically defined as comprising three interrelated components: (a) client and therapist agreement on treatment goals; (b) client and therapist agreement on the tasks that will be used to achieve those goals (in this case, CBT); and (c) a dyadic bond that the client and therapist experience as

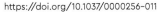

https://doi.org/10.1037/0000256-011

Deliberate Practice in Cognitive Behavioral Therapy, by J. F. Boswell and M. J. Constantino

secure, warm, and friendly. Of course, such relational qualities can wax and wane during therapy, especially considering the natural strains of therapeutic work or other dyadic misattunements that might *rupture* (in one participant, the other, or both) a sense of coordinated collaboration or close connection. When such ruptures occur, they can relate to maladaptive treatment processes and outcomes. Importantly, though, they can also represent potential change opportunities that, if handled skillfully, can be therapeutic. That is, rupture–repair can be a therapy change mechanism that operates instead of, or alongside, the putative mechanisms of the treatment being delivered. In this case, rather than persist with CBT in the face of rupture markers, which might involve trying to convince the client of CBT's merits, research supports a contextual shift from CBT to a more humanistic and interpersonal stance and strategy.

To responsively apply such strategies first requires noticing markers of alliance rupture, which (when originating with the client) can be generally classified into two types. The first, *withdrawal markers*, represent the pursuit of relatedness at the expense of one's need for self-definition or assertion (i.e., being reluctant to confront because of fear of losing the relationship). The second, *confrontation markers*, represent the expression of self-definition at the expense of relatedness. Whatever the type, the marker represents an important message about the state of the relationship and treatment that a clinician would be wise to explore via the interpersonal strategy of metacommunication, or bringing immediate awareness to bear on the relational process as it unfolds. In the context of such communication, the clinician can also engage humanistic strategies of expressing empathy and taking at least partial responsibility for the relationship strain in the service of validating the client's experience and offering to work collaboratively to shift the dyadic experience. Such temporary and contextual departure from CBT can be facilitative, both on its own as a corrective interpersonal experience and by restoring the working relationship to the point of returning to the CBT plan.

Examples of Therapists Responding to Therapeutic Alliance Ruptures

Example 1

CLIENT: [*frustrated*] Well, I'm not really sure about it, but I guess I'll give the thought record another shot if you think that's best.

THERAPIST: Well, we certainly can do one together. However, I get the feeling that maybe you're just agreeing to do it because I suggested it. Like you're going along with it but maybe aren't so sure it makes sense right now? Is that on or off base?

Example 2

CLIENT: [*exasperated*] I feel like you've been hearing me wrong since we started. You don't seem to understand what I mean. Are you even listening?

THERAPIST: I can hear your frustration with me, which makes complete sense given that it feels like I've not been listening to you. I fear that I've probably been too focused on how to *solve* the problem, that I neglected to *hear* the problem accurately. That's on me, and I will try to do better. Can you say more about what I've gotten wrong?

Example 3

CLIENT: [*frustrated*] Whelp, the homework was another big swing and miss. Made no sense. Can we not do that one again?

THERAPIST: I can see that the homework is adding more stress. In fact, I realize that I did not explain its rationale clearly. It may also be that this assignment was less relevant to your most pressing needs. I apologize, and I'd like to discuss what does seem more relevant and personally suitable.

INSTRUCTIONS FOR EXERCISE 9
Step 1: Role-Play and Feedback
• The client says the first beginner client statement. The therapist improvises a response based on the skill criteria. • The trainer (or, if not available, the client) provides brief feedback based on the skill criteria. • The client then repeats the same statement, and the therapist again improvises a response. The trainer (or client) again provide brief feedback.
Step 2: Repeat
• Repeat Step 1 for all the statements in the current difficulty level (beginner, intermediate, or advanced).
Step 3: Assess and Adjust Difficulty
• The therapist completes the Deliberate Practice Reaction Form (see Appendix A) and decides whether to make the exercise easier or harder or to stay at the same difficulty level.
Step 4: Repeat for Approximately 15 Minutes
• Repeat Steps 1 to 3 for at least 15 minutes. • The trainees then switch therapist and client roles and start over.

Optional Variation for Exercise 9

In the final round of the exercise, the person playing the client improvises an alliance rupture that they have directly experienced from a real training case, and the person playing the therapist then attempts to begin the rupture–repair process. The client can then share if the therapist's response was experienced as empathic and collaborative. Note that the client should be careful only to talk about topics that they feel comfortable sharing.

SKILL CRITERIA FOR EXERCISE 9
1. Momentarily step away from the CBT change agenda.
2. Warmly invite the client to discuss their subjective experience.
3. Empathize with the client's thoughts and feelings and invite further disclosure of unhelpful or invalidating occurrences.
4. "Disarm" the client's negative affect toward you or CBT by finding some truth in their disclosures.

> **Now it's your turn! Follow Steps 1 and 2 from the instructions.**

Remember: The goal of the role-play is for trainees to practice improvising responses to the client statements in a manner that (a) uses the skill criteria and (b) feels authentic for the trainee. **Example therapist responses for each client statement are provided at the end of this exercise. Trainees should attempt to improvise their own responses before reading the example responses.**

BEGINNER-LEVEL CLIENT STATEMENTS FOR EXERCISE 9
Beginner Client Statement 1
[**Frustrated**] Well, I'm not really sure about it, but I guess I'll give the thought record another shot if you think that's best.
Beginner Client Statement 2
[**Withdrawn**] I'm not sure where to start, or what to prioritize on today's agenda. Sorry.
Beginner Client Statement 3
[**Sad, withdrawn**] I just don't know what to say or do anymore . . . to you—or anyone.
Beginner Client Statement 4
[**Exasperated**] I feel like you've been hearing me wrong since we started. You don't seem to understand what I mean. Are you even listening?
Beginner Client Statement 5
[**Surprised**] That was a really abrupt ending last session. I know we only have an hour, but I was kind of in the middle of something. That's been on my mind ever since. I even considered not coming today . . . I guess I've been a little pissed off about it.

 Assess and adjust the difficulty here (see Step 3 in the exercise instructions).

INTERMEDIATE-LEVEL CLIENT STATEMENTS FOR EXERCISE 9
Intermediate Client Statement 1
[**Challenging**] Are you all here today? No offense, doc, but your mind seems elsewhere.
Intermediate Client Statement 2
[**Frustrated**] Whelp, the homework was another big swing and miss. Made no sense. Can we not do that one again?
Intermediate Client Statement 3
[**Frustrated**] I just don't think you're equipped to help me. The whole "cognitive triad" thing, or whatever you called it, seems bogus.
Intermediate Client Statement 4
[**Angry**] Now you just seem to be playing a psychologist . . . like the cliché ones on TV. But I guess you're the expert, so tell me what's next please.
Intermediate Client Statement 5
[**Irritated**] My mother was trying to remind me to "check in" on my thoughts and breathing yesterday. So annoying. People are always trying to solve my problems without possibly being able to understand what I'm going through.

✋ **Assess and adjust the difficulty here (see Step 3 in the exercise instructions).**

ADVANCED-LEVEL CLIENT STATEMENTS FOR EXERCISE 9
Advanced Client Statement 1
[**Angry**] My partner cheated on me. And, no, there is no alternative explanation, so stop asking that! He cheated, so our relationship was a lie!
Advanced Client Statement 2
[**Anxious**] I did the measure you asked me to fill out. Honestly, I think I might have rated you lower than usual, but I'm not sure I want to talk about it.
Advanced Client Statement 3
[**Angry**] You're the worst. You keep asking me to interpret the situation in different ways, like my perspective is always wrong. It's like you're calling me a liar. My last therapist would not have called me a liar.
Advanced Client Statement 4
[**Defeated**] To be honest, I wouldn't expect you to ever really get me.
Advanced Client Statement 5
[**Irritated**] Well, I guess the homework you're suggesting makes some sense, but I'm also easily irritated lately . . . especially when things are unclear for me and when they're overwhelming.

 Assess and adjust the difficulty here (see Step 3 in the exercise instructions). If appropriate, follow the instructions to make the exercise even more challenging (see Appendix A).

Example Therapist Responses: Responding to Therapeutic Alliance Ruptures

Remember: Trainees should attempt to improvise their own responses before reading the example responses. **Do not read the following responses verbatim unless you are having trouble coming up with your own responses!**

EXAMPLE RESPONSES TO BEGINNER-LEVEL CLIENT STATEMENTS FOR EXERCISE 9
Example Response to Beginner Client Statement 1
Well, we certainly can do one together. However, I get the feeling that maybe you're just agreeing to do it because I suggested it. Like you're going along with it but maybe aren't so sure it makes sense right now? Is that on- or off base?
Example Response to Beginner Client Statement 2
Oh, I see. Putting agendas aside for a moment, I'm having a sense that you are somewhat distant me from today . . . less engaged than typical. Is that your sense too?
Example Response to Beginner Client Statement 3
That sounds really hard, like being at your wit's end. Can you help me understand what it feels like for you? I'm really invested in understanding your experience so that we can get on the same page of how to use our time effectively.
Example Response to Beginner Client Statement 4
I can hear your frustration with me, which makes complete sense given that it feels like I've not been listening to you. I fear that I've probably been too focused on how to *solve* the problem, that I neglected to *hear* the problem accurately. That's on me, and I will try to do better. Can you say more about what I've gotten wrong?
Example Response to Beginner Client Statement 5
I really appreciate you coming today *and* bringing this up. I bet it wasn't easy, but it sounds like I really hurt you. You're absolutely right that in holding us to our time, I missed the boat on what you needed. If you're willing, I'd like to discuss this now, as it seems like a really important relationship issue for us.

EXAMPLE RESPONSES TO INTERMEDIATE-LEVEL CLIENT STATEMENTS FOR EXERCISE 9

Example Response to Intermediate Client Statement 1

I was definitely not aware of having that effect on you, but I'm really glad you pointed it out. I'd like to take a moment to notice my experience; it's certainly possible that I've been less attentive today. Have there been other times you've noticed this?

Example Response to Intermediate Client Statement 2

I can see that the homework is adding more stress. In fact, I realize that I did not explain its rationale clearly. It may also be that this assignment was less relevant to your most pressing needs. I apologize, and I'd like to discuss what does seem more relevant and personally suitable.

Example Response to Intermediate Client Statement 3

It must be troubling to have such doubts, especially a few sessions into our work. Let's put our CBT frame aside for now. What's it like to see me as incapable of helping?

Example Response to Intermediate Client Statement 4

That cannot feel good. Maybe it even feels like I'm being disingenuous. As for expertise, I know that you know yourself better than anyone, so if I'm falling short in your eyes, that's *the* most important perspective. Can we discuss that?

Example Response to Intermediate Client Statement 5

That stinks. Actually, it's occurring to me that maybe it feels like I do that sometimes too? Maybe when suggesting an agenda or homework assignment? Or when we explore your thoughts together in session? Does that happen with us?

EXAMPLE RESPONSES TO ADVANCED-LEVEL CLIENT STATEMENTS FOR EXERCISE 9

Example Response to Advanced Client Statement 1

I can feel that you're very angry at me right now. My words must have hurt you; can you tell me more about this?

Example Response to Advanced Client Statement 2

I was just noticing that your trust in me has gone down some. I wonder if you could help me appreciate what that's like for you? I'd far prefer that to just persisting with our agenda when you may have diminishing faith in it or me.

Example Response to Advanced Client Statement 3

It seems that in suggesting different ways to interpret your situation, it felt like I was calling you a liar. That must have hurt you terribly. I apologize for being insensitive with my words.

Example Response to Advanced Client Statement 4

I imagine that creates a real bind for you. I know you come here to get help, but then the person who is trying to help is limited. What does that feel like?

Example Response to Advanced Client Statement 5

It seems that what's frustrating to you is not only that the homework is unclear, but perhaps that I've asked you to do too much. This is definitely a misstep on my part, and I'd really like to work together to find activities that are clear and not overwhelming. Can we discuss that together today?

Responding to Client Resistance

Preparations for Exercise 10

1. Read the instructions in Chapter 2.

2. Download the Deliberate Practice Reaction Form at https://www.apa.org/pubs/books/deliberate-practice-cognitive-behavioral-therapy (refer to Clinician and Practitioner Resources; also available in Appendix A). The optional diary form in Appendix B can also be downloaded from this site.

Skill Description

Skill Difficulty Level: Advanced

As noted, therapist flexibility and the ongoing tailoring of psychotherapy to the specific client and context represents evidence-based practice in its most complex, fullest form (see Chapter 3 on responsivity in cognitive behavioral therapy (CBT) for a full discussion and synthesis of the research literature). Complementing the skill of CBT fidelity-consistent modification and flexibility (Exercise 8), there is also growing evidence that CBT is more effective when therapists fully, although temporarily, "depart" from standard CBT skills in the face of certain in-session process markers or moments. Instead, depending on the marker, the therapist can use specific and evidence-informed CBT fidelity-*inconsistent* strategies until the salient (and often hindering) process has been adequately addressed; such resolution would then precipitate a return to standard CBT. In this skill, we focus on the responsive use of *client-centered* skills to address client *resistance* that may emerge during a course of CBT.

Namely, research supports a contextual shift from CBT to motivational interviewing (MI) strategies and "spirit" when a client demonstrates resistance to the direction of the treatment or to the provider. Resistance, a regularly occurring clinical process, can stem from a few common precipitants. For example, it may reflect a client's diminishing belief

https://doi.org/10.1037/0000256-012

in the personally relevant logic and/or efficacy of CBT, despite being motivated to reduce symptoms and improve functioning. Alternatively, resistance may be the manifestation of a client's understandable ambivalence about change and moving away from what is familiar (even if maladaptive). Such resistances can take different direct forms (e.g., homework noncompliance, explicitly disagreeing with the treatment rationale, criticizing the therapist) or indirect forms (e.g., missing sessions; in-session withdrawing, interrupting, or sidetracking), but the general experience is palpable client opposition to the current session agenda and/or the general direction of treatment. Importantly, though, resistance is usually a valid client message that the treatment is misaligned with their ideas about improvement, that they are ambivalent about changing, and/or that the therapeutic relationship is misattuned. Whatever the reason, persisting with the current plan is unlikely to help, whereas engaging more client-centered, MI principles, precisely in this context, can be facilitative.

Examples of Therapists Responding to Client Resistance

Example 1

CLIENT: [*pessimistic*] I know I agreed to this approach, and I understand what we're trying to do here, but I'm starting to doubt it's a good fit.

THERAPIST: I'm so glad you told me this, as your outlook on therapy is central to it working. Let's shift gears for a moment, put aside our agenda, and just discuss what has or has not felt like a fit for you. How does that sound?

Example 2

CLIENT: [*ambivalent*] I apologize for missing sessions, but I just wasn't sure about coming back. I'm not convinced I need to change all that much . . . if anything

THERAPIST: I see. I imagine it would be hard to come to session, *especially* if the goals no longer, or maybe never, fit what you want or need. And it sounds like maybe you're still sorting that out. Putting what we've done to date off to the side, can you say more about how you're feeling?

Example 3

CLIENT: [*sad*] I guess I'm feeling hopeless. A part of me wants to change, but another part is afraid of who I'll be if I change too much.

THERAPIST: It must be so hard to carry around such internal tension. I don't think I fully appreciated both sides of that coin. For anything we do in here to be useful, we need to honor *all* parts of yourself. If it's OK with you, maybe we can just discuss your experiences for a while, without any agenda or direction. Your feelings are very important to me.

INSTRUCTIONS FOR EXERCISE 10
Step 1: Role-Play and Feedback
• The client says the first beginner client statement. The therapist improvises a response based on the skill criteria.   • The trainer (or, if not available, the client) provides brief feedback based on the skill criteria.   • The client then repeats the same statement, and the therapist again improvises a response. The trainer (or client) again provide brief feedback.
Step 2: Repeat
• Repeat Step 1 for all the statements in the current difficulty level (beginner, intermediate, or advanced).
Step 3: Assess and Adjust Difficulty
• The therapist completes the Deliberate Practice Reaction Form (see Appendix A) and decides whether to make the exercise easier or harder or to stay at the same difficulty level.
Step 4: Repeat for Approximately 15 Minutes
• Repeat Steps 1 to 3 for at least 15 minutes.   • The trainees then switch therapist and client roles and start over.

Optional Variation for Exercise 10

In the final round of the exercise, the person playing the client improvises an example of resistance (to either the therapist or the CBT model) that they have directly experienced from a real training case, and the person playing the therapist then attempts to address this resistance. The client can then share if the therapist's response was experienced as validating and collaborative. Note that the client should be careful only to talk about topics that they feel comfortable sharing.

SKILL CRITERIA FOR EXERCISE 10
1. Momentarily step away from the CBT change agenda.   2. Empathically explore the client's experience of treatment and you.   3. Validate clients' experience and "roll with" versus challenging their resistance.   4. Support clients' autonomy and elicit their motivation for pursuing valued directions.

Now it's your turn! Follow Steps 1 and 2 from the instructions.

Remember: The goal of the role-play is for trainees to practice improvising responses to the client statements in a manner that (a) uses the skill criteria and (b) feels authentic for the trainee. **Example therapist responses for each client statement are provided at the end of this exercise. Trainees should attempt to improvise their own responses before reading the example responses.**

BEGINNER-LEVEL CLIENT STATEMENTS FOR EXERCISE 10
Beginner Client Statement 1
[**Anxious**] I really want to try testing some of my assumptions about what people think of me, but I'm just not sure I'm ready.
Beginner Client Statement 2
[**Pessimistic**] I know I agreed to this approach, and I understand what we're trying to do here, but I'm starting to doubt it's a good fit.
Beginner Client Statement 3
[**Reluctant**] I have to admit to not doing the homework. I don't think I "distort" my thoughts any more than the next person, so the assignment seemed a bit, well, silly—pardon my bluntness.
Beginner Client Statement 4
[**Ambivalent**] I apologize for missing sessions, but I just wasn't sure about coming back. I'm not convinced I need to change all that much—if anything.
Beginner Client Statement 5
[**Ambivalent**] Well, I went to do the homework, but then it occurred to me that I shouldn't try to reduce my worry too much. I mean it's stressful, but there are times it actually helps me stay on top of things . . . to be accountable.

 Assess and adjust the difficulty here (see Step 3 in the exercise instructions).

INTERMEDIATE-LEVEL CLIENT STATEMENTS FOR EXERCISE 10

Intermediate Client Statement 1

[**Assertive**] I do feel bad for missing sessions. I need to be in therapy. I need to get this stress under control. I just don't think we've attacked it the right way.

Intermediate Client Statement 2

[**Sad**] I guess I'm feeling hopeless. A part of me wants to change, but another part is afraid of who I'll be if I change too much.

Intermediate Client Statement 3

[**Frustrated**] I don't like it when you ask me if I have "catastrophic thoughts." Aren't catastrophes reserved for wars and natural disasters? So, no, I don't think I catastrophize. Please don't ask again.

Intermediate Client Statement 4

[**Angry**] I mean, of course, relaxation would be nice, but who can shut off their mind like that? I'm not even sure I'd want to . . . I might just end up lazy and complacent! I don't know . . . it's so frustrating.

Intermediate Client Statement 5

[**Relieved**] I'm glad you could see my reluctance about cognitive behavioral therapy! I think it started to feel more like a class than a treatment, which was unhelpful. I do want to work on feeling better—and thinking better [laughs]—but sometimes I don't have a clear agenda or direction. In those times, just taking some space to talk freely helps me a lot.

 Assess and adjust the difficulty here (see Step 3 in the exercise instructions).

ADVANCED-LEVEL CLIENT STATEMENTS FOR EXERCISE 10
Advanced Client Statement 1
[**Withdrawn**] Honestly, I don't know about CBT . . . almost seems a bit condescending.
Advanced Client Statement 2
[**Angry**] You seem so concerned with just finishing what's on your list before time runs out. I feel like I'm just a plug-and-play client!
Advanced Client Statement 3
[**Angry**] Honestly, I just don't see how you can help me. I mean, sure, if I had your life maybe I could sit around and relax at the end of everyday too, but I don't! In my life, I don't get to relax. So, I just don't see how you're going to be able to fix that for me.
Advanced Client Statement 4
[**Defeated**] You know, I've felt a lot better these past few weeks, and I honestly wonder if it's because I stopped doing those exercises you gave me. I mean, maybe writing down my thoughts and trying to relax is making me worse . . . maybe this is just who I am, and this is the best that I can feel, and I just need to learn to live with that.
Advanced Client Statement 5
[**Angry**] Actually, no, I don't want to set an agenda. I don't think that I want to keep doing this stuff. I just don't see the point!

 Assess and adjust the difficulty here (see Step 3 in the exercise instructions). If appropriate, follow the instructions to make the exercise even more challenging (see Appendix A).

Example Therapist Responses: Responding to Client Resistance

Remember: Trainees should attempt to improvise their own responses before reading the example responses. **Do not read the following responses verbatim unless you are having trouble coming up with your own responses!**

EXAMPLE RESPONSES TO BEGINNER-LEVEL CLIENT STATEMENTS FOR EXERCISE 10
Example Response to Beginner Client Statement 1
And that's fine. Readiness is key. What if today we simply start by discussing what being "ready" would look or feel like to you?
Example Response to Beginner Client Statement 2
I'm so glad you told me this, as your outlook on therapy is central to it working. Let's shift gears for a moment, put aside our agenda, and just discuss what has or has not felt like a fit for you. How does that sound?
Example Response to Beginner Client Statement 3
No pardon needed. I truly see where you're coming from. The idea that thinking in extremes might contribute to your concerns doesn't really fit *your* experience. It makes sense, then, that the homework was off base. I wonder how it feels for me to have assigned it?
Example Response to Beginner Client Statement 4
I see. I imagine it would be hard to come to session, *especially* if the goals no longer, or maybe never, fit what you want or need. And it sounds like maybe you're still sorting that out. Putting what we've done to date off to the side, can you say more about how your feeling?
Example Response to Beginner Client Statement 5
First, I appreciate you sharing this, as I imagine it wasn't easy. Second, it must be difficult to hold such competing feelings simultaneously. On the one hand, a lot of worrying stinks, but, on the other, it can also serve a purpose. That seems to put you in a bind, and maybe we've been ignoring the side of you that sort of *values* your worrying. Does that fit your experience?

EXAMPLE RESPONSES TO INTERMEDIATE-LEVEL
CLIENT STATEMENTS FOR EXERCISE 10

Example Response to Intermediate Client Statement 1

I can absolutely appreciate that. In fact, perhaps I pushed *my* CBT agenda too forcefully. So, let's pause, or even stop, my direction. Instead, I wonder if you can help me understand directions that you'd be more optimistic about, whether it's something we've discussed before or a new focus altogether?

Example Response to Intermediate Client Statement 2

It must be so hard to carry around such internal tension. I don't think I fully appreciated both sides of that coin. For anything we do in here to be useful, we need to honor *all* parts of yourself. If it's okay with you, maybe we can just discuss your experiences for a while, without any agenda or direction. Your feelings are very important to me.

Example Response to Intermediate Client Statement 3

It seems like my words upset you, and I totally get it. Here I am using a CBT term that I *assumed* would be relevant you, when in fact it's not. I really should not have made that assumption, and I'll do better to check in. In fact, I wonder if you find *any* part of focusing on your cognitions to be useful?

Example Response to Intermediate Client Statement 4

If I'm hearing you, it sounds like the idea of practicing relaxation is a frustrating one. Do I have that right? To me, it's most important that *you* value the types of things we do in therapy, so maybe we can discuss whether this task has any value to you right now.

Example Response to Intermediate Client Statement 5

I'm glad I asked too. I just sensed that we were not well aligned, and I'm so glad I understand why. We can absolutely balance the structured and unstructured activities, as I too would prefer not to fall into a "lesson" mode. So, how would you like to proceed now, in this moment? I want to meet you where it's most useful, and please let me know whenever that's not occurring, in case I miss it.

EXAMPLE RESPONSES TO ADVANCED-LEVEL CLIENT STATEMENTS FOR EXERCISE 10

Example Response to Advanced Client Statement 1

I can understand that. It must be upsetting to feel like I am talking down to you, and I can see how some of the things we do might feel like that. I apologize, and I hope we can work together to think about next steps that meet your needs in a way that feels useful and not condescending. I'm really committed to that.

Example Response to Advanced Client Statement 2

I really appreciate your courage in pointing out this really important feeling. I imagine it has been painful to feel like I've lost you in some of the details of the work. Very importantly, I'd really like to change that.

Example Response to Advanced Client Statement 3

I'm so glad that you told me how you've been feeling. It sounds like I'm not understanding what it's like to be *you* and that some of the suggestions that I've made have been off the mark for the demands that exist in your life. I can definitely see how that would be incredibly frustrating. I'd really like to understand your perspective better. I think that doing so will help us work together to come up with some things that will be more personally helpful *for you*. How does that sound?

Example Response to Advanced Client Statement 4

I can hear in your voice how painful it is to feel like this might be the best you can ever feel. And, it sounds like one of the major reasons you're feeling this way is that the exercises I've given you may be making things worse instead of better. So, I want to say that different strategies work for different people, and there are all kinds of strategies that we can try to help *you* get to where *you* would like to be. Can we discuss what that might look for you?

Example Response to Advanced Client Statement 5

Okay, let's pause the agenda, then. This is *your* therapy, and you are the best judge of what does and doesn't make sense for you. With that in mind, why don't we pause the stuff we've been working on and maybe you can tell me how you've been feeling . . . about the treatment and me.

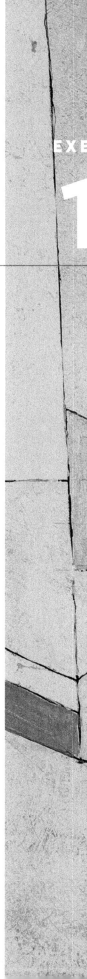

Annotated Cognitive Behavioral Therapy Practice Session Transcripts

It is now time to put all the skills you have learned together! This exercise presents transcripts from two typical therapy sessions with the same client. The first transcript reflects a typical early cognitive behavioral therapy (CBT) session. The second transcript reflects a typical midphase session. Each therapist statement is annotated to indicate which CBT skill from Exercises 1 through 10 is used. This transcript provides an example of how therapists can interweave different CBT skills in response to clients. Trainees may also elect to use parts or all of this exercise for practice. To assist with this, Appendix B includes a deliberate practice therapist diary form that can also be downloaded from the series companion website (https://www.apa.org/pubs/books/deliberate-practice-cognitive-behavioral-therapy; refer to Clinician and Practitioner Resources).

Instructions

As in the previous exercises, one trainee can play the client while the other plays the therapist. As much as possible, the trainee who plays the client should try to adopt an authentic emotional tone as if they are a real client. The first time through, both partners can read verbatim from the transcript. After one complete run-through, try it again. This time, the client can read from the script while the therapist can improvise to the degree that they feel comfortable. At this point, you may also want to reflect on it with a supervisor and go through it again. Before you start, it is recommended that both therapist and client read the entire transcript through on your own, until the end. The purpose of the sample transcripts is to give trainees the opportunity to try out what it is like to offer the CBT responses in a sequence that mimics live therapy sessions.

https://doi.org/10.1037/0000256–013

Deliberate Practice in Cognitive Behavioral Therapy, by J. F. Boswell and M. J. Constantino

Note to Therapists

First, remember to be aware of your vocal quality, tone, and nonverbal behavior. Second, as noted throughout this book, certain skills may be more relevant at different points in a course of CBT. In this first annotated transcript, we highlight an early treatment session example and focus more prominently on beginner (Exercises 1–4) and intermediate (Exercises 5–7) skills. In the second annotated transcript, we highlight a middle treatment session that more explicitly integrates intermediate and advanced (Exercises 8–10) skills. Interestingly, among the covered skills, the advanced skills (Adherence Flexibility, Responding to Therapeutic Alliance Ruptures, and Responding to Client Resistance) may become relevant at any point in the course CBT or a given session. Furthermore, both negotiating a session agenda and assigning and reviewing between-session activities are relevant for most CBT sessions. Across both transcripts, however, the therapist should not feel restricted to these when considering alternative responses.

Annotated Cognitive Behavioral Therapy Transcript 1

THERAPIST 1: Hello, again. It's nice to see you. We spent our last appointment discussing what has brought you here, your concerns, and some of your history. Based on our discussion, it sounds like you are most concerned about panic attacks, and your mood has also been pretty down of late, starting to feel a bit hopeless. Am I summarizing what we've discussed accurately?

CLIENT 1: Yes. I'd say my biggest concern right now is the panic, but I can definitely see how that's connected to my mood.

THERAPIST 2: Right. That's an insightful connection. So, based on that, my tentative agenda for today is to introduce and discuss a plan for working on those concerns, including beginning to set some short-term and longer term goals. Time permitting, I'd like to introduce a monitoring strategy. However, if there is anything else that you want to prioritize today, I want to make sure that we budget our time for that. (Skill 3: Negotiating a Session Agenda)

CLIENT 2: I'm not sure what to add. Your plan sounds fine; I'm happy to defer to you.

THERAPIST 3: OK. We can follow that plan and adjust as needed. I always want to be sensitive to unilaterally dictating how we spend our time in session. I'll have some ideas for our agenda each week, but it's best to discuss and plan it together. I can appreciate that therapy may be a bit of a mystery, so it might be less clear at this point what to prioritize without a bit more guidance. Does this make sense? (Skill 3: Negotiating a Session Agenda; Skill 8: Adherence Flexibility)

CLIENT 3: Sure. So how is this supposed to work?

THERAPIST 4: Great question. In cognitive behavioral therapy, or CBT, we'll be looking at your cognitions—that is, thoughts and your behaviors—to identify whether I can teach you some skills for managing them that will help you address your panic, anxiety, and low mood. Does that help answer your question? (Skill 1: Explaining Treatment Rationale for CBT)

CLIENT 4: Yeah, I've heard people talk about CBT and how it's supposed to be good.

THERAPIST 5: Yes, CBT is generally quite helpful for people struggling with anxiety and depression. This is a well-researched approach with substantial support for its effectiveness; the support is particularly strong for panic disorder. Of course, each person is unique and experiences things differently. So, we'll tailor what we do to best fit your needs and preferences, and make sure that we prioritize checking in to see what seems to be working or not working for you. (Skill 1: Explaining Treatment Rationale for CBT; Skill 2: Establishing Goals)

CLIENT 5: How long will it take for this to work?

THERAPIST 6: Another good question. The short answer is, it depends. Part of what I'd like us to discuss today is defining more concretely what it would look like or feel like if this is working or not working. I don't want to put words in your mouth, but I assume that having fewer panic attacks would be a pretty straightforward indication. (Skill 1: Explaining Treatment Rationale for CBT; Skill 2: Establishing Goals)

CLIENT 6: Yep!

THERAPIST 7: I realize it might be frustrating to hear that the number of sessions "depends." CBT is generally built on a shorter term model that has a track record of effectiveness. CBT approaches for panic typically involve 10 to 12 sessions. However, each person is unique, and we'll assess progress in various ways and adjust as needed. I expect that you'll start to notice improvements in mood that coincide with progress in the areas of panic and anxiety, but we might also need to integrate other strategies that more directly address your mood. Is that tentative timeframe consistent or inconsistent with what you were expecting? (Skill 1: Explaining Treatment Rationale for CBT)

CLIENT 7: Honestly, I don't know what to expect. I guess I'm a little relieved to hear that I won't be in therapy forever.

THERAPIST 8: [laughs] No, you won't be in therapy forever. In fact, an implicit goal of cognitive behavioral therapies is to teach clients how to become their own therapists; people can learn different ways of understanding and responding to their experience that they can take with them and apply outside of the therapy context. Of course, as we've already touched on, what this looks like and the time that it will take depends on your goals and preferences. (Skill 1: Explaining Treatment Rationale for CBT; Skill 2: Establishing Goals)

CLIENT 8: I just don't want to feel anxious anymore. I'm tired of it.

THERAPIST 9: I know it's exhausting, and no one can blame you for wanting that. In cases like yours, we want to get the anxiety to more manageable levels, and that includes significantly reducing, if not entirely eliminating, your panic attacks. Is it more accurate to say that you have a goal of *reducing* anxiety? Or do you want to *eliminate* it altogether; *never* feeling anxious? (Skill 2: Establishing Goals)

CLIENT 9: Well . . . never feeling anxious sounds pretty appealing to me, but I understand that that probably isn't realistic.

THERAPIST 10: Hmm. You're right that it probably isn't realistic. What if I said that anxiety isn't inherently bad and, in fact, can be pretty helpful and adaptive? (Skill 1: Explaining Treatment Rationale for CBT; Skill 7: Working With Emotions)

CLIENT 10: I think I know what you're getting at. Anxiety can help us focus, prepare for things.

THERAPIST 11: Exactly! To be clear, I'm not minimizing the suffering that occurs when anxiety is frequent and intense. We do want to get the frequency and intensity down to more manageable and adaptive levels. Would you want to make that one of your goals? (Skill 1: Explaining Treatment Rationale for CBT; Skill 2 Establishing Goals)

CLIENT 11: Definitely.

THERAPIST 12: OK. And related to this, I assume we'll want to aim for a decrease in panic attacks and panic-related symptoms, correct? (Skill 2: Establishing Goals)

CLIENT 12: Yes. I guess it's just hard to imagine anything changing because I've been dealing with this for so long. I feel so hopeless.

THERAPIST 13: I can see how it's hard to picture how things might be different, and, at this point, there might be a part of you that's overwhelmed by the work that's ahead. *And* there is another part that brought you here, and that reality is not trivial and gives me hope *for* you. As we've already touched on, perhaps this feeling of hopelessness is itself a problem worth working on—to reduce or overcome as a goal in here. Do you have thoughts on that? (Skill 2: Establishing Goals)

CLIENT 13: I would agree; it's not that I have *no* hope. This helps me feel more optimistic that things can change.

THERAPIST 14: That's really important, and we can work with that optimism. I want to take a moment to frame what we've talked about so far; goals include getting anxiety to a more manageable level, reducing panic attack frequency, and increasing hope. These could be considered both long-term—that is, what we would want to see by the end of our work together—and medium-term goals. I wonder if we can make these even more concrete. What would you be doing differently if we were on the right track on these things? (Skill 2: Establishing Goals)

CLIENT 14: Hmm. Well . . . that's just the thing. I feel like my life is on pause right now. I'm not doing much of anything; it's like the world is shrinking around me. I suppose . . . if I didn't have to worry about panic attacks or anxiety, I'd go out more and do more things like have coffee with friends, exercise, go to movies.

THERAPIST 15: Mmhmm. First, I want to highlight and table something that you just said— "if I didn't have to worry about panic attacks." The worry about potential panic attacks and anxiety is interfering. Take going to the movies, for example. Is it the case that when you're at home, you worry about having a panic attack, and that leads you to avoid going to the movies? (Skill 5: Working With Cognitions; Skill 6: Working With Behaviors)

CLIENT 15: Absolutely. That actually happened over the weekend when a friend texted me. I get so worked up that I actually start to panic at home, which sucks. If I'm panicking that much just thinking about the movies, then I'm definitely going to have a panic attack at the movies, so I'm just not going. I mean, that's clearly a problem. And then I just feel more depressed and defeated.

THERAPIST 16: I see. You're painting a pretty clear picture for us. The fact that you can recognize the subsequent impact on our mood is pretty insightful. I'd like to understand what happens in this situation. The text from your friend comes in, and . . . (Skill 6: Working With Behaviors; Skill 7: Working With Emotions)

CLIENT 16: I see the text; for a split second, I get excited about the invitation. I then almost immediately think, "Oh, I can't go."

THERAPIST 17: You think to yourself "I can't go." Any other thoughts? (Skill 5: Working With Cognitions)

CLIENT 17: Um. "I'll have a panic attack." If I even make it into the theater, I won't make it through without needing to leave.

THERAPIST 18: Has that scenario actually happened before? (Skill 5: Working With Cognitions)

CLIENT 18: Yes, it did happen once, which was enough.

THERAPIST 19: OK. So, you're having these thoughts. What about physical symptoms? Is anything happening in your body? (Skill 5: Working With Cognitions; Skill 7: Working With Emotions)

CLIENT 19: Yeah, pretty simultaneously, my heart starts racing, I get really hot and start sweating, I get short of breath. I wouldn't call it a full-blown panic attack, but it does escalate until I text back and decline with some lame excuse.

THERAPIST 20: OK, so you're noticing specific thoughts and physical sensations; it isn't entirely clear which comes first, but it sounds like they influence one another and kind of ramp up the intensity until you do something, like decline or cancel. (Skill 5: Working With Cognitions; Skill 6: Working With Behaviors; Skill 7: Working With Emotions)

CLIENT 20: That's exactly it. That's pretty much the same scenario for other situations too.

THERAPIST 21: And then you send the text to decline, and what happens? (Skill 6: Working With Behaviors)

CLIENT 21: Immediate relief. The symptoms start to go away, although not completely. But then I just feel bad. Like, "what a loser . . ."

THERAPIST 22: So declining the invitation, or avoiding the movie, instantly reduces the intensity of the anxiety. Shortly after, however, there is another set of thoughts and feelings—telling yourself "I'm a loser" and feeling more, what, sad than anxious? (Skill 5: Working With Cognitions; Skill 6: Working With Behaviors; Skill 7: Working With Emotions)

CLIENT 22: Yeah, that feels more like sad or depressed, in that moment. And gets back to that feeling of hopelessness.

THERAPIST 23: Got it. OK, you're already thinking like a CBT therapist. Let's put a framework on what you've just described. There is an event—something that we often label an antecedent—and then you have a response that's comprised of an interaction among particular types of thoughts, physical sensations, and behaviors. In the moment, that mix of components is experienced more globally as "bad" or "anxious." The thoughts and feelings are aversive—and understandably so—and based on learned experience; the most efficient way to stop or remove that negative state is to avoid—in this case, decline the invitation to the movies. The consequence of that involves a new set of thoughts, physical feelings, and behaviors. Perhaps most importantly, that avoidance brings a subjective sense of relief. Am I getting this right? (Skill 1: Explaining Treatment Rationale for CBT; Skill 5: Working With Cognitions; Skill 6: Working With Behaviors; Skill 7: Working With Emotions)

CLIENT 23: Mmhmm.

THERAPIST 24: OK, I'm going to map these parts out on this form [walks through form with client]. That feeling of relief is part of what we call *negative reinforcement*. It's the same principle at play when you have a headache and take an aspirin or ibuprofen. You know that when you take that medication, that will eliminate the headache. Even if not completely in your awareness, you know that when you decline that invitation, avoid the movies, avoid the coffee date, you will decrease the anxiety and reduce worry about a potential panic attack. It seems like a pretty logical and effective way to feel better and avoid expected danger. At a basic level, this learning process is adaptive. However, there are also costs, right? (Skill 6: Working With Behaviors)

CLIENT 24: I don't want to just avoid ever leaving my apartment! What kind of life is that? And I just end up getting more depressed.

THERAPIST 25: Right. Your frustration is clear. The good news is that I'm confident that this approach will help you. Getting back to goals, would it make sense to identify doing more of things like accepting invitations to get out of the house or avoiding the anxiety-driven urge to avoid, as a reasonable marker of progress? (Skill 2: Establishing Goals)

CLIENT 25: Definitely. That would be great.

THERAPIST 26: Excellent. Then I have a suggestion for a few things that you can do between today and our next appointment. Can we finish by discussing that before we stop today? (Skill 4: Assigning and Reviewing Between-Session Activities)

CLIENT 26: Sure.

THERAPIST 27: First, I suggest that you review this document that explains a bit more about the "panic cycle," which is the experience that you described quite clearly in your example here today. [Hands client the document] Second, I'm giving you two blank versions of the form that we completed in here today, where we broke down, labeled, and recorded the different parts of the panic response to the movie invitation [hands client the forms]. On one form, I suggest thinking back to either the first or the most intense panic attack that you experienced and breaking the components and experiences down on the form. On the second form, if you happen to experience a panic attack in the next week, then break it down and record it in the same way—antecedent or situation, thoughts, physical sensations, and behaviors, as well as what you noticed immediately afterward. How does this sound? (Skill 4: Assigning and Reviewing Between-Session Activities)

CLIENT 27: That sounds doable, I guess; but how, exactly, will this help me?

THERAPIST 28: I appreciate that the usefulness of completing these forms might not be clear. In short, recall that we started by recognizing feeling "bad," "anxious," "panicky." That is the more common *subjective* experience. We want to start by introducing a different way of noticing and reflecting on your experience. Isolating the components and how they relate to one another will help us to better understand your patterns; in turn, that will help us tailor our treatment plan. The forms can help provide a structure or prompt for that, as well as document what happened during the week, which is useful for the next session. Does that make sense? (Skill 10: Responding to Client Resistance)

CLIENT 28: Yeah, that makes sense. Basically a way to practice independently what we did together today?

THERAPIST 29: Once again, you've said it better and more concisely than me.

CLIENT 29: [laughs]

THERAPIST 30: Do you anticipate anything might make it difficult to complete these steps over the next week? It's also important to remember that we're just getting started; this isn't something that you're expected to be a pro at right away, and this isn't something that gets "graded." (Skill 4: Assigning and Reviewing Between-Session Activities)

CLIENT 30: I'll definitely give it a try. I guess I'm wondering what I should do if I don't have a panic attack between today and the next session?

THERAPIST 31: Well, first, that would be great. Second, then you could use one form to record the first panic attack that you can recall and the second form to record a previous panic attack that sticks out in your memory. Or—and I don't want to overwhelm you with options—you could record your experience at a time when you are feeling more depressed. Do those options make sense? (Skill 4: Assigning and Reviewing Between-Session Activities)

CLIENT 31: Yes, that makes sense.

THERAPIST 32: OK, great. It seems like you're ahead of the game at this. Breaking things down and seeing how the different parts of our experience are connected helps us understand the problem and what might be done to address it. Once we get the basics of this monitoring down, we'll start building on it with other strategies. And you'll see how thoughts, feelings, and behaviors are connected and why what we do in here tends to boil down to strategies that more directly address thoughts, feelings, and behaviors. (Skill 1: Explaining Treatment Rationale for CBT)

Annotated Cognitive Behavioral Therapy Transcript 2

THERAPIST 1: Here's what I'm thinking for our agenda today, and, as always, let me know your preferences and anything you want to add or prioritize. We can start by discussing your experience with the monitoring. Depending somewhat on where that takes us, I'd like to focus more explicitly on the physical sensations associated with your panic attacks today. This will include doing some exercises, and based on what we learn from those, we can come up with a plan for the next week. How does that sound? (Skill 3: Negotiating a Session Agenda; Skill 4: Assigning and Reviewing Between-Session Activities)

CLIENT 1: That sounds good. I forgot my monitoring forms, but I think I'm getting the hang of that. To be honest . . . [nervous laughter] . . . I'm already getting anxious about the exercises you mentioned.

THERAPIST 2: Oh, OK. Why don't we just focus on that for the moment? What do you notice in your body right now? (Skill 7: Working With Emotions; Skill 8: Adherence Flexibility; Skill 10: Responding to Client Resistance)

CLIENT 2: My heart is starting to race.

THERAPIST 3: Anything else? (Skill 7: Working With Emotions)

CLIENT 3: Feeling in the pit of my stomach, getting hot.

THERAPIST 4: OK. I know it isn't easy, but try to sit with those sensations right now. What thoughts are you noticing? (Skill 5: Working With Cognitions; Skill 7: Working With Emotions)

CLIENT 4: Umm. That I can't handle this. I'm going to have a panic attack. I'm going to pass out in this office . . .

THERAPIST 5: OK. You clearly are getting the hang of monitoring, nice work. Notice any behaviors or urges? (Skill 6: Working With Behaviors; Skill 7: Working With Emotions)

CLIENT 5: I guess restlessness; I don't really want to be here right now. I'm not sure if this counts, but I'm also working pretty hard to calm down. Maybe that's a thought—"I gotta get this together."

THERAPIST 6: Yes, I'd label the latter a thought. So your mind is working hard to control, what, your symptoms? (Skill 5: Working With Cognitions; Skill 7: Working With Emotions)

CLIENT 6: Um, yes. To control the panic symptoms—get them under control so I don't full-blown panic.

THERAPIST 7: I see. Not for nothing, but you're doing a pretty good job of continuing the session—you haven't run out of the room and we're carrying on a coherent conversation. (Skill 5: Working With Cognitions; Skill 6: Working With Behaviors; Skill 7: Working With Emotions)

CLIENT 7: I suppose that's right. It's taking a lot of effort . . .

THERAPIST 8: I appreciate that. We've already discussed this at some length, but is it fair to say what's happening now is pretty typical? (Skill 5: Working With Cognitions; Skill 6: Working With Behaviors; Skill 7: Working With Emotions; Skill 10: Responding to Client Resistance)

CLIENT 8: Definitely. In other contexts, though, this would probably escalate to a full-blown attack.

THERAPIST 9: Can you say more about that? The importance of context? (Skill 6: Working With Behaviors; Skill 7: Working With Emotions)

CLIENT 9: I guess there's something about being in the session, in this office, that makes this feel a bit more manageable than when I feel this way outside of here.

THERAPIST 10: That makes sense and will be important to keep in mind for our work in here. We want this to generalize to your everyday life. If you don't have specific questions or concerns about the monitoring, I think we can actually fold most of that work into the rest of the session. Would that be OK? (Skill 4: Assigning and Reviewing Between-Session Activities; Skill 8: Adherence Flexibility)

CLIENT 10: Sure.

THERAPIST 11: OK. You've already provided a lot of useful information today, which serves as a good segue. Do you remember our discussion of the panic cycle and how panic is actually learned fear of physical sensations? (Skill 6: Working With Behaviors; Skill 7: Working With Emotions)

CLIENT 11: Yes.

THERAPIST 12: Great. Based on the panic symptoms that you've endorsed and what you described so far today, we already have a decent working understanding of the nature of this fear. That's important because everybody is a little bit different in their experience of panic symptoms. I could be wrong, but I have a hunch that your reaction to mentioning "exercises" on today's agenda might be related to our plan to focus heavily on exposure in here. (Skill 1: Explaining Treatment Rationale for CBT; Skill 2: Establishing Goals; Skill 10: Responding to Client Resistance)

CLIENT 12: Probably. Things are already getting more intense as you talk about it.

THERAPIST 13: Things, meaning the sensations that you mentioned before? (Skill 7: Working With Emotions)

CLIENT 13: Yep.

THERAPIST 14: OK. Well, the idea would be to work directly with those sensations today. Recall that there are different types of exposure. For example, you've mentioned that you try to avoid going to crowded movie theatres because you might have panic symptoms, and we've talked about the importance of facing that situation as an alternative to avoiding it. With panic attacks, the sensation of a racing heart is similar to the movie theatre. We similarly want you to face that physical sensation as an alternative to avoiding or working desperately to control it. When the exposure focuses on an internal physical sensation—racing heart, nausea, dizziness, etc.—that's called *interoceptive exposure*. (Skill 1: Explaining the Treatment Rationale for CBT; Skill 2: Establishing Goals; Skill 6: Working With Behaviors; Skill 7: Working With Emotions)

CLIENT 14: I read about this and I don't like it . . .

THERAPIST 15: That's important. Can you help me understand more about that? (Skill 9: Responding to Therapeutic Alliance Ruptures; Skill 10: Responding to Client Resistance)

CLIENT 15: I mean . . . it makes me more anxious and panicky thinking about. I'm not sure I can do it, at least not right now. I know it's not logical but . . . I could lose it.

THERAPIST 16: Lose it, meaning feel out of control? Pass out? (Skill 7: Working With Emotions)

CLIENT 16: Yes, all that.

THERAPIST 17: If we just hit the pause button for a moment, I think it's important to recognize the process that's unfolding right in front of us. Concerns about future symptoms bring on a specific set of symptoms; in awareness, these in turn just provide evidence that there is something dangerous happening or about to happen. You say it isn't logical. At one level, that might be true. However, it's perfectly understandable given how strong emotions motivate certain thoughts and behaviors. (Skill 5: Working With Cognitions; Skill 7: Working With Emotions; Skill 9: Responding to Therapeutic Alliance Ruptures)

CLIENT 17: I know . . . [seems distant, irritated]

THERAPIST 18: Mmhmm. Yes, I know you know it well. I want to be clear that, in pointing this out, I don't mean to be patronizing. It's also not my intention to minimize your distress or work from the assumption that being aware of these patterns will, on its own, directly lead to something different. I have ideas about what would be most helpful, but I also want to be sensitive to what you need and keep this work collaborative. (Skill 9: Responding to Therapeutic Alliance Ruptures)

CLIENT 18: I understand. I appreciate that. I actually want you to push me a bit—I signed up for that. It also occurs to me that this is a common reaction for me. I get irritated when people encourage me to "just push forward." They're just trying to be helpful, but . . . I don't know.

THERAPIST 19: I don't want to put words in your mouth . . . they're just trying to be helpful, but they don't . . . really understand? (Skill 9: Responding to Therapeutic Alliance Ruptures)

CLIENT 19: Yeah. They don't know how bad it feels [quiet, does not make eye contact]

THERAPIST 20: What's happening right now? It seems like there was a shift. (Skill 7: Working With Emotions; Skill 9: Responding to Therapeutic Alliance Ruptures)

CLIENT 20: [tearing up] I'm not sure. Suddenly feeling sad, weirdly. Maybe . . . hopeless again.

THERAPIST 21: I wonder if the experience of others not understanding . . . maybe that disconnect brings up these feelings? (Skill 7: Working With Emotions; Skill 9: Responding to Therapeutic Alliance Ruptures)

CLIENT 21: I think that's right. It's also that I am the one being unreasonable.

THERAPIST 22: I see. So there is also maybe placing the blame on yourself, a sense of guilt? (Skill 5: Working With Cognitions; Skill 7: Working With Emotions)

CLIENT 22: Yes, guilt. There it is again.

THERAPIST 23: OK. Now, let's stay *here* for a moment. What do you notice in your body? (Skill 7: Working With Emotions; Skill 8: Adherence Flexibility)

CLIENT 23: My body? I feel kind of heavy, tired; chest feels tight; stomach is queasy. I want to curl up in a ball.

THERAPIST 24: I see. Shoulders slumping . . . I can see that heaviness playing out. . . . Notice how physical sensations aren't just relevant to anxiety or panic; these experiences are also important for our work. Let's take that feeling of heaviness, for example. On a scale from 0 to 10, with 10 being the most intense, how would you rate the intensity of the heaviness? (Skill 7: Working With Emotions; Skill 8: Adherence Flexibility)

CLIENT 24: Umm. Probably a 6. I'd say when it's really bad, usually more like a 7 or 8.

THERAPIST 25: OK. How much are you bothered by that feeling of heaviness on the same 0 to 10 scale? (Skill 7: Working With Emotions)

CLIENT 25: Bothered . . . do you mean like annoyed?

THERAPIST 26: More or less. Subjective sense of distress, annoyance. (Skill 7: Working With Emotions)

CLIENT 26: Probably a 7.

THERAPIST 27: OK, so pretty bothered or distressed by this heavy feeling. Now, on the same 0-to-10 scale, how similar is this feeling of heaviness to other times when you feel sad or guilty? (Skill 7: Working With Emotions)

CLIENT 27: Oh, that's a 10, easy. When I'm feeling depressed, I feel totally weighed down . . . not sure how else to describe it.

THERAPIST 28: This is incredibly helpful, thanks. It might be easier to see how physical sensations connect to panic, but the same principle holds here. Feeling heavy and weighed down is associated with feeling sad, guilty, or a generally depressed mood. It also naturally leads to a specific set of behaviors or action tendencies—to curl up, withdraw, retreat. (Skill 6: Working With Behaviors; Skill 7: Working With Emotions)

CLIENT 28: Yeah. I feel like my life right now is just ping-ponging back and forth between panic and depression.

THERAPIST 29: Mmhmm. I know you want to prioritize working on the panic attacks, and we'll continue to do so. But, as we've talked about, we can feed two birds with one scone. In fact, what we just did with your feelings of sadness and guilt—the ratings of intensity, distress, and similarity—is pretty close to the exercise that I had planned for today. (Skill 2: Establishing Goals; Skill 8: Adherence Flexibility)

CLIENT 29: Really?

THERAPIST 30: Yes. The only differences are that I was planning for us to focus on anxiety and panic and had a slightly more structured approach in mind. (Skill 8: Adherence Flexibility)

CLIENT 30: I see. Sorry for getting us off track.

THERAPIST 31: Whose therapy is this anyway? [slight smile] It seems like you're still in the self-blame zone? (Skill 9: Responding to Therapeutic Alliance Rupture)

CLIENT 31: Ugh. Yeah, that seems true.

THERAPIST 32: OK. From my perspective, there isn't anything to feel sorry about here. In fact, we ended up covering some really important ground, and, because of this, I think we're working toward a better understanding of this experience of sadness and guilt as it relates to your panic attacks. It's also important to remind ourselves that this is not a linear process. . . . With that said, can you guess where we're going with this? (Skill 8: Adherence Flexibility; Skill 9: Responding to Therapeutic Alliance Ruptures)

CLIENT 32: Hmm. Take a look at my panic symptoms and go through those rating steps?

THERAPIST 33: Exactly. And outside of evoking them naturally, as happened when I brought up the exercises at the start of the session, and you noticed your reactions, we have some more structured assessment steps to identify what's going to be most relevant and helpful to you, specifically. (Skill 3: Negotiating a Session Agenda)

CLIENT 33: What's involved in the more structured assessment?

THERAPIST 34: Good question. One example is practicing hyperventilation—intentionally bringing on the physical symptoms associated with that and conducting a similar type of assessment. (Skill 3: Negotiating a Session Agenda; Skill 7: Working With Emotions)

CLIENT 34: Intentionally hyperventilate?!

THERAPIST 35: I know it seems strange. Similar to the sensations of feeling weighed down, provoking panic symptoms allows us to more directly assess their nature and similarity to typical experience. Certain symptoms will be more or less relevant to you, in particular, and we want to "diagnose" those. Then, recall that we can think about racing heart just like we think about going to the movies. Targeted interoceptive exposure can help extinguish the distress that you experience when you perceive heart rate changes. After some work on this, the levels of intensity might end up being in a similar range because these symptoms are part of our natural, biological response; however, we want to help you get less caught up in them, short-circuit the cycle, and help you make it to the movies. Does that make sense? (Skill 1: Explaining Treatment Rationale for CBT; Skill 7: Working With Emotions; Skill 10: Responding to Client Resistance)

CLIENT 35: Yeah, that makes sense.

THERAPIST 36: In the time we have remaining, are you open to trying this? (Skill 8: Adherence Flexibility)

CLIENT 36: Yes. And no [chuckles]. I mean, yes, but I'm nervous.

THERAPIST 37: I would fully expect that, and we'll take it one step at a time. So, when I say hyperventilate, this is what I mean [demonstrates hyperventilation by breathing in and out forcefully and rapidly]. When I say "begin," we will hyperventilate together until I say stop. It's important to keep going until I say stop. It will likely be uncomfortable. If you feel compelled to stop, I ask you to jump back into it as soon as possible and continue until I stop. Please try to stay with it. All set? (Skill 7: Working With Emotions; Skill 10: Responding to Client Resistance)

CLIENT 37: As much as I can be.

THERAPIST 38: OK. Begin [both begin hyperventilating; when the client appears to struggle or slows down, the therapist gestures for the client to keep going and stay with it] (Skill 7: Working With Emotions; Skill 8: Adherence Flexibility)

CLIENT 38: [about 30 seconds in] I can't. [trying to catch breath] I can't do it anymore. I'm going to pass out.

THERAPIST 39: I know it's hard. Try to keep going for a few more seconds. I'm with you on this [continues for another 30 seconds; client does reattempt but seems to be holding back a bit]. OK. Now let's breathe normally, keep our eyes open, and look straight ahead. What did you notice? (Skill 6: Working With Behaviors; Skill 7: Working With Emotions; Skill 8: Adherence Flexibility; Skill 10: Responding to Client Resistance)

CLIENT 39: Racing heart; difficult to breathe; throat started to hurt; dizzy.

THERAPIST 40: OK. How intense, 0 to 10? (Skill 7: Working With Emotions)

CLIENT 40: A 10!

THERAPIST 41: How much *distress*, 0 to 10? (Skill 7: Working With Emotions)

CLIENT 41: Well, I stopped, so probably a 9 or 10.

THERAPIST 42: Similarity with a typical panic attack? (Skill 7: Working With Emotions)

CLIENT 42: Pretty similar, though not entirely. I would say racing heart, shortness of breath, and dizziness are definitely similar; other sensations maybe less so.

THERAPIST 43: Great. You did a fantastic job. Did you know that you made it a whole additional 30 seconds? (Skill 7: Working With Emotions)

CLIENT 43: No way. Wow.

THERAPIST 44: Yep. By the way, I always find that pretty intense myself. I also get a racing heart. I also notice that I get overheated and tingly, and then suddenly get kind of cold and clammy. The cold air also bothers my throat. I've done this hundreds of times and those symptoms really don't change for me. (Skill 7: Working With Emotions; Skill 10: Responding to Client Resistance)

CLIENT 44: Right, but you aren't as bothered by them.

THERAPIST 45: I think that's the important difference. Don't misunderstand; I don't particularly love it, but I've learned that this is the expected response, it dissipates relatively quickly, and it has yet to lead to anything catastrophic. (Skill 5: Working With Cognitions; Skill 7: Working With Emotions)

CLIENT 45: Makes sense. I'm noticing that things are normalizing already.

THERAPIST 46: Yep. Noticing the clock, let's think about what to work on between today and the next session. You're now an expert at intentional hyperventilation. It seems the symptoms that were evoked from this are largely similar to a typical panic attack, so that means that we want to keep focusing on this. I'd like you to set aside some time each day over the next week. Hyperventilate for 1 minute and record your experience on this form here [shares the form]. I'd like you to repeat that at least five times in a row, within the same sitting, likely around 15 minutes of work start-to-finish. What do you think about that? Is that feasible? (Skill 4: Assigning and Reviewing Between-Session Activities)

CLIENT 46: It's definitely feasible in terms of the time commitment, but I'm not sure that I can go the full minute.

THERAPIST 47: That's an important point. First, it's important to aim for a minute, and, just like today, if you do end up stopping at any point, get back into it as quickly as possible. It will also be useful to pay attention to the thoughts that come up before, during, and after each trial. One of the most important things is when your brain is telling you to "stop!," you keep going beyond that red line. That "stop!" could show up after 15 seconds, 30 seconds, or 45 seconds, but you keep going. (Skill 4: Assigning and Reviewing Between-Session Activities; Skill 5: Working With Cognitions; Skill 7: Working With Emotions; Skill 10: Responding to Client Resistance)

CLIENT 47: I'll definitely try my best.

THERAPIST 48: It's also important to set a timer with an alarm that is not immediately visible during the exercise. People often end up watching the time for reassurance, and that can undermine progress. Is that feasible? (Skill 4: Assigning and Reviewing Between-Session Activities; Skill 6: Working With Behaviors; Skill 7: Working With Emotions)

CLIENT 48: Sure, I can set my watch and set it aside.

THERAPIST 49: You really did some amazing work today.

CLIENT 49: Thanks.

Mock Cognitive Behavioral Therapy Sessions

In contrast to highly structured and repetitive deliberate practice exercises, a mock cognitive behavioral therapy (CBT) session is an unstructured and improvised role-play therapy session. Like a jazz rehearsal, mock sessions let you practice the art and science of *appropriate responsiveness* (Hatcher, 2015; Stiles & Horvath, 2017), putting your psychotherapy skills together in way that is helpful to your mock client. This exercise outlines the procedure for conducting a mock CBT session. It offers different client profiles you may choose to adopt when enacting a client. The last recommendation gives you the option to play yourself, a choice we have found to be highly rewarding.

Mock sessions are also an opportunity for trainees to practice the following:

- using psychotherapy skills responsively
- navigating challenging choice-points in therapy
- choosing which interventions to use
- tracking the arc of a therapy session and the overall big-picture therapy treatment
- guiding treatment in the context of the client's preferences
- determining realistic goals for therapy in the context of the client's capacities
- knowing how to proceed when the therapist is unsure, lost, or confused
- recognizing and recovering from therapeutic errors
- discovering your personal therapeutic style
- building endurance for working with real clients

Mock Cognitive Behavioral Therapy Session Overview

For the mock session, **you will perform a role-play of an initial therapy session.** As is true with the exercises to build individual skills, the role-play involves three people: One trainee role-plays the therapist, another trainee role-plays the client, and a trainer (a professor or a supervisor) observes and provides feedback. This is an open-ended role-play, as is commonly done in training. However, this differs in two important ways from the role-plays used in more traditional training. First, the therapist will use their

https://doi.org/10.1037/0000256-014

Deliberate Practice in Cognitive Behavioral Therapy, by J. F. Boswell and M. J. Constantino

hand to indicate how difficult the role-play feels. Second, the client will attempt to make the role-play easier or harder to ensure the therapist is practicing at the right difficulty level.

Preparation

1. Read the instructions in Chapter 2.

2. Download the Deliberate Practice Reaction Form at https://www.apa.org/pubs/ books/deliberate-practice-cognitive-behavioral-therapy (refer to Clinician and Practitioner Resources; also available in Appendix A). The optional diary form in Appendix B can also be downloaded from this site.

3. Designate one student to role-play the therapist and one student to role-play the client. The trainer will observe and provide corrective feedback.

4. Every student will need their own copy of the Deliberate Practice Reaction Form on a separate piece of paper so that they can access it quickly.

Mock Cognitive Behavioral Therapy Session Procedure

1. The trainees will role-play an initial (first) therapy session. The trainee role-playing the client selects a client profile from the end of this exercise.

2. Before beginning the role-play, the therapist raises their hand to their side, at the level of their chair seat (see Figure E12.1). They will use this hand throughout the whole role-play to indicate how challenging it feels to them to help the client. Their starting

FIGURE E12.1. Ongoing Difficulty Assessment Through Hand Level

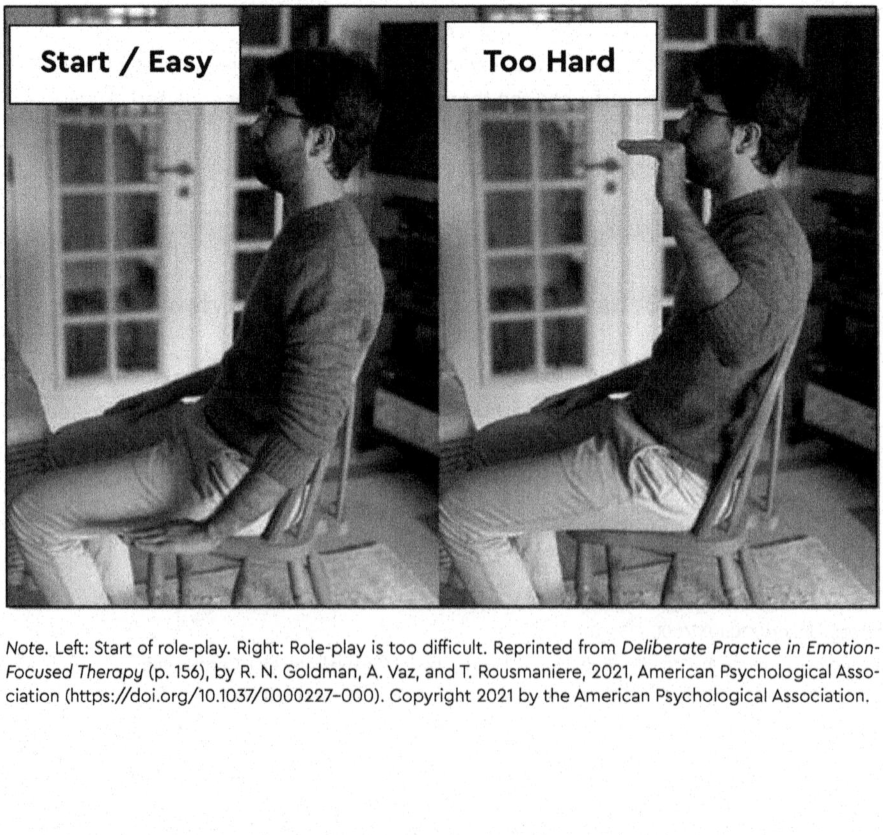

Note. Left: Start of role-play. Right: Role-play is too difficult. Reprinted from *Deliberate Practice in Emotion-Focused Therapy* (p. 156), by R. N. Goldman, A. Vaz, and T. Rousmaniere, 2021, American Psychological Association (https://doi.org/10.1037/0000227-000). Copyright 2021 by the American Psychological Association.

hand level (chair seat) indicates that the role-play feels easy. By raising their hand, the therapist indicates that the difficulty is rising. If their hand rises above their neck level, it indicates that the role-play is too difficult.

3. The therapist begins the role-play. The therapist and client should engage in the role-play in an improvised manner, as they would engage in a real therapy session. The therapist keeps their hand out at their side throughout this process. (This may feel strange at first!)

4. Whenever the therapist feels that the difficulty of the role-play has changed significantly, they should move their hand up if it feels more difficult; down if it feels easier. If the therapist's hand drops below the seat of their chair, the client should make the role-play more challenging; if the therapist's hand rises above their neck level, the client should make the role-play easier. Instructions for adjusting the difficulty of the role-play are described next in the Varying the Level of Challenge section.

5. The role-play continues for at least 15 minutes. The trainer may provide corrective feedback during this process if the therapist gets significantly off track. However, trainers should exercise restraint and keep feedback as short and tight as possible, as this will reduce the therapist's opportunity for experiential training.

6. After the role-play is finished, the therapist and client switch roles and begin a new mock session.

7. After both trainees have completed the mock session as a therapist, the trainer completes an evaluation and trainees completes the self-evaluation form, and the three discuss the experience.

Varying the Level of Challenge

If the therapist indicates that the mock session is too easy, the person enacting the role of the client can use the following modifications to make it more challenging (see also Appendix A):

- The client can improvise with topics that are more evocative or make the therapist uncomfortable, such as expressing currently held strong feelings (see Figure A.2).

- The client can use a distressed voice (e.g., angry, sad, sarcastic) or unpleasant facial expression. This increases the emotional tone.

- Blend complex mixtures of opposing feelings (e.g., love and rage).

- Become confrontational, questioning the purpose of therapy or the therapist's fitness for the role.

  If the therapist indicates that the mock session is too hard:

- The client can be guided by Figure A.2 to
  - present topics that are less evocative,
  - present material on any topic but without expressing feelings, or
  - present material concerning the future or the past or events outside therapy.

- The client can ask the questions in a soft voice or with a smile. This softens the emotional stimulus.

- The therapist can take short breaks during the role-play.

- The trainer can expand the "feedback phase" by discussing CBT or general psychotherapy theory.

Mock Session Client Profiles

Following are six client profiles for trainees to use during mock sessions, presented in order of difficulty. After these profiles is a third advanced profile, where clients have the option of playing themselves. Trainees playing as themselves can be very challenging and should only be done if they are comfortable doing so and only after completing the other profiles. The choice of client profile may be determined by the trainee playing the therapist or the trainee playing the client, or assigned by the trainer.

The most important aspect of role-plays is for trainees to convey the emotional tone indicated by the client profile (e.g., "angry," "sad"). The demographics of the client (e.g., age, gender) and specific content of the client profiles are not important. Thus, trainees should adjust the client profile to be most comfortable and easy for the trainee to role-play. A trainee may change the client profile from female to male or from 45 to 22 years old, for example.

Beginner Profile: An Anxious and Depressed Client

Lisa is a 35-year-old Asian American civil service worker whose mother suffers from early-onset dementia. She has been experiencing a mix of strong emotions about this. For example, she reports feeling anxious and worried about her mother's finances and living situation, feeling angry about the related increased demands for her support and decision making, and experiencing sadness about the meaning of her mother's difficulties and their relationship moving forward. Simultaneously, Lisa is experiencing increased stress at work and is working long hours to accomplish more and avoid receiving a negative evaluation or making mistakes. Lisa wants help with her worsening anxiety, worry, and depressed mood.

- **Symptoms:** Excessive and difficult-to-control worry, depressed mood, and irritability.

- **Client's goals for therapy:** Lisa wants help managing her emotions related to her family situation, as well as skills for dealing with work-related stress.

- **Attitude toward therapy:** Lisa had a good experience with therapy in college and is optimistic about therapy helping again.

- **Strengths:** Lisa is very motivated for CBT and openly discloses to the therapist.

Beginner Profile: An Anxious and Lonely Client

Nicole is a 24-year-old African American nursing student. She only recently began her program of study in an unfamiliar city. Nicole is excited about the program; however, she is also feeling intimidated by the workload and getting to know so many new people. She has tried to arrange social outings with some of her peers in the program, but plans have fallen through because everyone reports being too busy with family and program responsibilities. She is coming to therapy because she is feeling anxious and lonely. Nicole is worried about her new program and that she will get demoralized and stop trying to make new friends.

- **Symptoms:** Loneliness, anxiety, and demoralization.

- **Client's goals for therapy:** Nicole wants to work on excessive worry about her new program, including concerns about whether she made the correct decision in pursuing this career. She also wants to build motivation to make more friends.

- **Attitude toward therapy:** Nicole briefly tried therapy several years ago but did not connect with her therapist and terminated after a few sessions. However, she reports being hopeful that this therapy (and therapist) will be helpful.

- **Strengths:** Nicole is psychologically minded and motivated to engage in the therapy tasks.

Intermediate Profile: An Angry and Substance-Abusing Client

Mike is a 40-year-old White construction worker who is having trouble managing his anger and alcohol use. He often experiences rage that leads to verbal and physical outbursts. On multiple occasions, these outbursts included damaging property on his construction site. Mike's father was verbally and physical abusive and encouraged Mike to do things like "punch a tree" to "get his anger out." Up to this point, his outbursts have not involved assaulting other people. Mike's alcohol consumption is currently "much less than before" and involves "two or three beers" after work each night. He acknowledges that he should probably "try to cut down." He is seeking therapy at the suggestion of his work supervisor, who informed him that another incident will likely result in his termination. Mike has difficulty identifying any of his emotions other than anger.

- **Symptoms:** Anger, destructive behaviors, and excessive alcohol use.

- **Client's goals for therapy:** Mike wants to learn how to better manage his anger, eliminate his destructive behaviors, and reduce his alcohol consumption while developing alternative stress management strategies.

- **Attitude toward therapy:** Mike is somewhat suspicious of therapy and skeptical about its ability to help. The feedback and suggestion of his work supervisor seem to be the primary, acute motivation for seeking help at this time.

- **Strengths:** Underneath his gruff demeanor, Mike is quite personable and openly discloses. Despite the pressure from his work supervisor, he is able to acknowledge that he probably needs to make some changes.

Intermediate Profile: A Depressed and Irritable Older Client

Pamela is a 68-year-old White semiretired office worker who suffers from depressed mood and irritability. She feels like she has "wasted" her whole life. She has never been married and lives alone in an apartment. Pamela used to be more engaged socially (e.g., at her church) and enjoyed aspects of her work. In recent years, however, she has disengaged from and avoided other people and social activities. She is also frustrated with work because her perspective does not seem to be valued. Furthermore, she would like to retire fully but cannot afford to do so at this time, which feels is "unfair" at her age. Pamela's mood is consistently low, and she feels hopeless. She is seeking therapy to address her persistent depressed mood, irritability, and hopelessness.

- **Symptoms:** Depressed mood, irritability, hopelessness, and loneliness.

- **Client's goals for therapy:** Pamela wants to improve her mood, decrease her social/interpersonal avoidance, and decrease her irritability.

- **Attitude toward therapy:** Pamela's general state of hopelessness leads her to have low expectations for therapy outcome. Despite this and no previous experience with therapy, a part of her believes that therapy could be helpful. She is rather negativistic but does not appear to be uniquely so toward therapy or the therapist.

- **Strengths:** She seems genuine and, at a basic level, open to giving therapy a try. She displays some insight into the nature of her problems.

Advanced Profile: A Traumatized and Interpersonally Distressed Client

Isabel is a 42-year-old Latinx receptionist in a medical office. She is the oldest of four siblings. Isabel and her siblings were sexually and physically abused by their father when they were children. Her father also beat her mother frequently. Her father is deceased. Isabel feels a lot of anger toward her deceased father, as well as her mother for not protecting her and her siblings. Her youngest sister recently committed suicide due to persistent struggling with the experience of abuse. Isabel also feels very guilty about not protecting her siblings from her father. She occasionally experiences flashbacks of her traumatic childhood experiences.

- **Symptoms:** Anger at her parents, guilt about not protecting siblings, grief about her sister's suicide, and posttraumatic stress.

- **Client's goals for therapy:** Isabel wants to resolve her guilt about her sister, and *possibly* address her trauma history.

- **Attitude toward therapy:** Isabel went to therapy in grade school but had a bad experience. When she told her therapist about her father's abuse, the therapist didn't seem to believe her. Isabel is very distrustful of therapists. In addition, she acknowledges that her history of trauma impacts her life to some extent, yet she is ambivalent about doing trauma-focused CBT.

- **Strengths:** Isabel is resilient and quick-thinking. She maintains strong connections with the other members of her family.

Advanced Profile: An Obsessive and Stuck Client

Paul is 48 years old, White, and unemployed. He has been on disability for approximately 10 years. He has a variety of obsessions and compulsive behaviors, including fears of contamination and excessive cleaning and handwashing. He also experiences significant social anxiety. He avoids most social situations and is ambivalent about pursuing a romantic relationship. He describes often feeling "paralyzed" by the idea of doing more with this life. As a child, he was sexually abused on one occasion by his mother's boyfriend yet has never endorsed clinical threshold posttraumatic stress symptoms.

- **Symptoms:** Obsessions and compulsions, social anxiety, and anhedonia.

- **Client's goals for therapy:** Paul wants to be less preoccupied with his contamination fears and to branch out more socially.

- **Attitude toward therapy:** Paul has been seen at the same university-based training clinic for about 6 years. He was recently transferred to you after working with a trainee whose practicum rotation ended. He rarely misses a session and reports finding therapy helpful.

- **Strengths:** Paul discloses openly and is capable of engaging in therapy.

Advanced Profile: Play Yourself

The last example suggests that therapists in training play themselves. When you choose to draw on your actual experience as a client, you learn an immense amount about what is helpful (or not). You also have an opportunity to explore your own experience in a productive manner. This is also highly beneficial to your therapist in training (the trainee seated across from you), as they get an opportunity to feel the impact of the various responses and evaluate from moment to moment whether they are achieving their aim. This also provides an opportunity for them to read and perceive your actual experience and base their chosen response on what you have presented. Thus, for example, when the client presents a real issue, the therapist can decide, in each moment, which response would be most fitting to achieve their aim. One important note here is that the person playing client should choose a personal issue or topic that they feel comfortable exploring and deepening. They need to monitor their own experience and choose how deep they wish to go. Finally, in this particular exercise, it is not recommended for the therapist to use their hand because it could be distracting to the client and prevent exploration.

Instructions

Work in pairs. One trainee playing the client chooses an issue from their own life that they wish to discuss that feels comfortable to explore in the training setting. Trainees may choose an issue that they have been struggling with recently and want to talk over, problem solve, or gain insight into. If you are playing yourself as client, you may want to think over in advance (a) what relational problems or issues, symptoms, or behaviors you wish to discuss; (b) what your goal for the session might be (exploration as a goal is valid!); and (c) what attitude toward your therapist you wish to convey (curiosity about your own experience is very valid).

Strategies for Enhancing the Deliberate Practice Exercises

Part III consists of one chapter, Chapter 3, that provides additional advice and instructions for trainers and trainees so that they can reap more benefits from the deliberate practice exercises in Part II. Chapter 3 offers six key points for getting the most out of deliberate practice, guidelines for practicing appropriately responsive treatment, evaluation strategies, methods for ensuring trainee well-being and respecting their privacy, and advice for monitoring the trainer–trainee relationship.

How to Get the Most Out of Deliberate Practice: Additional Guidance for Trainers and Trainees

In Chapter 2 and in the exercises themselves, we provided instructions for completing these deliberate practice exercises. This chapter provides guidance on big-picture topics that trainers will need to successfully integrate deliberate practice into their training program. This guidance is based on relevant research and the experiences and feedback from trainers at more than a dozen psychotherapy training programs who volunteered to test the deliberate practice exercises in this book. We cover topics including evaluation, getting the most from deliberate practice, trainee well-being, respecting trainee privacy, trainer self-evaluation, responsive treatment, and the trainee–trainer alliance.

Six Key Points for Getting the Most From Deliberate Practice

Following are six key points of advice for trainers and trainees to get the most benefits from the cognitive behavioral therapy (CBT) deliberate practice exercises. The following advice is gleaned from experiences vetting and practicing the exercises, sometimes in different languages, with many trainees across many countries and on different occasions.

Key Point 1: Create Realistic Emotional Stimuli

A key component of deliberate practice is using stimuli that provoke similar reactions to challenging real-life work settings. For example, pilots train with flight simulators that present mechanical failures and dangerous weather conditions; surgeons practice with surgical simulators that present medical complications with only seconds to respond. Training with challenging stimuli will increase trainees' capacity to perform therapy effectively under stress—for example, with clients they find challenging. The stimuli used for CBT deliberate practice exercises are role-plays of challenging client statements in therapy. **It is important that the trainee who is role-playing the client**

https://doi.org/10.1037/0000256-015

Deliberate Practice in Cognitive Behavioral Therapy, by J. F. Boswell and M. J. Constantino

perform the script with appropriate emotional expression and maintain eye-contact with the therapist. For example, if the client statement calls for sad emotion, the trainee should try to express sadness eye-to-eye with the therapist. We offer these suggestions regarding emotional expressiveness:

- The emotional tone of the role-play matters just as much as the words of each script. Trainees role-playing the client should feel free to improvise and change the words if it will help them be more emotionally expressive. Trainees do not need to stick 100% exactly to the script. In fact, to read off the script during the exercise can sound flat and prohibit eye contact. Rather, trainees in the client role should first read the client statement silently to themselves, then, when ready, say it in an emotional manner while looking directly at the trainee playing the therapist. This will help the experience feel more real and engaging for the therapist.

- Trainees whose first language isn't English may particularly benefit from reviewing and changing the words in the client statement script before each role-play so they can find words that feel congruent and facilitate emotional expression.

- Trainees role-playing the client should try to use tonal and nonverbal expressions of feelings. For example, if a script calls for anger, the trainee can speak with an angry voice and make fists with their hands; if a script calls for shame or guilt, the trainee could hunch over and wince; if a script calls for sadness, the trainee could speak in a soft or deflated voice.

- If trainees are having persistent difficulties acting believably when following a particular script in the role of client, it may help to first do a "demo round" by reading directly from paper and then, immediately after, dropping the paper to make eye contact and repeating the same client statement from memory. Some trainees reported that this helped them "become available as a real client" and made the role-play feel less artificial. Some trainees did three or four "demo rounds" to get fully into their role as a client.

Key Point 2: Customize the Exercises to Fit Your Unique Training Circumstances

Deliberate practice is less about adhering to specific *rules* than it is about using *training principles*. Every trainer has their own individual teaching style and every trainee their own learning process. Thus, the exercises in this book are designed to be flexibly customized by trainers across different training contexts within different cultures. Trainees and trainers are encouraged to continually adjust exercises to optimize their practice. The most effective training will occur when deliberate practice exercises are customized to fit the learning needs of each trainee and culture of each training site. In our experience with more than a dozen CBT trainers and trainees across many countries, we found that everyone spontaneously customized the exercises for their unique training circumstances. No two trainers followed the exact same procedure. Here are several examples:

- One supervisor used the exercises with a trainee who found all the client statements to be too hard, including the "beginning" stimuli. This trainee had multiple reactions in the "too hard" category, including nausea and severe shame and self-doubt. The trainee disclosed to the supervisor that she had experienced extremely harsh learning environments earlier in her life and found the role-plays to be highly evocative. To help, the supervisor followed the suggestions offered earlier to make the stimuli progressively easier until the trainee reported feeling "good challenge" on the Reaction Form (see Appendix A). Over many weeks of practice, the trainee developed a sense of safety and was able to practice with more difficult client statements. (Note that if the supervisor had proceeded at the too hard difficulty level, the trainee might have complied while hiding her negative reactions, become emotionally flooded and overwhelmed, leading to withdrawal and thus prohibiting her skill development and risking dropout from training.)

- Supervisors of trainees for whom English was not their first language adjusted the client statements to their own primary language.

- One supervisor used the exercises with a trainee who found all the stimuli to be too easy, including the advanced client statements. This supervisor quickly moved to improvising more challenging client statements from scratch by following the instructions on how to make client statements more challenging.

Key Point 3: Discover Your Own Unique Personal Therapeutic Style

Deliberate practice in psychotherapy can be likened to the process of learning to play jazz music. Every jazz musician prides themselves on their skillful improvisations, and the process of "finding your own voice" is a prerequisite for expertise in jazz musicianship. Yet improvisations are not a collection of random notes but rather the culmination of extensive deliberate practice over time. Indeed, the ability to improvise is built on many hours of dedicated practice of scales, melodies, harmonies, and so on. Much in the same way, psychotherapy trainees are encouraged to experience the scripted interventions in this book not as ends in themselves but as a means to promote skill in a systematic fashion. Over time, effective therapeutic creativity can be aided, instead of constrained, by dedicated practice in these therapeutic "melodies."

Key Point 4: Engage in a Sufficient Amount of Rehearsal

Deliberate practice uses rehearsal to move skills into procedural memory, which helps trainees maintain access to skills even when working with challenging clients. This only works if trainees engage in many repetitions of the exercises. Think of a challenging sport or musical instrument you have learned: How many rehearsals would a professional need to feel confident performing a new skill? Psychotherapy is no easier than those other fields!

Key Point 5: Continually Adjust Difficulty

A crucial element of deliberate practice is training at an optimal difficulty level—neither too easy nor too hard. To achieve this, do difficulty assessments and adjustments with the Deliberate Practice Reaction Form in Appendix A. **Do not skip this step!** If trainees don't feel any of the "Good Challenge" reactions at the bottom of the Deliberate Practice Reaction Form, then the exercise is probably too easy; if they feel any of the "Too Hard" reactions then the exercise could be too difficult for the trainee to benefit. Advanced CBT trainees and therapists may find all the client statements too easy. If so, they should follow the instructions in Appendix A on making client statements harder to make the role-plays sufficiently challenging.

Key Point 6: Put It All Together With the Practice Transcript and Mock Therapy Sessions

Some trainees may desire greater contextualization of the individual therapy responses associated with each skill, feeling the need to integrate the disparate pieces of their training in a more coherent manner with a simulation that mimics a real therapy session. The practice therapy transcripts are offered after the skill exercises because they tie all the skills together. The mock therapy sessions outlined in Exercise 12 serve the same function, allowing therapists to put their skill training into practice.

Responsive Treatment

The exercises in this book are designed not only to help trainees acquire specific CBT skills but also to use them in ways that are responsive to each individual client (Constantino et al., 2021). Across the psychotherapy literature, this stance has been referred to as *appropriate responsiveness*, wherein the therapist exercises flexible judgment, based in their perceptions of the unfolding context and needs of the client. Within a session, this responsiveness naturally guides the therapist to integrate strategies and interpersonal styles to achieve positive proximal and distal outcomes (Hatcher, 2015; Stiles et al., 1998). The effective therapist is responsive to the emerging context. As Stiles and Horvath (2017) argued, a therapist is effective *because* he or she is appropriately responsive. Doing the "right thing" may be different each time and means providing each client with an individually tailored response.

Appropriate responsiveness counters a misconception that deliberate practice rehearsal is designed to promote robotic repetition of therapy techniques. Psychotherapy researchers have shown that overadherence to a particular model while neglecting client preferences reduces therapy effectiveness (e.g., Castonguay et al., 1996; Henry et al., 1993). Therapist flexibility, on the other hand, has been shown to improve outcomes (e.g., Kendall & Beidas, 2007; Kendall & Frank, 2018; Owen & Hilsenroth, 2014). It is thus of paramount importance for trainees to develop the necessary perceptual skills to be able to attune to what the client is experiencing in the moment and form their response based on the client moment-by-moment context (Constantino et al., 2021; Hatcher, 2015; Hill & Knox, 2013). Supervisors should help the supervisee to attune themselves specifically to the unique and specific needs of clients during sessions. Importantly, this attunement emphasizes both intervention delivery and the process of clinical judgment.

It is also important that deliberate practice occur within a context of wider CBT learning. As noted in Chapter 1, training should be combined with supervision of actual therapy recordings, theoretical learning, and observation of competent CBT psychotherapists. When the trainer or trainee determines that the trainee is having difficulty acquiring CBT skills, it is important to assess carefully what is missing or needed. Assessment should then lead to the appropriate remedy as the trainer and trainee collaboratively determine what is needed.

Responsiveness in Cognitive Behavioral Therapy

Although this book focuses on deliberate practice for learning specific CBT skills, we carefully guard against the overly prescriptive or mechanical application of such skills. Rather, both indirectly when describing core CBT methods (e.g., negotiating a session agenda) and directly when describing more pantheoretical, momentary "departures" from CBT (e.g., responding to therapeutic alliance ruptures), we underscore the need to practice CBT with collaborative flexibility; implement well-timed personalization of treatment to the clients' idiographic concerns and needs; and maintain ongoing therapist attunement to the person, relationship, or context. All of these elements can fall under the general rubric of *therapist responsiveness*. In this chapter, we briefly outline several ways in which clinicians learning central CBT skills can also learn (through the same deliberate practice methods) to apply key responsivity proficiencies during a course of psychotherapy. As noted, sometimes these responsiveness strategies will be nested within the CBT-specific interventions (as is highlighted in Exercises 1–7); other times, they will represent temporary movements away from CBT when clients or process markers call for it (as is highlighted in Exercises 8–10).

Importantly, our balanced focus on core CBT and core responsiveness elements is grounded in evidence (see Constantino et al., 2020, 2021). Namely, in addition to the general efficacy of CBT for various conditions (i.e., when delivered as a package of theory-specified interventions, it promotes meaningful improvement in the average client), growing research also supports the need for contextual responsivity. Put differently, one treatment size or shape does not fit all clients, or even the same client at all times. To provide just a few empirical examples, theory-*common* client factors (e.g., outcome expectation), therapist factors (e.g., self-disclosure), and relationship factors (e.g., alliance quality) have been shown to facilitate adaptive client outcomes (Norcross & Lambert, 2019; Norcross & Wampold, 2019), whereas overadherence to theory-*specific* factors (e.g., CBT interventions) can hinder client improvement (Castonguay et al., 1996). Moreover, even standard levels of adherence to theory-prescribed techniques tend not to predict outcome, in part because clients likely have different needs at different times. That is, whereas some clients may need a lot of CBT-specific strategies to improve, others may need just a few to achieve the same amount of gain. Still others may need an average amount of CBT techniques, or even some mixture of CBT with other interventions that may be considered outside of the cognitive behavioral model. Or a given client may need a lot of different CBT interventions at the outset of treatment but later may only need the one or two key interventions with which they resonated. With all of these permutations, it is likely unsurprising that simply using more of a group of theory-prescribed interventions does not have a linear association with outcome (Stiles, 2013).

Additionally, some research shows that within-case *adherence flexibility*, or the natural integration of some "off-brand" interventions (even when aiming to deliver a specific treatment with fidelity), can promote better therapy process (Goldman et al., 2013) and outcomes (Katz et al., 2019) for that particular case. Moreover, when therapists balance adhering to a treatment agenda with providing clients emotional support and a sense of agency, it can boost client improvement (Elkin et al., 2014). Finally, several studies of CBT, in particular, have tested non-CBT departure strategies for addressing specific types of negative relational process. For example, whether addressing alliance ruptures (Constantino et al., 2008) or client resistances (Westra et al., 2016), assimilating such modules as temporary deviances from the CBT agenda causally improved outcomes over simply sticking with traditional CBT when facing these relational challenges. Although this empirical synthesis is necessarily brief, it demonstrates growing support for the therapeutic value of therapist responsiveness, in its varied forms, as well as the need to guard against overadherence or mechanical prescription when setting out to deliver a generally empirically supported treatment like CBT.

As noted, responsivity can take different shapes as a course of treatment unfolds over time. At whatever stage, though, it holds that this metaconstruct involves being responsive *to* something (for which there is often a telling clue or marker) and being responsive *with* something (like a decision or intervention type). Also as noted earlier in this chapter, and as highlighted across the exercises in Part II, the responsive action (or "right thing at the right time") can occur while still largely upholding the CBT-specific skill. Alternatively, timely responsiveness could draw on theory and research to prompt a therapist to do something less CBT-like in a given moment. We provide pertinent examples of each form as we discuss a developmental course of CBT: (a) launching CBT on the right foot, (b) persisting with the current CBT plan when it is indicated by process or adaptive gains, and (c) shifting away from the current CBT plan when it is indicated by process or stunted gains (or even indicators of harm; see also Constantino et al., 2021).

Responsive Launching of Cognitive Behavioral Therapy

Although this book is about learning *central* CBT skills, the exercises illustrate that there are numerous treatment foci that can fall under the overarching labels *cognitive* and *behavioral*. For example, at the most basic level, some interventions focus more on underlying thoughts (Exercise 5), whereas as others focus more on overt behaviors (Exercise 6). Responsive launching could mean presenting a CBT rationale and treatment plan that aligns well with a client's own understanding of their problems and what might be most effective to treat them. For clients who see their cognitions driving, say, their depression, a CBT rationale and treatment plan that centers on challenging and changing thought patterns may be most compelling. For clients who think more concretely in terms of problematic behaviors, a CBT rationale and treatment plan that emphasizes something like exposure or contingency management may be the most hope inspiring. The key point is that when outlining a shape that a course of CBT can take, it can be personalized to the client, while still representing CBT proper (King & Boswell, 2019). Further, research supports the need to do this: Two distinct meta-analyses have indicated that (a) the more clients perceive treatment as personally credible (Constantino, Coyne, et al., 2018) and (b) the higher their expectation for its success (Constantino, Vîslă, et al., 2018), the better their actual posttreatment outcomes.

Other very early markers could call for responsiveness that is less CBT-like. Again, one of the primary goals of this volume is to use deliberate practice for learning CBT skills; however, we hope it goes without saying that their use presupposes a given client will be a good candidate for CBT and be ready to benefit from what it has to offer them. For example, early motivational language can signal a client's readiness for a change-oriented intervention. Whereas some clients may immediately use change-talk (i.e., language that favors adaptive behavior change that CBT can address), others might use some counterchange-talk (i.e., language that favors maintaining the problem feature, or at least an ambivalence or fear of relinquishing what is familiar). This latter group of clients may require a different first step than an explicitly change-oriented treatment agenda. For example, therapists could use motivational interviewing to support and validate clients' experiences and valued directions, even if a course of CBT will ultimately commence later (ideally once a client-valued change direction has been established; Boswell, Bentley, & Barlow, 2015). This approach would epitomize adherence flexibility (Exercise 8), which is another main goal of this volume. Indeed, research supports the need for attuning and flexibly adapting to clients' early motivational language. For example, in one study, clients with higher versus lower change-talk improved more rapidly when receiving CBT, whereas those with higher versus lower counterchange-talk had a lower likelihood of response to standard CBT (Goodwin et al., 2019).

Responsiveness as Persisting With the Current Cognitive Behavioral Therapy Plan

Presuming that CBT is off and running on a reasonably good foot and that the client has found it realistically credible and hope-inspiring, ongoing therapist responsiveness could simply mean continuing to use CBT strategies that are helping (or least continue to be seen as promising). This movement would be consistent with *plan compatibility*, or therapist actions that align with the idiographic case conceptualization (Silberschatz, 2017). Importantly, such responsiveness would also mean that both therapist and client would be cognizant that such alignment could shift and that resulting plans might need to change—that is, plan compatibility may need to be redefined and such revisions should remain front and center in the therapeutic dialogue throughout treatment. Empirically supporting this "more of the same" action, Silberschatz (2017) demonstrated that when an initial case formulation resonates with a client, the more a therapist behaves in a way that is compatible with that conceptualization, the better the treatment outcome.

Another marker for persisting with the current CBT plan is when a client seems to trust and rely on the therapist's direction. For some clients, they are looking for guidance, and their deference to the therapist can be adaptive in that they fully trust what the therapist is offering and are quite willing to see where it leads. Indeed, there is some research to suggest that when CBT promotes greater trusting reliance in clients, those clients derive more benefit from it (Coyne et al., 2019). Thus, such friendly deference can be a green light for continuing as planned, as opposed to other client interpersonal stances that would suggest a yellow or red light (as discussed in the next section).

Responsiveness as Shifting Away From the Current Cognitive Behavioral Therapy Plan (at Least Temporarily)

Responsiveness in this form suggests a notable shift in a key moment away from the original or current plan. For example, within the CBT framework, this could be as straightforward as trying a different CBT homework assignment when a previous one failed to compel the client. Or if a client's belief in the CBT rationale, as currently outlined, or expected outcome are waning (even if they had been high initially), then the therapist may need to respond by limiting CBT to those elements that the client continues to find compelling (e.g., working with core schema but not behavioral activation; Boswell & Schwartzman, 2018).

Most notably, though, such a context-responsive shift may require a specific move away from CBT, at least for a period of time, to some theoretically and empirically more appropriate response. For example, if a client is ambivalent about change or no longer trusts the therapist's CBT direction, this could manifest interpersonally as resistance to the treatment or provider—or both. Research now tells us that putting CBT on the shelf in the face of resistance and instead opting for more client-centered, motivational interviewing strategies that privilege validation and respect for client autonomy can improve the efficacy of standard CBT (which, in its traditional form, might handle resistance by trying to convince clients of its merits; Westra et al., 2016). We highlight in Exercise 10 how to use deliberate practice to learn such responsive skills vis-à-vis resistance markers. Similarly, in Exercise 9, we teach the skills of humanistic and interpersonal alliance rupture–repair strategies that have been shown to be efficacious in specifically addressing diminished client–therapist agreement on therapy tasks and goals or a disrupted bond (Eubanks et al., 2018), including during the course of CBT. These two threads of research are also generally consistent with research indicating that meeting a client's reactance with ongoing directiveness (a hallmark of CBT) will only exacerbate that client's perceived threat to their freedom; rather, it is more effective to match client reactance with less controlling and more freedom-granting interventions (that may be less CBT-typical; Beutler et al., 2018). Importantly, once these salient clinical issues are worked through, or resolved, another responsive move can be a return to CBT provided that it matches the client's post–resistance/rupture/reactance needs.

Responsiveness and Cultural Diversity

It is important to highlight that cultural misattunement can also mark the need for therapist responsiveness. Like the previous examples, responsive maneuvers toward greater attunement can be nested within traditional CBT skills or may need to replace them. Regarding the former, it is possible that clients will see CBT as well-matched to their understanding of their mental health issues and how they conceive of change. However, traditional CBT, although likely helpful, might also be incomplete. For example, it may be that a client also hopes, needs, or expects spirituality to be a part of the clinical change process. A failure to accommodate spirituality into the CBT plan could result in any number of maladaptive processes (e.g., a reduced sense of trust in the therapist) or outcomes (e.g., premature termination).

In other cases, the client may expect something more than a CBT addition or tweak. They may, for example, seek a traditional healing practice within their culture. Whereas this may precipitate a complex decision-making chain, for the purposes of the current book, the skilled CBT therapist can put their own CBT plans on the shelf to explore cultural needs and meanings. Although not explicitly addressed in this book, we find the theory and research on multicultural orientation to be a compelling means to guiding cultural responsiveness in a theory-neutral manner (see Davis et al., 2016). Namely, therapists can apply the evidence-informed multicultural orientation pillars of cultural humility (e.g., relinquishing one's sense of superiority by being open and curious about the client's identities), cultural opportunity (e.g., attending to negative process or cultural missteps with a willingness to learn from the client), and cultural comfort (e.g., exhibiting a sense of ease working with diverse people).

Our hope is that this section demonstrates our interest in teaching the skills of *both* CBT and contextual responsiveness. We view this as an important and largely new way of thinking about training that neither eschews theory-specific contributions to effective clinical practice nor overemphasizes them at the expense of personalized treatment (Boswell et al., 2020). Moreover, we believe that both sets of skills are evidence-informed and can be facilitated through deliberate practice training methods. Finally, in addition to the individual skills presented in Exercises 1 through 10, there are examples of responsive launching on the right foot, persisting with the current CBT plan, and shifting away from the current CBT plan (at least temporarily) in the annotated psychotherapy sessions that we provide in Exercise 11. We hope these examples of therapist pliability will help you use CBT, as well as other methods in this training series, in a way that embraces psychotherapy's inherent complexities and meets people at their most personally salient needs at a given time.

Being Mindful of Trainee Well-Being

Although negative effects that some clients experience in psychotherapy have been well documented (Barlow, 2010), negative effects of training and supervision on trainees have received less attention (Castonguay et al., 2010). Soberingly, though, M. V. Ellis and colleagues (2014) found that 93% of the supervisees experienced "inadequate supervision," and more than half had experienced "harmful supervision."

To support strong self-efficacy, trainers must ensure that trainees are practicing at a correct difficulty level. The exercises in this book feature guidance for frequently assessing and adjusting the difficulty level, so that trainees can rehearse at a level that precisely targets their personal skill threshold. Trainers and supervisors must be mindful to provide an appropriate challenge. One risk to trainees that is particularly pertinent to this book occurs when using role-plays that are too difficult. The Reaction Form in Appendix A is provided to help trainers ensure that role-plays are done at an appropriate challenge level. Trainers or trainees may be tempted to skip the difficulty assessments and adjustments out of their motivation to focus on rehearsal to make fast progress and quickly acquire skills. Across all our test sites, however, we found that skipping the difficulty assessments and adjustments caused more problems and hindered skill acquisition more than any other error. Thus, trainers are advised to remember that **one of their most important responsibilities is to remind trainees to do the difficulty assessments and adjustments.**

Additionally, the Reaction Form serves a dual purpose of helping trainees develop the important skills of self-monitoring and self-awareness (Bennett-Levy, 2019). This will help trainees adopt a positive and empowered stance regarding their own self-care and should facilitate career-long professional development.

Respecting Trainee Privacy

The deliberate practice exercises in this book may stir up complex or uncomfortable personal reactions within trainees, including, for example, memories of past traumas. Exploring psychological and emotional reactions may make some trainees feel vulnerable. Therapists of every career stage, from trainees to seasoned therapists with decades of experience, commonly experience shame, embarrassment, and self-doubt in this process. Although these experiences can be valuable for building trainees' self-awareness, it is important that training remain focused on professional skill development and not blur into personal therapy (e.g., M. V. Ellis et al., 2014). Therefore, one trainer role is to remind trainees to maintain appropriate boundaries.

Trainees must have the final say about what to disclose or not disclose to their trainer. Trainees should keep in mind that the goal is for the trainee to expand their own self-awareness and psychological capacity to stay active and helpful while experiencing uncomfortable reactions. The trainer does not need to know the specific details about the trainee's inner world for this to happen.

Trainees should be instructed to share only personal information that they feel comfortable sharing. The Reaction Form and difficulty assessment process are designed to help trainees build their self-awareness while retaining control over their privacy. Trainees can be reminded that the goal is for them to learn about their own inner world. They do not necessarily have to share that information with trainers or peers (Bennett-Levy & Finlay-Jones, 2018). Likewise, trainees should be instructed to respect the confidentiality of their peers.

Trainer Self-Evaluation

As we have noted, the exercises in this book were tested at a wide range of training sites around the world, including graduate courses, practicum sites, and private practice offices. Although trainers reported that the exercises were highly effective for training, some also said that they felt disoriented by how different deliberate practice feels compared with their traditional methods of clinical education. Many felt comfortable evaluating their trainees' performance but were less sure about their own performance as trainers.

The most common concern we heard from trainers was "My trainees are doing great, but I'm not sure if I am doing this correctly!" To address this concern, we recommend trainers perform periodic self-evaluations along the following five criteria:

1. Observe trainees' work performance.
2. Provide continual corrective feedback.
3. Ensure rehearsal of specific skills is just beyond the trainees' current ability.
4. Ensure that the trainee is practicing at the right difficulty level (neither too easy nor too challenging).
5. Continuously assess trainee performance with real clients.

Criterion 1: Observe Trainees' Work Performance

Determining how well we are doing as trainers means first having valid information about how well trainees are responding to training. This requires that we directly observe trainees practicing skills in order to provide corrective feedback and evaluation. One risk of deliberate practice is that trainees gain competence in performing therapy skills in role-plays, but those skills do not transfer to trainees' work with real clients. Thus, trainers will ideally also have the opportunity to observe samples of trainees' work with real clients, either live or via recorded video. Session notes and narrative accounts of therapy are not reliable methods for accurately assessing trainees' performance and identifying their clinical challenges (Goodyear & Nelson, 1997). Haggerty and Hilsenroth (2011) described this challenge:

> Suppose a loved one has to undergo surgery and you need to choose between two surgeons, one of whom has never been directly observed by an experienced surgeon while performing any surgery. He or she would perform the surgery and return to his or her attending physician and try to recall, sometimes incompletely or inaccurately, the intricate steps of the surgery they just performed. It is hard to imagine that anyone, given a choice, would prefer this over a professional who has been routinely observed in the practice of their craft. (p. 193)

Criterion 2: Provide Continual Corrective Feedback

Trainees need corrective feedback to learn what they are doing well and doing poorly, as well as how to improve their skills. Feedback should be as specific and incremental as possible. Examples of specific feedback are "Your voice sounds rushed. Try slowing down by pausing for a few seconds between your statements to the client" and "That's excellent how you are making eye contact with the client." Examples of vague and nonspecific feedback are "Try to build better rapport with the client" and "Try to be more open to the client's feelings."

Criterion 3: Rehearse Specific Skills Just Beyond the Trainees' Current Ability (Zone of Proximal Development)

Deliberate practice emphasizes skill acquisition via behavioral rehearsal. Trainers should endeavor not to get caught up in client conceptualization at the expense of focusing on skills. For many trainers, this requires significant discipline and self-restraint. It is simply more enjoyable to talk about psychotherapy theory (e.g., case conceptualization, treatment planning, nuances of psychotherapy models, similar cases the supervisor has had) than watch trainees rehearse skills. Trainees have many questions and supervisors have an abundance of experience; the allotted supervision time can easily be filled sharing knowledge. The supervisor gets to sound smart, while the trainee doesn't have to struggle with acquiring skills at their learning edge. Although answering questions is important, trainees' intellectual knowledge about psychotherapy can quickly surpass their procedural ability to perform psychotherapy, particularly with clients they find challenging. Here's a simple rule of thumb: The trainer provides the knowledge, but the behavioral rehearsal provides the skill (Rousmaniere, 2019).

Criterion 4: Practice at the Right Difficulty Level (Neither Too Easy nor Too Challenging)

Deliberate practice involves *optimal strain*: practicing skills just beyond the trainee's current skill threshold so that he or she can learn incrementally without becoming overwhelmed (Ericsson, 2006).

Trainers should use difficulty assessments and adjustments throughout deliberate practice to ensure that trainees are practicing at the right difficulty level. Note that some trainees are surprised by their unpleasant reactions to exercises (e.g., disassociation, nausea, blanking out) and may be tempted to "push through" exercises that are too hard. This can happen out of fear of failing a course, fear of being judged as incompetent, or negative self-impressions by the trainee (e.g., "This shouldn't be so hard"). Trainers should normalize the fact that there will be wide variation in perceived difficulty of the exercises and encourage trainees to respect their own personal training process.

Criterion 5: Continuously Assess Trainee Performance With Real Clients

The goal of deliberately practicing psychotherapy skills is to improve trainees' effectiveness at helping real clients. One of the risks in deliberate practice training is that the benefits will not generalize: Trainees' acquired competence in specific skills may not translate into work with real clients. Thus, it is important that trainers assess the impact of deliberate practice on trainees' work with real clients. Ideally, this is done through triangulation of multiple data points:

1. Client data (verbal self-report and routine outcome monitoring data)
2. Supervisor's report
3. Trainee's self-report

If the trainee's effectiveness with real clients is not improving after deliberate practice, the trainer should do a careful assessment of the difficulty. If the supervisor or trainer feels it is a skill acquisition issues, they may want to consider adjusting the deliberate practice routine to better suit the trainee's learning needs or style.

Guidance for Trainees

The central theme of this book has been that skill rehearsal is not automatically helpful. Deliberate practice must be done well for trainees to benefit (Ericsson & Pool, 2016). In this chapter and in the exercises, we offer guidance for effective deliberate practice. We would also like to provide additional advice specifically for trainees. That advice is drawn from what we have learned at our volunteer deliberate practice test sites around the world. We cover how to discover your own training process, active effort, and playfulness during deliberate practice; taking breaks; the trainee's right to control self-disclosure to trainers; monitoring training results, monitoring complex reactions toward the trainer; and the trainee's own personal therapy.

Individualized Cognitive Behavioral Therapy Training: Finding Your Zone of Proximal Development

Deliberate practice works best when training targets each trainee's personal skill thresholds. Also termed the *zone of proximal development*, a term first coined by Vygotsky in reference to developmental learning theory (Zaretskii, 2009), this is the area just beyond the trainee's current ability but that is possible to reach with the assistance of a teacher or coach (Wass & Golding, 2014). **If a deliberate practice exercise is either too easy or too hard, the trainee will not benefit.** To maximize training productivity, elite performers follow a "challenging but not overwhelming" principle: Tasks that are too far beyond their capacity will prove ineffective and even harmful, but it is equally true that mindlessly repeating what they already can do confidently will prove equally fruitless. Because of this, deliberate practice requires ongoing assessment of the trainee's current skill and concurrent difficulty adjustment to consistently target a "good enough" challenge. Thus, if you are practicing Exercise 10, Responding to Client Resistance, and it just feels too difficult, consider moving back to a more comfortable skill such as Explaining the Treatment Rationale for CBT (Exercise 1) or Negotiating a Session Agenda (Exercise 3) that they may feel they have already mastered.

Active Effort

It is important for trainees to maintain an active and sustained effort while doing the deliberate practice exercises in this book. Deliberate practice really helps when trainees push themselves up to and past their current ability. This is best achieved when trainees take ownership of their own practice by guiding their training partners to adjust role-plays to be as high on the difficulty scale as possible without hurting themselves. This will look different for every trainee. Although it can feel uncomfortable or even frightening, this is the zone of proximal development where the most gains can be made. Simply reading and repeating the written scripts will provide little or no benefit. Trainees are advised to remember that their effort from training should lead to more confidence and comfort in session with real clients.

Stay the Course: Effort Versus Flow

Deliberate practice only works if trainees push themselves hard enough to break out of their old patterns of performance, which then permits growth of new skills (Ericsson & Pool, 2016). Because deliberate practice constantly focuses on the current edge of one's performance capacity, it is inevitably a straining endeavor. Indeed, professionals are unlikely to make lasting performance improvements unless there is sufficient engagement in tasks that are just at the edge of one's current capacity (Ericsson, 2003, 2006). From athletics or fitness training, many of us are familiar with this process of being pushed out of our comfort zones followed by adaptation. The same process applies to our mental and emotional abilities.

Many trainees might feel surprised to discover that deliberate practice for CBT feels harder than psychotherapy with a real client. This may be because, when working with a real client, a therapist can get into a state of *flow* (Csikszentmihalyi, 1997), in which work feels effortless. CBT therapists in training may find it difficult to continually rehearse responses, feeling they "are just repeating themselves" or have captured the experience and response as best as they can and are ready to move forward. In such cases, therapists may want to vary the stimuli and their focus, and try different ones for a short time, in part to increase a sense of confidence and mastery.

Discover Your Own Training Process

The effectiveness of deliberate practice is directly related to the effort and ownership trainees exert while doing the exercises. Trainers can provide guidance, but it is important for trainees to learn about their own idiosyncratic training processes over time. This will let them become masters of their own training and prepare for a career-long process of professional development. The following are a few examples of personal training processes trainees discovered while engaging in deliberate practice:

- One trainee noticed that she is good at persisting while an exercise is challenging, but also that she requires more rehearsal than other trainees to feel comfortable with a new skill. This trainee focused on developing patience with her own pace of progress.

- One trainee noticed that he could acquire new skills rather quickly, with only a few repetitions. However, he also noticed that his reactions to evocative client statements could jump very quickly and unpredictably from the "good challenge" to "too hard" categories, so he needed to attend carefully to the reactions listed in the Reaction Form.

- One trainee described herself as "perfectionistic" and felt a strong urge to "push through" an exercise even when she had anxiety reactions in the "too hard" category, such as nausea and disassociation. This caused the trainee not to benefit from the exercises and risk becoming demoralized. This trainee focused on going slower, developing self-compassion regarding her anxiety reactions, and asking her training partners to make role-plays less challenging.

One reason the exercises in this book feature self-evaluations is to facilitate the process of trainee self-discovery. Trainees are encouraged to reflect deeply on their own experiences using the exercises to learn the most about themselves and their personal learning processes.

Playfulness and Taking Breaks

Psychotherapy is serious work that often involves painful feelings. However, practicing psychotherapy can also be fun. Trainees should remember that one of the main goals of deliberate practice is to experiment with different approaches and styles of therapy. If deliberate practice ever feels rote, boring, or routine, it probably isn't going to help advance trainees' skill. In this case, trainees should try to liven it up. A good way to do this is introduce an atmosphere of playfulness. For example, trainees can

- use different vocal tones, speech pacing, body gestures, or other languages. This can expand trainees' communication range.

- practice while simulating being masked, visually or auditorily. This can increase sensitivity in the other senses.

- practice while standing up or walking around outside. This can help trainees get new perspectives on the process of therapy.

The supervisor can also ask trainees if they would like to take a 5- to 10-minute break between questions, particularly if the trainees are dealing with difficult emotions and are feeling stressed out.

Additional Deliberate Practice Opportunities

This book focuses on deliberate practice methods that involve active, live engagement between trainees and a supervisor. Importantly, deliberate practice can extend beyond these focused training sessions. For example, a trainee might read the client stimuli quietly or aloud and practice their responses independently between sessions with a supervisor. In such cases, it is important for the trainee to say their therapist responses aloud, rather than rehearse silently in one's head. Alternatively, two trainees can practice as a pair, without the supervisor. Although the absence of a supervisor limits one source of feedback, the peer trainee who is playing the client can serve this role, as they can when a supervisor is present. Importantly, these additional deliberate practice opportunities are intended to take place between focused training with a supervisor; the use of homework fits perfectly with the CBT approach. To optimize the quality of the deliberate practice when conducted independently or without a supervisor, we have developed a Deliberate Practice Therapist Diary Form that can be found in Appendix B and can also be downloaded from the book's companion website (https://www.apa.org/pubs/books/deliberate-practice-cognitive-behavioral-therapy; refer to Clinician and Practitioner Resources). This form provides a template for the trainee to record their experience of the deliberate practice activity, and, ideally, it will aid in the consolidation of learning. This form is not necessarily intended to be used as part of the evaluation process with the supervisor, but trainees are certainly welcome to bring their experience with the independent practice into the next meeting with the supervisor.

Monitoring Training Results

Although trainers will likely evaluate trainees using a competency-focused model, trainees are also encouraged to take ownership of their own training process and look for results of deliberate practice themselves. Trainees should experience the results of deliberate practice within a few training sessions. A lack of results can be demoralizing for trainees and result in trainees applying less effort and focus in deliberate practice. Trainees who are not seeing results should openly discuss this problem with their trainer and experiment with adjusting their deliberate practice process. Results can include client outcomes and improving the trainee's own work as a therapist, their personal development, and their overall training.

Client Outcomes

The most important result of deliberate practice is an improvement in trainees' client outcomes. This can be assessed via routine outcome monitoring (Boswell, Kraus, et al., 2015; Lambert, 2010), qualitative data (McLeod, 2017), and informal discussions with clients. However, trainees should note that an improvement in client outcome due to deliberate practice can sometimes be challenging to achieve quickly. For example, a client with severe chronic symptoms may not respond quickly to any treatment, regardless of how effectively a trainee practices. For some clients, an increase in patience and self-compassion regarding their symptoms, rather than an immediate decrease in symptoms, may be a sign of progress. Thus, trainees are advised to keep their expectations for client change realistic in the context of their client's symptoms, history, and presentation. It is important that trainees not try to force their clients to improve in therapy so that the trainee feels like they are making progress in their training (Rousmaniere, 2016).

Trainee's Work as a Therapist

One important result of deliberate practice is change within the trainee regarding their work with clients. For example, trainees at test sites reported feeling more comfortable sitting with evocative clients, more confident addressing uncomfortable topics in therapy, and more responsive to a broader range of clients.

Trainee's Personal Development

Another important result of deliberate practice is personal growth within the trainee. For example, trainees at test sites reported becoming more in touch with their own feelings, increased self-compassion, and enhanced motivation to work with a broader range of clients.

Trainee's Training Process

Another valuable result of deliberate practice is improvement in the trainees' training process. For example, trainees at test sites reported becoming more aware of their personal training style, preferences, strengths, and challenges. Over time, trainees should grow to feel more ownership of their training process. Training to be a psychotherapist is a complex process that occurs over many years. Experienced, expert therapists still report continuing to grow well beyond their graduate school years (Orlinsky & Ronnestad, 2005). Furthermore, training is not a linear process. In learning to be a CBT therapist, one can, at times, feel that they are making excellent progress, that one had really turned a corner and would not look back, only to be confronted the next day with a huge feeling of disappointment and setback when confronted with a new client, or new problem. Remember to be easy on yourself. And trust the process!

The Trainee–Trainer Alliance: Monitoring Complex Reactions Toward the Trainer

Trainees who engage in deliberate practice often report experiencing complex feelings toward their trainer. For example, one trainee said, "I know this is helping, but I also don't look forward to it!" Another trainee reported feeling both appreciation and frustration toward her trainer simultaneously. Trainees are advised to remember intensive training they have done in other fields, such as athletics or music. When a coach pushes a trainee to the edge of their ability, it is common for trainees to have complex reactions toward them.

   This does not necessarily mean that the trainer is doing anything wrong. In fact, intensive training inevitably stirs up reactions toward the trainer, such as frustration, annoyance, disappointment, or anger, that coexist with the appreciation they feel. In fact, if trainees do not experience complex reactions, it is worth considering whether the deliberate practice is sufficiently challenging. But what we asserted earlier about rights to privacy apply here as well. Because professional mental health training is hierarchical and evaluative, trainers should not require or even expect trainees to share complex reactions they may be experiencing toward them. Trainers should stay open to their sharing, but the choice always remains with the trainee.

Trainee's Own Therapy

When engaging in deliberate practice, many trainees discover aspects of their inner world that may benefit from attending their own psychotherapy. For example, one trainee discovered that her clients' anger stirred up her own painful memories of abuse, another trainee found himself disassociating while practicing empathy skills, and another trainee experienced overwhelming shame and self-judgment when she couldn't master skills after just a few repetitions.

Although these discoveries were unnerving at first, they ultimately were very beneficial, as they motivated the trainees to seek out their own therapy. Many therapists attend their own therapy. In fact, Norcross and Guy (2005) found in their review of 17 studies that about 75% of the more than 8,000 therapist participants have attended their own therapy. Orlinsky and Ronnestad (2005) found that more than 90% of therapists who attended their own therapy reported it as helpful.

QUESTIONS FOR TRAINEES

1. Are you balancing the effort to improve your skills with patience and self-compassion for your learning process?
2. Are you attending to any shame or self-judgment arising from training?
3. Are you being mindful of your personal boundaries and also respecting any complex feelings you may have toward your trainers?

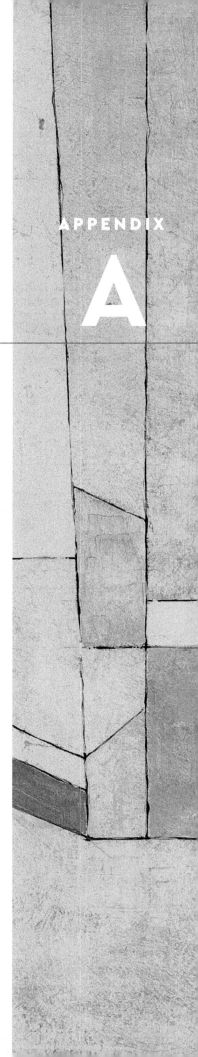

Difficulty Assessments
and Adjustments

Deliberate practice works best if the exercises are performed at a good challenge level that is neither too hard nor too easy. To ensure that trainees are practicing at the correct difficulty, they should do a *difficulty assessment and adjustment* after each level of client statement is completed (beginner, intermediate, and advanced). To do this, use the following instructions and the Deliberate Practice Reaction Form (Figure A.1), which is also available at https://www.apa.org/pubs/books/deliberate-practice-cognitive-behavioral-therapy (refer to Clinician and Practitioner Resources). **Do not skip this process!**

How to Assess Difficulty

The *therapist* completes the Deliberate Practice Reaction Form (Figure A.1). If they

- answer either Question 1 or 2 on the Reaction Form as "too hard," follow the instructions to make the exercise easier;

- answer both Questions 1 and 2 as "too easy" and "no," proceed to the next level of harder client statements or follow the instructions to make the exercise harder; or

- answer both Questions 1 and 2 as "good challenge" and "no," do not proceed to the harder client statements but rather repeat the same level.

Making Client Statements Easier

If the therapist ever answers either Question 1 or 2 on the Reaction Form as "too hard," use the next-level easier client statements (e.g., if you were using Advanced client statements, switch to Intermediate). But if you already were using Beginner client statements, use the following methods to make the client statements even easier:

- The person playing the client can use the same Beginner client statements but this time in a softer, calmer voice and with a smile. This softens the emotional tone.

- The client can improvise with topics that are less evocative or make the therapist more comfortable, such as talking about topics without expressing feelings, the future/past (avoiding here and now), or any topic outside therapy (see Figure A.2).

FIGURE A.1. Deliberate Practice Reaction Form

Question 1: How challenging was it to fulfill the skill criteria for this exercise?

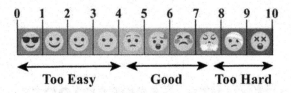

Question 2: Did you have any reactions in "good challenge" or "too hard" categories? (yes/no)					
Good Challenge			**Too Hard**		
Emotions and Thoughts	Body Reactions	Urges	Emotions and Thoughts	Body Reactions	Urges
Manageable shame, self-judgment, irritation, anger, sadness, etc.	Body tension, sighs, shallow breathing, increased heart rate, warmth, dry mouth	Looking away, withdrawing, changing focus	Severe or overwhelming shame, self-judgment, rage, grief, guilt, etc.	Migraines, dizziness, foggy thinking, diarrhea, disassociation, numbness, blanking out, nausea, etc.	Shutting down, giving up

Too Easy	Good Challenge	Too Hard
⬇	⬇	⬇
Proceed to next difficulty level	**Repeat the same difficulty level**	**Go back to previous difficulty level**

Note. Reprinted from *Deliberate Practice in Emotion-Focused Therapy* (p. 180), by R. N. Goldman, A. Vaz, and T. Rousmaniere, 2021, American Psychological Association (https://doi.org/10.1037/0000227–000). Copyright 2021 by the American Psychological Association.

FIGURE A.2. How to Make Client Statements Easier or Harder in Role-Plays

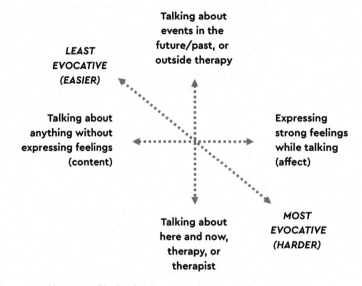

Note. Figure created by Jason Whipple, PhD.

- The therapist can take a short break (5–10 minutes) between questions.

- The trainer can expand the "feedback phase" by discussing cognitive behavioral therapy or psychotherapy theory and research. This should shift the trainees' focus toward more detached or intellectual topics and reduce the emotional intensity.

Making Client Statements Harder

If the therapist answers both Questions 1 and 2 on the Reaction Form as "too easy," proceed to next-level harder client statements. If you were already using the Advanced client statements, the client should make the exercise even harder, using the following guidelines:

- The person playing the client can use the Advanced client statements again with a more distressed voice (e.g., very angry, sad, sarcastic) or unpleasant facial expression. This should increase the emotional tone.

- The client can improvise new client statements with topics that are more evocative or make the therapist uncomfortable, such as expressing strong feelings or talking about the here and now, therapy, or the therapist (see Figure A.2).

Note. The purpose of a deliberate practice session is not to get through all the client statements and therapist responses but to spend as much time as possible practicing at the correct difficulty level. This may mean that trainees repeat the same statements or responses many times, which is okay as long as the difficulty remains in the "good challenge" level.

Deliberate Practice
Diary Form

This book focuses on deliberate practice methods that involve active, live engagement between trainees and a supervisor. Importantly, deliberate practice can extend beyond these focused training sessions. For example, a trainee might read the client stimuli quietly or aloud and practice their responses independently between sessions with a supervisor. In such cases, it is important for the trainee to speak aloud rather than rehearse silently in one's head. Alternatively, two trainees can practice without the supervisor. Although the absence of a supervisor limits one source of feedback, the peer trainee who is playing the client can serve this role, as they can when a supervisor is present. Importantly, these additional deliberate practice opportunities are intended to take place between focused training with a supervisor; the use of homework fits perfectly with the cognitive behavioral therapy approach. To optimize the quality of the deliberate practice when conducted independently or without a supervisor, we have developed a deliberate practice therapist diary form that can also be downloaded from the book companion website (https://www.apa.org/pubs/books/deliberate-practice-cognitive-behavioral-therapy; refer to Clinician and Practitioner Resources). This form provides a template for the trainee to record their experience of the deliberate practice activity and, hopefully, will aid in the consolidation of learning. This form is not necessarily intended to be used as part of the evaluation process with the supervisor, but trainees are certainly welcome to bring their experience with the independent practice into the next meeting with the supervisor.

Use this form to consolidate learning from the deliberate practice exercises. Please protect your personal boundaries by only sharing information that you are comfortable disclosing.

Name: _____ Date: _____

Exercise: _____

Question 1. What was unhelpful or didn't go well this deliberate practice session? In what way?

Question 2. What was helpful or worked well this deliberate practice session? In what way?

Question 3. What did you learn about yourself, your current skills, and skills you'd like to keep improving? Feel free to share any details, but only those you are comfortable disclosing.

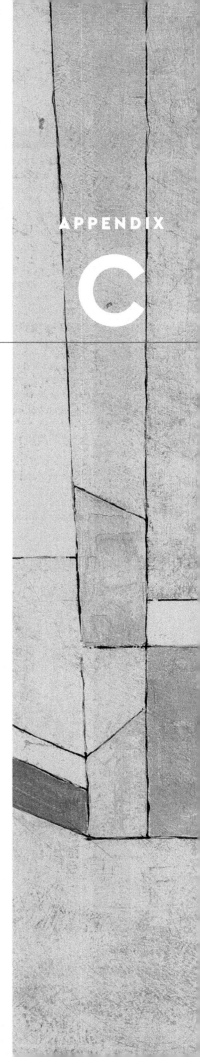

Sample Cognitive Behavioral Therapy Syllabus With Embedded Deliberate Practice Exercises

This appendix provides a sample one-semester, three-unit course dedicated to teaching cognitive behavioral therapy (CBT). This course is appropriate for graduate students (master's and doctoral) at all levels of training, including first-year students who have not yet worked with clients. We present it as a model that can be adopted to a specific program's contexts and needs. For example, instructors may borrow portions of it to use in other courses, in practica, in didactic training events at externships and internships, in workshops, and in continuing education for postgraduate therapists.

Course Title: Cognitive Behavioral Therapy: Theory and Deliberate Practice

Course Description

This course teaches theory, principles, and core skills of cognitive behavioral therapy (CBT). As a course with both didactic and practicum elements, it will review the theory and research on emotion, psychotherapy change processes, and foster the use of deliberate practice to enable students to acquire 10 key CBT skills.

Course Objectives

Students who complete this course will be able to

1. Describe the core theory, research, and skills of CBT
2. Apply the principles of deliberate practice for career-long clinical skill development
3. Demonstrate key CBT skills
4. Evaluate how they can fit CBT skills into their developing therapeutic framework
5. Employ CBT with clients from diverse cultural backgrounds
6. Describe the ways in which CBT is an evidenced-based practice

Date	Lecture and Discussion	Skills Lab	Homework (for next class)
Week 1	Introduction to cognitive behavioral therapy (CBT) theory, history, and research; process and outcome research	Lecture on principles of deliberate practice; deliberate practice research	Tolin (2016, Chapter 1); Dobson and Dozois (2019, Chapters 1–3)
Week 2	Developing a CBT working alliance; providing a treatment rationale	Exercise 1: Explaining the Treatment Rationale for Cognitive Behavioral Therapy	Tolin (2016, Chapters 5 & 6); Persons (2012, Chapter 6); Exercise 1
Week 3	Developing a CBT working alliance; establishing treatment goals	Exercise 2: Establishing Goals	Castonguay et al. (2010); Tolin (2016, Chapter 7); Persons (2012, Chapters 6 & 8); Exercise 2
Week 4	Negotiating session agendas	Exercise 3: Negotiating a Session Agenda	Persons (2012, Chapter 10); Exercise 3
Week 5	Assigning and reviewing between-session activities (i.e., homework); integrating experience monitoring within and between sessions	Exercise 4: Assigning and Reviewing Between-Session Activities	Kazantzis et al. (2005, Chapters 1–4); Exercise 4
Week 6	Working with cognitions	Exercise 5: Working With Cognitions	Tolin (2016, Chapters 13–17); Exercise 5
Week 7	Working with behaviors	Exercise 6: Working With Behaviors	Tolin (2016, Chapters 8–12); Exercise 6
Week 8	Working with emotions	Exercise 7: Working With Emotions	Tolin (2016, Chapters 18 & 19); Persons (2012, Chapter 4); Exercise 7
Week 9	Midterm paper due, self-evaluation, skill coaching feedback	Transcript Session or Mock Session	Reading and exercise identified by mock or real session
Week 10	Flexibility within fidelity	Exercise 8: Adherence Flexibility	Persons (2012, Chapters 11 & 12); Dobson and Dozois (2019, Chapter 13 by Norcross et al.); Exercise 8
Week 11	Identifying and responding to therapeutic alliance ruptures	Exercise 9: Responding to Therapeutic Alliance Ruptures	Eubanks et al. (2018); Constantino et al. (2010); Holtforth and Castonguay (2005); Exercise 9
Week 12	Identifying and responding to client resistance	Exercise 10: Responding to Client Resistance	Aviram et al. (2016); Westra and Aviram (2013); Westra et al. (2016); Westra and Constantino (2019); Exercise 10
Week 13	Transdiagnostic CBT principles and strategies	Exercises 5–7: Working With Cognitions, Behaviors, and Emotions	Boswell (2013); Barlow et al. (2017); Dobson and Dozois (2019, Chapter 16 by Norton et al.); Exercises 5–7
Week 14	Working with difficult clients; managing negative reactions	Exercises 8–10: Adherence Flexibility, Responding to Therapeutic Alliance Ruptures, and Responding to Client Resistance	Castonguay et al. (2010); Wolf et al. (2013, Chapter 2 by Levendusky & Rosmarin, & Conclusions & Guidelines); Exercises 8–10
Week 15	Final paper due, final exam, self-evaluation, skill coaching feedback	Transcript Session or Mock Session	None

Format of Class

Course time is split evenly between learning CBT theory and acquiring CBT skills:

Lecture/Discussion Class: Each week, there will be one Lecture/Discussion class for 1.5 hours focusing on CBT theory and related research.

CBT Skills Lab: Each week there will be one CBT Skills Lab for 1.5 hours. Skills Labs are for practicing CBT skills using the exercises in this book. The exercises use therapy simulations (role-plays) with the following goals:

1. Build trainees' skill and confidence for using CBT skills with real clients
2. Provide a safe space for experimenting with different therapeutic interventions, without fear of making mistakes
3. Provide plenty of opportunity to explore and "try on" different styles of therapy, so trainees can ultimately discover their own personal, unique therapy style

Mock Sessions: Twice in the semester (weeks 9 and 15), trainees will do a psychotherapy mock session in the CBT Skills Lab. In contrast to highly structured and repetitive deliberate practice exercises, a psychotherapy mock session is an unstructured and improvised role-played therapy session. Mock sessions let trainees

1. Practice using CBT skills responsively.
2. Experiment with clinical decision making in an unscripted context.
3. Discover their personal therapeutic style.
4. Build endurance for working with real clients.

Homework

Homework will be assigned each week and will include reading, 1 hour of skills practice with an assigned practice partner, and occasional writing assignments. For the skills practice homework, trainees will repeat the exercise they did for that week's CBT Skills Lab. Because the instructor will not be there to evaluate performance, trainees should instead complete the Deliberate Practice Reaction Form, as well as the Deliberate Practice Diary Form, for themselves as a self-evaluation.

Writing Assignments

Students are to write two papers: one due at midterm and one due at the last day of class. Some possible topics for the papers are as follows:

- exploration of one aspect of CBT theory, research, or technique
- a partial transcript of one of the trainees' therapy cases with a real client, with discussion from a CBT perspective

Vulnerability, Privacy, Confidentiality, and Boundaries

This course is aimed at developing CBT skills, self-awareness, and interpersonal skills in an experiential framework and as relevant to clinical work. This course is not psychotherapy or a substitute for psychotherapy. Students should interact at a level of self-disclosure that is personally comfortable and helpful to their own learning. Although becoming aware of internal emotional and psychological processes is necessary for a therapist's development, it is not necessary to reveal all that information to the trainer. It is important for students to sense their own level of safety and privacy. Students are not evaluated on the level of material that they choose to reveal in the class.

Multicultural Orientation

This course is taught in a multicultural context, defined as "how the cultural worldviews, values, and beliefs of the client and therapist interact and influence one another to co-create a relational experience that is in the spirit of healing" (Davis et al., 2018, p. 3). Core features of the multicultural orientation include cultural comfort, humility, and responding to cultural opportunities (or previously missed opportunities). Throughout this course, students are encouraged to reflect on their own cultural identity and improve their ability to attune with their clients' cultural identities (Hook et al., 2017). For further guidance on this topic and deliberate practice exercises to improve multicultural skills, see the forthcoming book *Deliberate Practice in Multicultural Counseling* (to be published by the American Psychological Association [APA]).

Confidentiality

Due to the nature of the material covered in this course, there are occasions when personal life experience may be relevant for the learning environment. You will not be required to share personal experiences (see below), but you might consider doing so when you are comfortable. Additionally, to create a safe learning environment that is respectful of client and therapist information and diversity and to foster open and vulnerable conversation in class, students are required to agree to strict confidentiality within and outside of the instruction setting.

Self-Revealing Information

In accordance with the *Ethical Principles of Psychologists and Code of Conduct* (APA, 2017), students are **not required to disclose personal information**. Because this class is about developing both interpersonal and CBT competence, following are some important points so that students are fully informed as they make choices to self-disclose:

- Students choose how much, when, and what to disclose. Students are not penalized for the choice not to share personal information.

- The learning environment is susceptible to group dynamics much like any other group space, and therefore students may be asked to share their observations and experiences of the class environment with the singular goal of fostering a more inclusive and productive learning environment.

Evaluation

Self-Evaluation: At the end of the semester (Week 15), trainees will perform a self-evaluation. This will help trainees track their progress and identify areas for further development. The Guidance for Trainees section in Chapter 3 of this book highlights potential areas of focus for self-evaluation.

Grading Criteria

As designed, students would be accountable for the level and quality of their performance in

- the Discussion classes
- the Skills Lab (exercises and mock sessions)
- homework
- midterm and final papers
- a final exam

Required Readings

Aviram, A., Westra, H. A., Constantino, M. J., & Antony, M. M. (2016). Responsive management of early resistance in cognitive-behavioral therapy for generalized anxiety disorder. *Journal of Consulting and Clinical Psychology, 84*(9), 783–794. https://doi.org/10.1037/ccp0000100

Barlow, D. H., Farchione, T. J., Sauer-Zavala, S., Murray Latin, H., Ellard, K. K., Bullis, J. R., Bentley, K. H., Boettcher, H. T., & Cassiello-Robbins, C. (2017). *Unified protocol for transdiagnostic treatment of emotional disorders: Therapist guide* (2nd ed.). Oxford University Press.

Boswell, J. F. (2013). Intervention strategies and clinical process in transdiagnostic cognitive-behavioral therapy. *Psychotherapy, 50*(3), 381–386. https://doi.org/10.1037/a0032157

Castonguay, L. G., Constantino, M. J., McAleavey, A. A., & Goldfried, M. R. (2010). The therapeutic alliance in cognitive-behavioral therapy. In J. C. Muran & J. P. Barber (Eds.), *The therapeutic alliance: An evidence-based guide to practice* (pp. 150–171). Guilford Press.

Constantino, M. J., Castonguay, L. G., Zack, S., & DeGeorge, J. (2010). Engagement in psychotherapy: Factors contributing to the facilitation, demise, and restoration of the therapeutic alliance. In D. Castro-Blanco & M. S. Carver (Eds.), *Elusive alliance: Treatment engagement strategies with high-risk adolescents* (pp. 21–57). American Psychological Association. https://doi.org/10.1037/12139-001

Dobson, K. S., & Dozois, D. J. A. (Eds.). (2019). *Handbook of cognitive-behavioral therapies* (4th ed.). Guilford Press.

Eubanks, C. F., Muran, J. C., & Safran, J. D. (2018). Repairing alliance ruptures. In J. C. Norcross & B. E. Wampold (Eds.), *Psychotherapy relationships that work: Evidence-based responsiveness* (3rd ed., pp. 549–579). Oxford University Press.

Holtforth, M. G., & Castonguay, L. G. (2005). Relationship and techniques in cognitive-behavioral therapy—A motivational approach. *Psychotherapy: Theory, Research, Practice, Training, 42*(4), 443–455. https://doi.org/10.1037/0033-3204.42.4.443

Kazantzis, N., Deane, F., Ronan, K. R., & L'Abate, L. (Eds.). (2005). *Using homework assignments in cognitive behavior therapy.* Routledge/Taylor & Francis.

Persons, J. B. (2012). *The case formulation approach to cognitive-behavior therapy.* Guilford Press.

Tolin, D. F. (2016). *Doing CBT: A comprehensive guide to working with behaviors, thoughts, and emotions.* Guilford Press.

Westra, H. A., & Aviram, A. (2013). Core skills in motivational interviewing. *Psychotherapy, 50*(3), 273–278. https://doi.org/10.1037/a0032409

Westra, H. A., & Constantino, M. J. (2019). Integrative psychotherapy for generalized anxiety disorder. In J. C. Norcross & M. R. Goldfried (Eds.), *Handbook of psychotherapy integration* (3rd ed., pp. 284–302). Oxford University Press.

Westra, H. A., Constantino, M. J., & Antony, M. M. (2016). Integrating motivational interviewing with cognitive-behavioral therapy for severe generalized anxiety disorder: An allegiance-controlled randomized clinical trial. *Journal of Consulting and Clinical Psychology, 84*(9), 768–782. https://doi.org/10.1037/ccp0000098

Wolf, A. W., Goldfried, M. R., & Muran, J. C. (Eds.). (2013). *Transforming negative reactions to clients: From frustration to compassion.* American Psychological Association.

Supplemental Readings

Beck, J. S. (2005). *Cognitive therapy for challenging problems: What to do when the basics don't work.* Guilford Press.

Castonguay, L. G., & Beutler, L. E. (Eds.). (2006). *Principles of therapeutic change that work.* Oxford Press.

Castonguay, L. G., Constantino, M. J., Boswell, J. F., & Kraus, D. (2010). The therapeutic alliance: Research and theory. In L. Horowitz & S. Strack (Eds.), *Handbook of interpersonal psychology: Theory, research, assessment, and therapeutic interventions* (pp. 509–518). John Wiley & Sons.

Constantino, M. J., Coyne, A. E., & Muir, H. J. (2020). Evidence-based therapist responsivity to disruptive clinical process. *Cognitive and Behavioral Practice, 27*(4), 405–416. https://doi.org/10.1016/j.cbpra.2020.01.003

Constantino, M. J., Goodwin, B. J., Muir, H. J., Coyne, A. E., & Boswell, J. F. (2021). Contextual-responsive psychotherapy integration applied to cognitive behavioral therapy. In J. C. Watson & H. Wiseman (Eds.), *The responsive psychotherapist: Attuning to clients in the moment.* American Psychological Association.

Davis, D. E., DeBlaere, C., Owen, J., Hook, J. N., Rivera, D. P., Choe, E., Van Tongeren, D. R., Worthington, E. L., & Placeres, V. (2018). The multicultural orientation framework: A narrative review. *Psychotherapy, 55*(1), 89–100. https://doi.org/10.1037/pst0000160

Goldfried, M. R., & Davison, G. C. (1994). *Clinical behavior therapy.* John Wiley & Sons.

Goodwin, B. J., Coyne, A. E., & Constantino, M. J. (2018). Extending the context-responsive psychotherapy integration framework to cultural processes in psychotherapy. *Psychotherapy, 55*(1), 3–8. https://doi.org/10.1037/pst0000143

Hayes, S. C., & Hofmann, S. G. (Eds.). (2018). *Process-based CBT: The science and core clinical competencies of cognitive-behavioral therapy.* Context Press.

Hays, P. A. (2009). Integrating evidence-based practice, cognitive-behavior therapy, and multicultural therapy: Ten steps for culturally competent practice. *Professional Psychology: Research and Practice, 40*(4), 354–360. https://doi.org/10.1037/a0016250

Hook, J. N., Davis, D. D., Owen, J., & DeBlaere, C. (2017). *Cultural humility: Engaging diverse identities in therapy.* American Psychological Association. https://doi.org/10.1037/0000037-000

Leahy, R. L. (Ed.). (2003). *Roadblocks in cognitive-behavioral therapy: Transforming challenges into opportunities for change.* Guilford Press.

Martell, C. R., Dimidjian, S., & Herman-Dunn, R. (2010). *Behavioral activation for depression: A clinician's guide.* Guilford Press.

Miller, S. D., Prescott, D., & Maeschalck, S. (2017). *Reaching for excellence: Feedback-informed treatment in practice.* American Psychological Association.

Safran, J. D., & Muran, J. C. (2000). *Negotiating the therapeutic alliance: A relational treatment guide.* Guilford Press.

Swift, J. K., & Greenberg, R. P. (2015). Foster the therapeutic alliance. In J. K. Swift & R. P. Greenberg, *Premature termination in psychotherapy: Strategies for engaging clients and improving outcomes* (pp. 137–147). American Psychological Association. https://doi.org/10.1037/14469-010

Westra, H. A., Norouzian, N., Poulin, L., Coyne, A. E., Constantino, M. J., Hara, K., Olson, D., & Antony, M. M. (2020). Testing a deliberate practice workshop for developing appropriate responsivity to resistance markers. *Psychotherapy.* Advance online publication. https://doi.org/10.1037/pst0000311

References

American Psychiatric Association. (2013). *Diagnostic and statistical manual of mental disorders (DSM-5)*. American Psychiatric Association Publishing.

American Psychological Association. (2017). *Ethical principles of psychologists and code of conduct* (2002, Amended June 1, 2010, and January 1, 2017). https://www.apa.org/ethics/code/

Anderson, T., Ogles, B. M., Patterson, C. L., Lambert, M. J., & Vermeersch, D. A. (2009). Therapist effects: Facilitative interpersonal skills as a predictor of therapist success. *Journal of Clinical Psychology*, 65(7), 755–768. https://doi.org/10.1002/jclp.20583

Aviram, A., Westra, H. A., Constantino, M. J., & Antony, M. M. (2016). Responsive management of early resistance in cognitive-behavioral therapy for generalized anxiety disorder. *Journal of Consulting and Clinical Psychology*, 84(9), 783–794. https://doi.org/10.1037/ccp0000100

Bailey, R. J., & Ogles, B. M. (2019). Common factors as a therapeutic approach: What is required? *Practice Innovations*, 4(4), 241–254. https://doi.org/10.1037/pri0000100

Barlow, D. H. (2002). *Anxiety and its disorders: The nature and treatment of anxiety and panic* (2nd ed.). Guilford Press.

Barlow, D. H. (Ed.). (2008). *Clinical handbook of psychological disorders* (4th ed.). Guilford Press.

Barlow, D. H. (2010). Negative effects from psychological treatments: A perspective. *American Psychologist*, 65(1), 13–20. https://doi.org/10.1037/a0015643

Barlow, D. H., Allen, L. B., & Choate, M. L. (2004). Toward a unified treatment for emotional disorders. *Behavior Therapy*, 35(2), 205–230. https://doi.org/10.1016/S0005-7894(04)80036-4

Barlow, D. H., Ellard, K. K., Fairholme, C. P., Farchione, T. J., Boisseau, C. L., Allen, L. B., & Ehrenreich-May, J. (2011). *Unified protocol for transdiagnostic treatment of emotional disorders: Client workbook*. Oxford University Press.

Barlow, D. H., Farchione, T. J., Sauer-Zavala, S., Murray Latin, H., Ellard, K. K., Bullis, J. R., Bentley, K. H., Boettcher, H. T., & Cassiello-Robbins, C. (2017). *Unified protocol for transdiagnostic treatment of emotional disorders: Therapist guide* (2nd ed.). Oxford University Press.

Beck, A. T. (1976). *Cognitive therapy and the emotional disorders*. New American Library.

Beck, A. T., Rush, A. J., Shaw, B. F., & Emery, G. (1979). *Cognitive therapy of depression*. The Guilford Press.

Beck, J. (2006). *Cognitive therapy* [Systems of Psychotherapy video series]. American Psychological Association. https://www.apa.org/pubs/videos/4310736

Beck, J. S. (2005). *Cognitive therapy for challenging problems: What to do when the basics don't work*. Guilford Press.

Bennett-Levy, J. (2019). Why therapists should walk the talk: The theoretical and empirical case for personal practice in therapist training and professional development. *Journal of Behavior Therapy and Experimental Psychiatry, 62*, 133–145. https://doi.org/10.1016/j.jbtep.2018.08.004

Bennett-Levy, J., & Finlay-Jones, A. (2018). The role of personal practice in therapist skill development: A model to guide therapists, educators, supervisors and researchers. *Cognitive Behaviour Therapy, 47*(3), 185–205. https://doi.org/10.1080/16506073.2018.1434678

Beutler, L. E., Edwards, C., & Someah, K. (2018). Adapting psychotherapy to patient reactance level: A meta-analytic review. *Journal of Clinical Psychology, 74*(11), 1952–1963. https://doi.org/10.1002/jclp.22682

Boswell, J. F. (2013). Intervention strategies and clinical process in transdiagnostic cognitive-behavioral therapy. *Psychotherapy, 50*(3), 381–386. https://doi.org/10.1037/a0032157

Boswell, J. F., Bentley, K. H., & Barlow, D. H. (2015). Motivation facilitation in the Unified Protocol for Transdiagnostic Treatment of Emotional Disorders. In H. Arkowitz, W. Miller, & S. Rollnick (Eds.), *Motivational interviewing in the treatment of psychological problems* (2nd ed., pp. 33–57). Guilford Press.

Boswell, J. F., Castonguay, L. G., & Wasserman, R. H. (2010). Effects of psychotherapy training and intervention use on session outcome. *Journal of Consulting and Clinical Psychology, 78*(5), 717–723. https://doi.org/10.1037/a0020088

Boswell, J. F., Constantino, M. J., & Goldfried, M. R. (2020). A proposed makeover of psychotherapy training: Contents, methods, and outcomes. *Clinical Psychology: Science and Practice, 27*(3), e12340. https://doi.org/10.1111/cpsp.12340

Boswell, J. F., Kraus, D. R., Miller, S. D., & Lambert, M. J. (2015). Implementing routine outcome monitoring in clinical practice: Benefits, challenges, and solutions. *Psychotherapy Research, 25*(1), 6–19. https://doi.org/10.1080/10503307.2013.817696

Boswell, J. F., & Schwartzman, C. (2018). An exploratory analysis of treatment augmentation in a single case. *Behavior Modification*. Advance online publication. https://doi.org/10.1177/0145445518796202

Boswell, J. F., Sharpless, B. A., Greenberg, L. S., Heatherington, L., Huppert, J. D., Barber, J. P., Goldfried, M. R., & Castonguay, L. G. (2011). Schools of psychotherapy and the beginnings of a scientific approach. In D. H. Barlow (Ed.), *Oxford handbook of clinical psychology* (pp. 98–127). Oxford University Press.

Castonguay, L. G. (2011). Psychotherapy, psychopathology, research and practice: Pathways of connections and integration. *Psychotherapy Research, 21*(2), 125–140. https://doi.org/10.1080/10503307.2011.563250

Castonguay, L. G., & Beutler, L. E. (Eds.). (2006). *Principles of therapeutic change that work.* Oxford Press.

Castonguay, L. G., Boswell, J. F., Constantino, M. J., Goldfried, M. R., & Hill, C. E. (2010). Training implications of harmful effects of psychological treatments. *American Psychologist, 65*(1), 34–49. https://doi.org/10.1037/a0017330

Castonguay, L. G., Constantino, M. J., McAleavey, A. A., & Goldfried, M. R. (2011). The alliance in cognitive behavioral therapy. In J. P. Barber & J. C. Muran (Eds.), *The therapeutic alliance: An evidence-based approach to practice and training* (pp. 150–171). Guilford Press.

Castonguay, L. G., Goldfried, M. R., Wiser, S., Raue, P. J., & Hayes, A. M. (1996). Predicting the effect of cognitive therapy for depression: A study of unique and common factors. *Journal of Consulting and Clinical Psychology, 64*(3), 497–504. https://doi.org/10.1037/0022-006X.64.3.497

Castonguay, L. G., & Hill, C. E. (Eds.). (2012). *Transformation in psychotherapy: Corrective experiences across cognitive behavioral, humanistic, and psychodynamic approaches.* American Psychological Association. https://doi.org/10.1037/13747-000

Clark, D. M. (1986). A cognitive approach to panic. *Behaviour Research and Therapy, 24*(4), 461–470. https://doi.org/10.1016/0005-7967(86)90011-2

Coker, J. (1990). *How to practice jazz.* Jamey Aebersold.

Constantino, M. J., Castonguay, L. G., Zack, S., & DeGeorge, J. (2010). Engagement in psychotherapy: Factors contributing to the facilitation, demise, and restoration of the therapeutic alliance. In D. Castro-Blanco & M. S. Carver (Eds.), *Elusive alliance: Treatment engagement strategies with high-risk adolescents* (pp. 21–57). American Psychological Association. https://doi.org/10.1037/12139-001

Constantino, M. J., Coyne, A. E., Boswell, J. F., Iles, B. R., & Vîslă, A. (2018). A meta-analysis of the association between patients' early perception of treatment credibility and their post-treatment outcomes. *Psychotherapy, 55*(4), 486–495. https://doi.org/10.1037/pst0000168

Constantino, M. J., Coyne, A. E., & Muir, H. J. (2020). Evidence-based therapist responsivity to disruptive clinical process. *Cognitive and Behavioral Practice, 27*(4), 405–416. https://doi.org/10.1016/j.cbpra.2020.01.003

Constantino, M. J., Goodwin, B. J., Muir, H. J., Coyne, A. E., & Boswell, J. F. (2021). Context-responsive psychotherapy integration applied to cognitive behavioral therapy. In J. C. Watson & H. Wiseman (Eds.), *The responsive psychotherapist: Attuning to clients in the moment* (pp. 151–169). American Psychological Association.

Constantino, M. J., Marnell, M. E., Haile, A. J., Kanther-Sista, S. N., Wolman, K., Zappert, L., & Arnow, B. A. (2008). Integrative cognitive therapy for depression: A randomized pilot comparison. *Psychotherapy: Theory, Research, Practice, Training, 45*(2), 122–134. https://doi.org/10.1037/0033-3204.45.2.122

Constantino, M. J., Vîslă, A., Coyne, A. E., & Boswell, J. F. (2018). A meta-analysis of the association between patients' early treatment outcome expectation and their posttreatment outcomes. *Psychotherapy, 55*(4), 473–485. https://doi.org/10.1037/pst0000169

Coyne, A. E., Constantino, M. J., & Muir, H. J. (2019). Therapist responsivity to patients' early treatment beliefs and psychotherapy process. *Psychotherapy, 56*(1), 11–15. https://doi.org/10.1037/pst0000200

Craske, M. G., Kircanski, K., Zelikowsky, M., Mystkowski, J., Chowdhury, N., & Baker, A. (2008). Optimizing inhibitory learning during exposure therapy. *Behaviour Research and Therapy, 46*(1), 5–27. https://doi.org/10.1016/j.brat.2007.10.003

Csikszentmihalyi, M. (1997). *Finding flow: The psychology of engagement with everyday life.* Basic Books.

Cuijpers, P., Reijnders, M., & Huibers, M. J. H. (2019). The role of common factors in psychotherapy outcomes. *Annual Review of Clinical Psychology, 15*(1), 207–231. https://doi.org/10.1146/annurev-clinpsy-050718-095424

Davis, D. E., DeBlaere, C., Brubaker, K., Owen, J., Jordan, T. A., II, Hook, J. N., & Van Tongeren, D. R. (2016). Microaggressions and perceptions of cultural humility in counseling. *Journal of Counseling and Development, 94*(4), 483–493. https://doi.org/10.1002/jcad.12107

Davis, D. E., DeBlaere, C., Owen, J., Hook, J. N., Rivera, D. P., Choe, E., Van Tongeren, D. R., Worthington, E. L., & Placeres, V. (2018). The multicultural orientation framework: A narrative review. *Psychotherapy, 55*(1), 89–100. https://doi.org/10.1037/pst0000160

DeRubeis, R. J., & Feeley, M. (1990). Determinants of change in cognitive therapy for depression. *Cognitive Therapy and Research, 14*(5), 469–482. https://doi.org/10.1007/BF01172968

Dobson, K. S. (2011). *Cognitive-behavioral therapy strategies* [Systems of Psychotherapy video series]. American Psychological Association. https://www.apa.org/pubs/videos/4310887

Dobson, K. S., & Dozois, D. J. A. (Eds.). (2019). *Handbook of cognitive-behavioral therapies* (4th ed.). Guilford Press.

Elkin, I., Falconnier, L., Smith, Y., Canada, K. E., Henderson, E., Brown, E. R., & McKay, B. M. (2014). Therapist responsiveness and patient engagement in therapy. *Psychotherapy Research, 24*(1), 52–66. https://doi.org/10.1080/10503307.2013.820855

Ellis, A. (1962). *Reason and emotion in psychotherapy.* Lyle Stuart.

Ellis, M. V., Berger, L., Hanus, A. E., Ayala, E. E., Swords, B. A., & Siembor, M. (2014). Inadequate and harmful clinical supervision: Testing a revised framework and assessing occurrence. *The Counseling Psychologist, 42*(4), 434–472. https://doi.org/10.1177/0011000013508656

Ericsson, K. A. (2003). Development of elite performance and deliberate practice: An update from the perspective of the expert performance approach. In J. L. Starkes & K. A. Ericsson (Eds.), *Expert performance in sports: Advances in research on sport expertise* (pp. 49–83). Human Kinetics.

Ericsson, K. A. (2004). Deliberate practice and the acquisition and maintenance of expert performance in medicine and related domains: Invited address. *Academic Medicine, 79*(10, Suppl.), S70–S81. https://doi.org/10.1097/00001888-200410001-00022

Ericsson, K. A. (2006). The influence of experience and deliberate practice on the development of superior expert performance. In K. A. Ericsson, N. Charness, P. J. Feltovich, & R. R. Hoffman (Eds.), *The Cambridge handbook of expertise and expert performance* (pp. 683–703). Cambridge University Press. https://doi.org/10.1017/CBO9780511816796.038

Ericsson, K. A., Hoffman, R. R., Kozbelt, A., & Williams, A. M. (Eds.). (2018). *The Cambridge handbook of expertise and expert performance* (2nd ed.). Cambridge University Press. https://doi.org/10.1017/9781316480748

Ericsson, K. A., Krampe, R. T., & Tesch-Römer, C. (1993). The role of deliberate practice in the acquisition of expert performance. *Psychological Review, 100*(3), 363–406. https://doi.org/10.1037/0033-295X.100.3.363

Ericsson, K. A., & Pool, R. (2016). *Peak: Secrets from the new science of expertise.* Houghton Mifflin Harcourt.

Eubanks, C. F., Muran, J. C., & Safran, J. D. (2018). Alliance rupture repair: A meta-analysis. *Psychotherapy, 55*(4), 508–519. https://doi.org/10.1037/pst0000185

Feeley, M., DeRubeis, R. J., & Gelfand, L. A. (1999). The temporal relation of adherence and alliance to symptom change in cognitive therapy for depression. *Journal of Consulting and Clinical Psychology, 67*(4), 578–582. https://doi.org/10.1037/0022-006X.67.4.578

Fisher, A. J., & Boswell, J. F. (2016). Enhancing the personalization of psychotherapy with dynamic assessment and modeling. *Assessment, 23*(4), 496–506. https://doi.org/10.1177/1073191116638735

Fisher, R. P., & Craik, F. I. M. (1977). Interaction between encoding and retrieval operations in cued recall. *Journal of Experimental Psychology: Human Learning and Memory, 3*(6), 701–711. https://doi.org/10.1037/0278-7393.3.6.701

Fluckiger, C., Del Re, A. C., Wampold, B. E., & Horvath, A. O. (2018). Alliance in adult psychotherapy: A meta-analytic synthesis. In J. C. Norcross & B. E. Wampold (Eds.), *Psychotherapy relationships that work: Evidence-based responsiveness* (3rd ed., pp. 24–78). Oxford University Press.

Foa, E. B., & Kozak, M. J. (1986). Emotional processing of fear: Exposure to corrective information. *Psychological Bulletin, 99*, 20–35.

Foa, E. B., Steketee, G., Grayson, J. B., & Doppelt, H. G. (1983). Treatment of obsessive-compulsives: When do we fail? In E. B. Foa & P. M. G. Emmelkamp (Eds.), *Failures in behavior therapy* (pp. 10–34). John Wiley & Sons.

Goldberg, S. B., Babins-Wagner, R., Rousmaniere, T., Berzins, S., Hoyt, W. T., Whipple, J. L., Miller, S. D., & Wampold, B. E. (2016). Creating a climate for therapist improvement: A case study of an agency focused on outcomes and deliberate practice. *Psychotherapy, 53*(3), 367–375. https://doi.org/10.1037/pst0000060

Goldberg, S. B., Baldwin, S. A., Merced, K., Caperton, D. D., Imel, Z. E., Atkins, D. C., & Creed, T. (2020). The structure of competence: Evaluating the factor structure of the Cognitive Therapy Rating Scale. *Behavior Therapy, 51*(1), 113–122. https://doi.org/10.1016/j.beth.2019.05.008

Goldberg, S. B., Rousmaniere, T. G., Miller, S. D., Whipple, J., Nielsen, S. L., Hoyt, W., & Wampold, B. E. (2016). Do psychotherapists improve with time and experience? A longitudinal analysis of outcomes in a clinical setting. *Journal of Counseling Psychology, 63*, 1–11. https://doi.org/10.1037/cou0000131

Goldfried, M. R., & Davison, G. C. (1976). *Clinical behavior therapy.* Holt, Rinehart, & Winston.

Goldfried, M. R., & Davison, G. C. (1994). *Clinical behavior therapy.* John Wiley & Sons.

Goldman, R. E., Hilsenroth, M. J., Owen, J. J., & Gold, J. R. (2013). Psychotherapy integration and alliance: Use of cognitive-behavioral techniques within a short-term psychodynamic treatment model. *Journal of Psychotherapy Integration, 23*(4), 373–385. https://doi.org/10.1037/a0034363

Goodwin, B. J., Constantino, M. J., Westra, H. A., Button, M. L., & Antony, M. M. (2019). Patient motivational language in the prediction of symptom change, clinically significant response, and time to response in psychotherapy for generalized anxiety disorder. *Psychotherapy, 56*(4), 537–548. https://doi.org/10.1037/pst0000269

Goodwin, B. J., Coyne, A. E., & Constantino, M. J. (2018). Extending the context-responsive psychotherapy integration framework to cultural processes in psychotherapy. *Psychotherapy, 55*(1), 3–8. https://doi.org/10.1037/pst0000143

Goodyear, R. K., & Nelson, M. L. (1997). The major formats of psychotherapy supervision. In C. E. Watkins, Jr. (Eds.), *Handbook of psychotherapy supervision* (pp. 328–344). John Wiley & Sons.

Haggerty, G., & Hilsenroth, M. J. (2011). The use of video in psychotherapy supervision. *British Journal of Psychotherapy, 27*(2), 193–210. https://doi.org/10.1111/j.1752-0118.2011.01232.x

Hatcher, R. L. (2015). Interpersonal competencies: Responsiveness, technique, and training in psychotherapy. *American Psychologist, 70*(8), 747–757. https://doi.org/10.1037/a0039803

Hayes, S. C., & Hofmann, S. G. (Eds.). (2018). *Process-based CBT: The science and core clinical competencies of cognitive-behavioral therapy.* Context Press.

Hays, P. A. (2009). Integrating evidence-based practice, cognitive-behavior therapy, and multicultural therapy: Ten steps for culturally competent practice. *Professional Psychology: Research and Practice, 40*(4), 354–360.

Henry, W. P., Strupp, H. H., Butler, S. F., Schacht, T. E., & Binder, J. L. (1993). Effects of training in time-limited dynamic psychotherapy: Changes in therapist behavior. *Journal of Consulting and Clinical Psychology, 61*(3), 434–440. https://doi.org/10.1037/0022-006X.61.3.434

Hill, C. E., Kivlighan, D. M. I. I. I., Rousmaniere, T., Kivlighan, D. M., Jr., Gerstenblith, J., & Hillman, J. (2020). Deliberate practice for the skill of immediacy: A multiple case study of doctoral student therapists and clients. *Psychotherapy, 57*(4), 587–597. https://doi.org/10.1037/pst0000247

Hill, C. E., & Knox, S. (2013). Training and supervision in psychotherapy: Evidence for effective practice. In M. J. Lambert (Ed.), *Handbook of psychotherapy and behavior change* (6th ed., pp. 775–811). John Wiley & Sons.

Hollon, S. D., Evans, M. D., Auerbach, A., DeRubeis, R. J., Elkin, I., Lowery, A., Kriss, M. R., Grove, W. M., Tuason, V. B., & Piasecki, J. M. (1988). *Development of a system for rating therapies for depression: Differentiating cognitive therapy, interpersonal psychotherapy and clinical management pharmacotherapy.* Unpublished manuscript, Department of Psychology, Vanderbilt University, Nashville.

Holtforth, M. G., & Castonguay, L. G. (2005). Relationship and techniques in cognitive-behavioral therapy—A motivational approach. *Psychotherapy: Theory, Research, Practice, Training, 42*(4), 443–455. https://doi.org/10.1037/0033-3204.42.4.443

Hook, J. N., Davis, D. D., Owen, J., & DeBlaere, C. (2017). *Cultural humility: Engaging diverse identities in therapy.* American Psychological Association. https://doi.org/10.1037/0000037-000

Katz, M., Hilsenroth, M. J., Gold, J. R., Moore, M., Pitman, S. R., Levy, S. R., & Owen, J. (2019). Adherence, flexibility, and outcome in psychodynamic treatment of depression. *Journal of Counseling Psychology, 66*(1), 94–103. https://doi.org/10.1037/cou0000299

Kazantzis, N., Deane, F. P., & Ronan, K. R. (2000). Homework assignments in cognitive and behavioral therapy: A meta-analysis. *Clinical Psychology: Science and Practice, 7*(2), 189–202. https://doi.org/10.1093/clipsy.7.2.189

Kazantzis, N., Deane, F., Ronan, K. R., & L'Abate, L. (Eds.). (2005). *Using homework assignments in cognitive behavior therapy.* Routledge/Taylor & Francis. https://doi.org/10.4324/9780203499825

Kazantzis, N., Whittington, C., Zelencich, L., Kyrios, M., Norton, P. J., & Hofmann, S. G. (2016). Quantity and quality of homework compliance: A meta-analysis of relations with outcome in cognitive behavior therapy. *Behavior Therapy, 47*(5), 755–772. https://doi.org/10.1016/j.beth.2016.05.002

Keijsers, G. P. J., Schaap, C. P. D. R., & Hoogduin, C. A. L. (2000). The impact of interpersonal patient and therapist behavior on outcome in cognitive-behavioral therapy. A review of empirical studies. *Behavior Modification, 24*(2), 264–297. https://doi.org/10.1177/0145445500242006

Kendall, P. C., & Beidas, R. S. (2007). Smoothing the trail for dissemination of evidence-based practices for youth: Flexibility within fidelity. *Professional Psychology, Research and Practice, 38*(1), 13–19. https://doi.org/10.1037/0735-7028.38.1.13

Kendall, P. C., & Frank, H. E. (2018). Implementing evidence-based treatment protocols: Flexibility within fidelity. *Clinical Psychology: Science and Practice, 25*(4), 1–12. https://doi.org/10.1111/cpsp.12271

Kendall, P. C., Gosch, E., Furr, J. M., & Sood, E. (2008). Flexibility within fidelity. *Journal of the American Academy of Child & Adolescent Psychiatry, 47*(9), 987–993.

King, B. R., & Boswell, J. F. (2019). Therapeutic strategies and techniques in early cognitive-behavioral therapy. *Psychotherapy, 56*(1), 35–40. https://doi.org/10.1037/pst0000202

Koziol, L. F., & Budding, D. E. (2012). Procedural learning. In N. M. Seel (Ed.), *Encyclopedia of the sciences of learning* (pp. 2694–2696). Springer. https://doi.org/10.1007/978-1-4419-1428-6_670

Lambert, M. J. (2010). Yes, it is time for clinicians to monitor treatment outcome. In B. L. Duncan, S. C. Miller, B. E. Wampold, & M. A. Hubble (Eds.), *Heart and soul of change: Delivering what works in therapy* (2nd ed., pp. 239–266). American Psychological Association. https://doi.org/10.1037/12075-008

Leahy, R. L. (Ed.). (2003). *Roadblocks in cognitive-behavioral therapy: Transforming challenges into opportunities for change.* Guilford Press.

Linehan, M. M. (1993). *Cognitive-behavioral treatment of borderline personality disorder.* Guilford Press.

Martell, C. R., Dimidjian, S., & Herman-Dunn, R. (2010). *Behavioral activation for depression: A clinician's guide.* Guilford Press.

McCarthy, K. S., Keefe, J. R., & Barber, J. P. (2016). Goldilocks on the couch: Moderate levels of psychodynamic and process-experiential technique predict outcome in psychodynamic therapy. *Psychotherapy Research, 26*(3), 307–317. https://doi.org/10.1080/10503307.2014.973921

McGaghie, W. C., Issenberg, S. B., Barsuk, J. H., & Wayne, D. B. (2014). A critical review of simulation-based mastery learning with translational outcomes. *Medical Education, 48*(4), 375–385. https://doi.org/10.1111/medu.12391

McLeod, J. (2017). Qualitative methods for routine outcome measurement. In T. G. Rousmaniere, R. Goodyear, D. D. Miller, & B. E. Wampold (Eds.), *The cycle of excellence: Using deliberate practice to improve supervision and training* (pp. 99–122). Wiley. https://doi.org/10.1002/9781119165590.ch5

Meichenbaum, D. (1977). *Cognitive behavior modification: An integrative approach.* Plenum Press.

Miller, S. D., Prescott, D., & Maeschalck, S. (2017). *Reaching for excellence: Feedback-informed treatment in practice.* American Psychological Association.

Mowrer, O. H. (1939). A stimulus-response analysis of anxiety and its role as a reinforcing agent. *Psychology Review, 46*, 553–565.

Muran, J. C., & Eubanks, C. F. (2020). *Therapist performance under pressure: Negotiating emotion, difference, and rupture.* American Psychological Association. https://doi.org/10.1037/0000182-000

Muse, K., & McManus, F. (2013). A systematic review of methods for assessing competence in cognitive-behavioural therapy. *Clinical Psychology Review, 33*(3), 484–499. https://doi.org/10.1016/j.cpr.2013.01.010

Nathan, P., & Gorman, J. (Eds.). (2007). *A guide to treatments that work* (3rd ed.). Oxford University Press.

Newman, C. F. (2016). *Cognitive-behavioral therapy supervision* [Psychotherapy Supervision video series]. American Psychological Association. https://www.apa.org/pubs/videos/4310957#

Norcross, J. C., & Guy, J. D. (2005). The prevalence and parameters of personal therapy in the United States. In J. D. Geller, J. C. Norcross, & D. E. Orlinsky (Eds.), *The psychotherapist's own psychotherapy: Patient and clinician perspectives* (pp. 165–176). Oxford University Press.

Norcross, J. C., & Lambert, M. J. (2019). *Psychotherapy relationships that work: Vol. 1. Evidence-based therapist contributions* (3rd ed.). Oxford University Press.

Norcross, J. C., Lambert, M. J., & Wampold, B. E. (2019). *Psychotherapy relationships that work* (3rd ed.). Oxford University Press.

Norcross, J. C., & Wampold, B. E. (Eds.). (2019). *Psychotherapy relationships that work: Vol. 2. Evidence-based therapist responsiveness* (3rd ed.). Oxford University Press. https://doi.org/10.1093/med-psych/9780190843960.001.0001

Olatunji, B. O. (2011). *Cognitive-behavioral therapy for clients with anxiety and panic* [Specific Treatments for Specific Populations video series]. American Psychological Association. https://www.apa.org/pubs/videos/4310884

Orlinsky, D. E., & Ronnestad, M. H. (2005). *How psychotherapists develop.* American Psychological Association.

Owen, J., & Hilsenroth, M. J. (2014). Treatment adherence: The importance of therapist flexibility in relation to therapy outcomes. *Journal of Counseling Psychology, 61*(2), 280–288. https://doi.org/10.1037/a0035753

Peluso, P. R., & Freund, R. R. (2018). Therapist and client emotional expression and psychotherapy outcomes: A meta-analysis. *Psychotherapy, 55*(4), 461–472. https://doi.org/10.1037/pst0000165

Persons, J. B. (2007). *Cognitive-behavior therapy* [Systems of Psychotherapy video series]. American Psychological Association. https://www.apa.org/pubs/videos/4310774

Persons, J. B. (2012). *The case formulation approach to cognitive-behavior therapy.* Guilford Press.

Power, M. J., & Dalgleish, T. (2008). *Cognition and emotion: From order to disorder* (2nd ed.). Psychology Press.

Rousmaniere, T. G. (2016). *Deliberate practice for psychotherapists: A guide to improving clinical effectiveness.* Routledge Press. https://doi.org/10.4324/9781315472256

Rousmaniere, T. G. (2019). *Mastering the inner skills of psychotherapy: A deliberate practice handbook.* Gold Lantern Press.

Rousmaniere, T. G., Goodyear, R., Miller, S. D., & Wampold, B. E. (2017). *The cycle of excellence: Using deliberate practice to improve supervision and training.* John Wiley & Sons. https://doi.org/10.1002/9781119165590

Safran, J. D., & Muran, J. C. (2000). *Negotiating the therapeutic alliance: A relational treatment guide.* Guilford Press.

Samoilov, A., & Goldfried, M. R. (2000). Role of emotion in cognitive-behavior therapy. *Clinical Psychology: Science and Practice, 7*(4), 373–385. https://doi.org/10.1093/clipsy.7.4.373

Sauer-Zavala, S., Gutner, C. A., Farchione, T. J., Boettcher, H. T., Bullis, J. R., & Barlow, D. H. (2017). Current definitions of "transdiagnostic" in treatment development: A search for consensus. *Behavior Therapy, 48*(1), 128–138. https://doi.org/10.1016/j.beth.2016.09.004

Silberschatz, G. (2017). Improving the yield of psychotherapy research. *Psychotherapy Research, 27*(1), 1–13. https://doi.org/10.1080/10503307.2015.1076202

Smith, S. M. (1979). Remembering in and out of context. *Journal of Experimental Psychology: Human Learning and Memory, 5*(5), 460–471.

Squire, L. R. (2004). Memory systems of the brain: A brief history and current perspective. *Neurobiology of Learning and Memory, 82*(3), 171–177. https://doi.org/10.1016/j.nlm.2004.06.005

Stiles, W. B. (2013). The variables problem and progress in psychotherapy research. *Psychotherapy, 50*(1), 33–41. https://doi.org/10.1037/a0030569

Stiles, W. B., Honos-Webb, L., & Surko, M. (1998). Responsiveness in psychotherapy. *Clinical Psychology: Science and Practice, 5*(4), 439–458. https://doi.org/10.1111/j.1468-2850.1998.tb00166.x

Stiles, W. B., & Horvath, A. O. (2017). *Appropriate responsiveness as a contribution to therapist effects.* In L. G. Castonguay & C. E. Hill (Eds.), *How and why are some therapists better than others? Understanding therapist effects* (pp. 71–84). American Psychological Association. https://doi.org/10.1037/0000034-005

Swift, J. K., & Greenberg, R. P. (2012). Premature discontinuation in adult psychotherapy: A meta-analysis. *Journal of Consulting and Clinical Psychology, 80*(4), 547–559. https://doi.org/10.1037/a0028226

Swift, J. K., & Greenberg, R. P. (2015). Foster the therapeutic alliance. In J. K. Swift & R. P. Greenberg, *Premature termination in psychotherapy: Strategies for engaging clients and improving outcomes* (pp. 137–147). American Psychological Association. https://doi.org/10.1037/14469-010

Taylor, J. M., & Neimeyer, G. J. (2017). Lifelong professional improvement: The evolution of continuing education. In T. G. Rousmaniere, R. Goodyear, S. D. Miller, & B. Wampold (Eds.), *The cycle of excellence: Using deliberate practice to improve supervision and training.* John Wiley & Sons.

Tolin, D. F. (2016). *Doing CBT: A comprehensive guide to working with behaviors, thoughts, and emotions.* Guilford Press.

Tracey, T. J. G., Wampold, B. E., Goodyear, R. K., & Lichtenberg, J. W. (2015). Improving expertise in psychotherapy. *Psychotherapy Bulletin, 50*(1), 7–13.

Vallis, T. M., Shaw, B. F., & Dobson, K. S. (1986). The cognitive therapy scale: Psychometric properties. *Journal of Consulting and Clinical Psychology, 54*(3), 381–385. https://doi.org/10.1037/0022-006X.54.3.381

Wass, R., & Golding, C. (2014). Sharpening a tool for teaching: The zone of proximal development. *Teaching in Higher Education, 19*(6), 671–684. https://doi.org/10.1080/13562517.2014.901958

Watson, J. B., & Raynor, R. (1920). Conditioned emotional reactions. *Journal of Experimental Psychology, 3*(1), 1–14. https://doi.org/10.1037/h0069608

Webb, C. A., DeRubeis, R. J., Amsterdam, J. D., Shelton, R. C., Hollon, S. D., & Dimidjian, S. (2011). Two aspects of the therapeutic alliance: Differential relations with depressive symptom change. *Journal of Consulting and Clinical Psychology, 79*(3), 279–283. https://doi.org/10.1037/a0023252

Westra, H. A. (2012). *Motivational interviewing in the treatment of anxiety.* Guilford Press.

Westra, H. A., & Aviram, A. (2013). Core skills in motivational interviewing. *Psychotherapy, 50*(3), 273–278. https://doi.org/10.1037/a0032409

Westra, H. A., & Constantino, M. J. (2019). Integrative psychotherapy for generalized anxiety disorder. In J. C. Norcross & M. R. Goldfried (Eds.), *Handbook of psychotherapy integration* (3rd ed., pp. 284–302). Oxford University Press. https://doi.org/10.1093/med-psych/9780190690465.003.0013

Westra, H. A., Constantino, M. J., & Antony, M. M. (2016). Integrating motivational interviewing with cognitive-behavioral therapy for severe generalized anxiety disorder: An allegiance-controlled randomized clinical trial. *Journal of Consulting and Clinical Psychology, 84*(9), 768–782. https://doi.org/10.1037/ccp0000098

Westra, H. A., Norouzian, N., Poulin, L., Coyne, A. E., Constantino, M. J., Hara, K., Olson, D., & Antony, M. M. (2020). Testing a deliberate practice workshop for developing appropriate responsivity to resistance markers. *Psychotherapy.* Advance online publication. https://doi.org/10.1037/pst0000311

Wolf, A. W., Goldfried, M. R., & Muran, J. C. (Eds.). (2013). *Transforming negative reactions to clients: From frustration to compassion.* American Psychological Association. https://doi.org/10.1037/13940-000

Wolpe, J. (1952). Experimental neuroses as learned behavior. *British Journal of Psychology, 43*(4), 243–268.

Young, J., & Beck, A. T. (1980). *Cognitive therapy scale: Rating manual* [Unpublished manuscript]. Center for Cognitive Therapy, University of Pennsylvania.

Zaretskii, V. (2009). The zone of proximal development: What Vygotsky did not have time to write. *Journal of Russian and East European Psychology, 47*(6), 70–93. https://doi.org/10.2753/RPO1061-0405470604

Index

About the Authors

James F. Boswell, PhD, is an associate professor of clinical psychology at the University at Albany, State University of New York. He is also an associate of the Center for the Elimination of Minority Health Disparities. He received his PhD in clinical psychology from The Pennsylvania State University. Dr. Boswell has received the Early Career Award from the American Psychological Foundation/American Psychological Association (APA) Division 29 (Society for the Advancement of Psychotherapy), the Outstanding Early Career Achievement Award from the Society for Psychotherapy Research, the David Shakow Early Career Award for Distinguished Scientific Contributions to Clinical Psychology, the Dissertation and Marvin R. Goldfried New Researcher Awards from the Society for the Exploration of Psychotherapy Integration, and a Rising Star designation from the Association for Psychological Science. He is also a Fellow of the APA and serves as president of the North American Society for Psychotherapy Research. Dr. Boswell has published extensively in the areas of psychotherapy process and outcome, measurement-based care, and practice-oriented research. His work has been funded by the Patient Centered Outcomes Research Institute, National Institute of Mental Health, Robert Wood Johnson Foundation, and APA. He is also a member of the Advisory Committee to the APA Mental and Behavioral Health Data Registry. In addition, he served as a technical expert panelist on the government-sponsored white paper prepared for the U.S. Department of Health and Human Services and the Office of the Assistant Secretary for Planning and Evaluation on Strategies for Measuring the Quality of Psychotherapy. Dr. Boswell is on the editorial board of the *Journal of Consulting and Clinical Psychology*, *Behaviour Research and Therapy*, *Behavior Therapy*, *Psychotherapy Research*, *Psychotherapy*, and the *Journal of Clinical Psychology*.

Michael J. Constantino, PhD, received his BA in psychology from SUNY Buffalo, and his MS and PhD from The Pennsylvania State University. He completed a predoctoral clinical internship at SUNY Upstate Medical University and a postdoctoral fellowship at the Stanford University Medical Center. Dr. Constantino is now a professor of psychological and brain sciences at the University of Massachusetts Amherst, where he directs the Psychotherapy Research Lab and serves as graduate program director. His professional and research interests center on patient, therapist, and dyadic factors in psychosocial treatments; pantheoretical principles of clinical change; and measurement-based care. He has published more than 150 articles and chapters in leading journals and books in the field, and he has received extramural grant and contract support for his research, including from the Patient-Centered Outcomes Research Institute, National Institute of Mental Health, Robert Wood Johnson Foundation, and APA. He is also coeditor of the book *Principles of Change: How Psychotherapists Implement Research Findings in Practice* (Oxford University Press) and the in-preparation *Handbook of Psychotherapy*, to be published by APA. Dr. Constantino has received several early- and midcareer research awards, including from the International Society for Psychotherapy Research, the Society for the Advancement of Psychotherapy (APA Division 29), and the Society for the Exploration of Psychotherapy Integration. Dr. Constantino is also an APA Fellow. Among other professional positions, he is associate editor for *Psychotherapy* and past-president of both APA Division 29 and the North American Society for Psychotherapy Research.

About the Series Editors

Tony Rousmaniere, PsyD, is a licensed psychologist on the clinical faculty at the University of Washington Department of Psychiatry and Behavioral Sciences in Seattle, where he also maintains a private practice. His research focus is clinical supervision and training for psychotherapists and graduate students. He hosts the clinical training website https://www.dpfortherapists.com/. Dr. Rousmaniere's work has been featured in mainstream press outlets, such as *The Atlantic*. In 2018, he won the Early Career Award from the Society for the Advancement of Psychotherapy (American Psychological Association [APA] Division 29) and the Outstanding Publication of the Year Award for the Cycle of Excellence from the Society of Counseling Psychology (APA Division 17).

Alexandre Vaz, MSc, is a clinician, professor, and psychotherapy researcher at the ISPA–University Institute in Lisbon, Portugal, and cofounder of the Deliberate Practice Institute. He has held multiple committee roles for the Society for Psychotherapy Research (SPR) and the Society for the Exploration of Psychotherapy Integration, including serving as editor of *The Integrative Therapist* newsletter and organizer and host to SPR's webinar series. Dr. Vaz is also the founder and host of *Psychotherapy Expert Talks*, an acclaimed interview series with distinguished psychotherapists and therapy researchers.